The
SCHOLAR
and the CROSS

Edith Stein in 1925

The SCHOLAR *and the* CROSS

The Life and Work of
EDITH STEIN

by

HILDA C. GRAEF

THE NEWMAN PRESS
WESTMINSTER, MARYLAND
1955

NIHIL OBSTAT
Georgius D. Smith, S.T.D., Ph.D., Censor deputatus

IMPRIMATUR
E. Morrogh Bernard, Vic. Gen.

Westmonasterii, die 18 Septembris, 1954

Library of Congress   Catalog Card Number 54–12447

Printed in England

PREFACE

THE present study of Edith Stein is, as regards the main outline of her life, largely based on biographical material contained in the Life[1] written by her former novice mistress and prioress Mother Teresia Renata de Spiritu Sancto, O.C.D. and I wish to acknowledge with my warmest thanks my indebtedness to her for the factual information she has assembled as an aid to those wishing to undertake further studies of this noble woman. I also wish to express my thanks to Messrs. Sheed & Ward, of London and New York, publishers of the English translation of Mother Renata's book (*Edith Stein*, 1952) for their permission to quote in English a number of passages from the original German edition of the book. Many friends of the Carmelite philosopher have placed letters and other hitherto unpublished material at my disposal. I owe a special debt of gratitude to the Dominican Third Order Sisters at Speyer, without whose help this book could hardly have been written, at least not in its present form; the greater part of the new material comes from them. I am scarcely less indebted to the Rev. Dr. J. H. Nota, S.J., professor at the Berchmanianum at Nijmegen, who not only allowed me to copy much precious material in his possession, but also went very carefully through the chapter dealing with her philosophy—for which I have also received welcome help from Fr. F. Copleston, S.J., Professor of Philosophy at Heythrop College—and made most valuable suggestions on the relations between Thomism and phenomenology. Fr. Erich Przywara, S.J., was equally generous in sending me writings of his on the subject and answering my many questions. Nor has Edith Stein's own Order failed to help me with the work. The Carmelite nuns at Cologne not only gave me generous hospitality in their new home (the old convent, where Edith Stein had lived, had been totally destroyed in air raids) but patiently answered my questions and told me their reminiscences. The Sisters at Echt (Holland) did the same, and

[1] *Edith Stein*, Glock & Lutz, Nürnberg, 1952.

my kind hostess there, Juffrouw Delsing, helped with her memories of Edith Stein's last years, as did her brother. For much valuable information I am also indebted to the Very Rev. Abbot Walzer, O.S.B., to the Rev. Professor Steffes, Münster, to Dr. Rudolf Allers, professor at Georgetown University, Washington, to Edith Stein's sister Dr. Erna Biberstein, her friend Mrs. Rose Bluhm, the Benedictine nuns of St. Lioba, the Sisters of Notre Dame at Bonn, and several of her former pupils and their parents. At the Husserl Archives at Louvain, where a great deal of the Edith Stein material is assembled, the director, Professor van Breda, O.F.M., made as much of it accessible to me as he could; but unfortunately it proved impossible to obtain access to a substantial part containing autobiographical notes of the time before her conversion, certain spiritual writings and some correspondence, for I was not able to secure the co-operation of the person in charge of this material in spite of urgent representations to the authorities of the Dutch province of the Carmelite Order. I had therefore regretfully to decide to write the book without this material, and apologize that for this reason the presentation is in some details not as complete as it might otherwise have been.

Oxford, 31 *March* 1954   HILDA C. GRAEF

CONTENTS

LIST OF ILLUSTRATIONS

PROLOGUE

Iɴ his Apocalypse St. John the Evangelist paints the arresting picture of the Woman persecuted by the great red dragon. To St. John the Woman, of course, is the Church, the same Church that is the first target of persecution today. But she is also our Lady, the ideal of all womanhood, therefore one may perhaps enlarge the significance, and see in the persecuted Woman the tenderness of love, the protection of motherhood, the self-sacrificing devotion which are woman's special vocation. And so the fight of our own day is once more linked with the fight against the Woman and against all she symbolizes.

This image of the Woman persecuted by the dragon struck me as I was studying the life that is to be described in these pages; for it is surely a part of the apocalyptic struggle between Woman and the powers of darkness, which we have been, and still are, witnessing in our age. Edith Stein, philosopher, teacher, and finally Carmelite nun, has both taught and lived the highest ideal of Christian womanhood. The dragon, this apocalyptic symbol of the totalitarian State, persecuted her as he has always persecuted the Woman, ground her to death in the machine of a modern dictatorship. But the Woman of the Apocalypse, though persecuted, did not die; and one of the martyrs of the early Church, St. Ignatius of Antioch, wrote: 'I am God's wheat, and I am ground by the teeth of wild beasts that I may be found pure bread. . . . Then shall I be truly a disciple of Jesus Christ, when the world shall not so much as see my body.'

CHAPTER ONE

CHILDHOOD AND SCHOOLDAYS

EDITH STEIN was born at Breslau, Silesia, on 12 October 1891, which in that year was the great Jewish Day of Atonement, a day of prayer and fasting, when the Chosen People made atonement to the Lord for their sins. Looking back on her life, which, throughout the years of her maturity, was so very much a life of penance and atonement, one cannot help feeling that this date was more than a coincidence, that it was, indeed, of symbolic significance.

She came from a large, devout Jewish family. Her father was one of twenty-three children (by three mothers), and her mother one of fifteen (by the same mother). Many of these were very gifted; one of her father's younger brothers was an actor and later a director of several theatres as well as a playwright. Among her mother's brothers were lawyers, judges, and doctors.

Her mother was a very remarkable woman. Indeed, if we would understand Edith and her vocation in the Church, we must first go to old Frau Stein, whose example and influence were perhaps the most formative factors in her life. One could hardly find a more suitable description of this truly 'valiant woman' than the one given in the Book of Proverbs:

> Far and from the uttermost coasts is the price of her. The heart of her husband trusteth in her. . . . She is like the merchant's ship: she bringeth her bread from afar. And she hath risen in the night, and given a prey to her household, and victuals to her maidens. She hath considered a field and bought it: with the fruit of her hands she hath planted a vineyard. . . . She hath opened her hand to the needy, and stretched out her hands to the poor. . . . She hath looked well to the parts of her house, and hath not eaten her bread idle. Her children rose up, and called her blessed: her husband, and he praised her.

Frau Stein became a widow when her youngest child, Edith, was not quite two years old, and there were six others. Her husband had a timber business which was just beginning to expand—what was she to do to bring up her seven children without his support? Her decision was soon made: she must herself take over the firm and try to combine this with her domestic duties as best she could. This, of course, did not mean that these latter were neglected: she was a German-Jewish *Hausfrau* who could tolerate neither untidiness nor bad food in her home, and who baked the bread for the family herself. It meant, however, that her smaller children had to be left to themselves more than would normally have been the case, and that the older ones had frequently to take the place of the mother.

When Frau Stein took over the business the firm's finances were not exactly satisfactory. She realized at once that only hard work and a sound technical knowledge could save her from ruin. With that energy which was later to be such an outstanding characteristic of her youngest daughter, she set herself to master the timber business, and soon had acquired such skill that she need only see some standing timber from a train to be able to estimate the value of its wood. Like the valiant woman in the passage just cited, she bought, not, it is true, fields, but whole forests, and her industry and keen business sense were soon to give her firm a solid reputation.

Her success, however, was due not only to her business acumen. For she, too, 'opened her hand to the needy, and stretched out her hands to the poor'. In winter she would give away large quantities of fuel to the poor; and when she knew some carpenter was in need she would give him back the money he had paid her for the wood. For Frau Stein belonged to that type of Jew, then unhappily becoming increasingly rare in Germany, who really practised his religion. Under William II, and even before, the segregation of the Jews from the rest of the population had almost ceased to exist, and intermarriages were very frequent. On the part of the Jews this resulted almost inevitably in the complete loss of their religion. They were generally baptized, but without any inner relationship to Christianity.

The Stein family were different. For Frau Stein her religion was her greatest treasure. She kept meticulously all the intricate prescriptions of Jewish religious ceremonial; grace at meals was said in Hebrew, and the pictures with which the walls of her home were decorated represented scenes from the Old Testament. Even in her extreme old age she would keep the Jewish fasts in all their rigour; where it was a question of serving God she would never have dreamt of allowing herself any mitigations. This strict discipline, too, she bequeathed to her youngest daughter, who needed no other moral education than the example of her mother. For her there was only one true evil in the world, and that was sin. There was only one standard of behaviour, which was the Law of God.

But this does not mean that Edith, who was a 'toddler' just through the hardest years of her mother's struggle, had a joyless childhood. On the contrary. Her mother loved her deeply, and her elder brothers and sisters adored her. For her intelligence showed itself when she was scarcely more than a baby, and her eldest brother used to carry her about in his arms and teach her the names of the German classical poets and their principal works, so that she could be produced at family parties as something like a child prodigy.

These early learned pursuits, however, did not prevent her from heartily joining in the games and amusements of a normal child, together with her sister Erna who was eighteen months older than herself, and her various little friends. The two little girls went for outings with neighbouring families, dressed up in their Sunday best, or had exciting games in the timber yard among the many big piles of wood, where they could play hide and seek so gloriously. At the numerous birthday parties, on the other hand, she could show off her precocious knowledge at such games as *Dichterquartett*, where it was a question of attributing the right works to their proper authors. Though she could not even read yet, she knew it all by heart, owing to the expert coaching of her elder brother and a phenomenal memory which she preserved throughout her life, and so she was able to prompt the other children many years her senior. Some of them, it is true, did not like this display of intellectual superiority on the part of a four-year-old; but for a lively intelligence to hide itself is an achievement of humility of which only full-grown saints are capable, and in her case the delight in displaying her knowledge was greatly encouraged by the pride her family took in her performances.

Thus it is not surprising that she should have awaited with impatience the great day when she could go to school, where she would be able both to gather in more knowledge and to measure herself against other children of her own age. When her sister Erna started school there was a scene in the nursery, for Edith wanted desperately to go with her. But the law for Prussian schools was that children were not to be admitted before the age of six, so despite her tears her desire could not be granted. The only compromise was to send her to a kindergarten. Now this was not exactly what Edith had wanted, and her pride was deeply hurt that she should have to play with the babies instead of learning to read and write with the bigger girls. So she was very pleased when on the first day of the kindergarten the rain was pouring down, and she declared firmly that she could not possibly go because her shoes would get too dirty. This excuse, however, did not impress her mother, who never allowed her fondness for her youngest daughter to interfere with her educational discipline, and to the kindergarten she had to go. She went, however, not on foot but had the privilege of being carried there in the arms of her big brother.

It soon became clear that the experiment was not successful. Edith, the precociously intelligent child, was too much out of her element among the kindergarten babies, nor did the teacher know how to occupy her suitably, as she was far too advanced for the ordinary amusements of her little flock. So the kindergarten was given up, and Edith had to stay at home for another year.

There was, however, to be one consolation for the disappointed little would-be scholar: her elder sister, Else, promised her that, if she herself passed her teacher's examination with distinction, she would plead with the headmaster of the Victoriaschule[1] that she should be admitted the moment she was six, though that would be in the middle of the German scholastic year, which begins at Easter. So she actually entered school on her sixth birthday, 12 October, and though all the other little girls had by then had six months of it, by Christmas she was already one of the best pupils.

Edith's brilliance continued to show itself throughout her

[1] In Germany girls' schools often have a headmaster.

schooldays; and her natural intelligence was aided by an iron will and an ambition that in those days sometimes repelled people. She excelled in languages and German literature, but science and mathematics were not her strong points, and for these subjects she sometimes had to rely on the promptings and other forbidden aid from her neighbour, whom she, in her turn, assisted in other subjects.

Edith had, however, to endure one great frustration throughout her schooldays: it was her coveted aim to be first, yet she never achieved this, but always occupied the second place. She herself attributed this to the headmaster's anti-Semitism, even then widespread in Germany, especially among the professional classes One little story, told by one of her school friends, seems to bear out this view. 'Prizes were distributed to celebrate the centenary of Schiller's death. Edith was doing particularly well at this time, and everyone expected her to get the prize. But instead, it was given to one Martha Ritter, the head of our class.' The headmaster was then asked why Edith had not won it, since 'the whole class considered that she deserved it rather than Martha Ritter. He laughed, but with the faintest touch of embarrassment . . . and said that the head of the class had to have it. It was the rule. There was, of course, no such rule, because it was an altogether exceptional occasion.'[1]

Thus, even in these early days the theme was sounded which was to be so fully developed in her later life. But now, in these carefree schooldays, these were only pinpricks hurting a keen intellect, hurting all the more because there was as yet no sign of acceptance. The brilliant Jewish girl, whose ambition in those days was very evident, was already made to realize that objective merit counts little where deep-seated prejudice is involved. The mystery of Israel, its election and its rejection, had already come to enter her life in the guise of such seemingly trivial incidents.

It may well be that these early disappointments influenced a decision that came as a great surprise to her family. Everyone had assumed that she would naturally follow the example of her sister Erna, and after finishing at the ordinary girls' school, go on to attend the recently introduced special courses in preparation

[1] *Life*, p. 8; English translation: *Edith Stein*, Sheed & Ward, London and New York, 1952. This account of her early days follows largely Mother Renata's book.

for the university. But when the time came, at Easter 1906, she suddenly made up her mind to leave school and to give up all idea of studying.

This seemed strange for a girl so naturally gifted and so much attracted to intellectual work. Since she was, however, very delicate and rather small and undeveloped for her age, her mother thought it might be a good thing to give her a complete break and decided to send her to her eldest sister, Else, who was by now married and living at Hamburg. As she had three small children she might find it a help to have Edith there to give a hand in the house and with the children when that was needed. Edith was not very good at domestic jobs, though she did all she was told to do thoroughly and conscientiously. To try to get out of some unpleasant duty or to do things superficially was against her nature as well as against her upbringing. A mother such as old Frau Stein would never have tolerated such negligence in her daughters. But Edith loved children and was very good with them; they probably provided a welcome compensation for the uncongenial domestic chores.

This new life with its greater opportunities for physical exercise, as well as the bracing sea air, brought about a very beneficial change in Edith. When her mother visited her some months later she hardly recognized her daughter, who had grown a good deal, put on weight and changed from her customary pallor to a healthy colour. At the same time she had come to realize that intellectual work was a necessity to her. So she took the opportunity of her mother's visit to tell her that after all she would like to continue her studies.

Frau Stein was naturally very pleased, and so Edith returned home and, to make up for the lost time, was coached by two students. In 1908 she passed the rather difficult entrance examination to the *Studienanstalt* with distinction and thus spent the next three years learning Latin and higher mathematics besides the other school subjects.

Her mother was proud of her brilliant youngest daughter, whose outstanding intellectual abilities were now recognized also by the school authorities. Yet she was not altogether happy about her. Edith's development appeared to become ever more one-sidedly intellectual. Besides, she now showed distinct leanings towards exaggerated feminism. Most of the gentler and more womanly elements seemed to be absent from this young girl vowed to the pursuit of learning. What disquieted Frau Stein particularly was the total lack of religion in her life. It is true that she accompanied her mother to the synagogue at the latter's wish whenever she was free to do so, but it was easy to see that she herself took no part in the service. As she confessed in later life, from her thirteenth to her twenty-first year she was an atheist.

This seems to be a hard saying for a young girl brought up in a devout Jewish family. Yet it is characteristic of her. For Edith was a person for whom there could be no compromise with truth. Having lost the unreasoning faith of childhood, she could not arrive at belief in the existence of God whether by philosophical proof or by religious experience. Therefore she refused to pretend to some vague private religion and said frankly that, for her, belief in God was impossible. Thus, though she was never in any sense a militant atheist, the fact remains that, once her childhood had passed, her Jewish beliefs were lost, and she was left without faith in God to guide her in a world of intellectual chaos.

But if she had lost her religion, there were fine traits in her character which now began to show themselves more clearly. She was, it is true, still very ambitious, but she no longer displayed her superiority with the unconcern of the child. She had become more silent, though she never excluded herself from the social life of her school friends, and her friendship was sought because she had a reputation for being discreet, averse to gossip. Already in these early days she had her own very definite views about things. One saying of hers that survives is typical. Criticizing a translation that to her seemed not sufficiently accurate, she said: 'A translator must be like a window pane which lets through all the light but remains itself invisible.'[1] It shows that she had already learned to appreciate the necessity of a certain self-effacement of the scholar before the subject of his research, an objectivity which was to stand her in good stead in her later years and which prevented her from the excesses of subjectivism so characteristic of much contemporary German philosophy. The

[1] *Life*, p. 21; 14. In this and all the following citations the first figure always refers to the sixth German edition of the book by Mother Theresia Renata, the second to the first edition of the English translation: *Edith Stein*, Sheed & Ward, London and New York, 1952.

insight reflected in these words is all the more remarkable, in that, when she spoke them, Edith could not have been more than about eighteen years of age and was thus passing through the most subjective phase of life.

Nor did this rare quality of her mind pass unrecognized. In the spring of 1911 she took her final examination corresponding to the English matriculation, at which, as had been expected, she achieved sufficiently high marks in the written papers to be excused the oral examination. When the headmaster made his farewell speech to the class he gave to each of his former pupils a little motto designed to bring out her most striking characteristics. When Edith's turn came he said, with a pun on her name: 'Strike the stone [in German *Stein*] and wisdom will leap forth.'[1] He can hardly have known at the time exactly how prophetic were these words.

[1] *Life*, pp. 21 f.; 15.

CHAPTER TWO

A PHILOSOPHER IN THE MAKING[1]

AFTER her examination Edith had at first intended to study at Heidelberg. She wanted to go there with her sister Erna; but this plan did not materialize, since Erna was just then preparing for a preliminary examination in the course of her medical studies. So it had to be Breslau.

Here she studied German language and literature, but in this study, as in every other subject that belonged to the philosophical faculty, philosophy had of necessity to be included, and to this Edith soon felt irresistibly attracted. She plunged with all the vigour of her twenty years into her new life, went to a large number of lectures and herself undertook to write several essays on the psychology of thought. In the articles and treatises she had to read in the course of these studies she constantly came across citations from Edmund Husserl's *Logical Investigations.* Eventually she felt she could no longer be satisfied with citations, and the suggestion of a friend sufficed to make her read the heavy work itself, which gave her intellectual life a new direction.

Husserl had produced almost a revolution in German philosophy, and this not because he was a revolutionary, but for the exactly opposite reason: he seemed to be a 'reactionary' who went so far as to go back to scholasticism and actually admit the existence of a knowable objective world; hence he called himself 'a common man where logic is concerned' (*Ein logischer Alltagsmensch*). Ever since Kant, at the end of the eighteenth century, had denied man any adequate knowledge of the world around him and affirmed that the 'thing in itself' is unknowable, German philosophers had increasingly tended to obliterate the outside world in their systems.

It was Husserl's great merit to have dispelled these mists of

---

[1] The contents of this chapter are partly taken from Edith Stein's own account reproduced in the *Life,* pp. 23–60; 17–55.

relativistic agnosticism by reaffirming the two old truths: the existence of objective truth and the existence of a knowable world in which we live. Significantly enough Husserl owed this old-new insight to two Catholic philosophers; to the Viennese professor Franz Brentano, who had once been a priest trained in the wisdom of the schools, but who had abandoned his vocation, and to Bernard Bolzano, who died in 1848. This latter, though not always orthodox in his thought, had never given up his priestly functions. He mercilessly castigated the absurdities of Hegelian dialectics.

It is strange, indeed, that two Catholic thinkers who had themselves strayed from the paths of orthodoxy, were to bring an unbelieving philosopher into contact with the fundamentals of Catholic thought. Husserl, in his turn, paved the way into the Church for more than one of his pupils, though he himself was destined to stay outside to the end of his life. He later said playfully that he ought to be canonized, seeing that so many of his students had become Catholics.

With the sense of the essential so characteristic of her, Edith Stein recognized at once that here was a philosopher of more than ordinary power and lucidity; that here was thought that corresponded with reality; and soon her mind was made up that she must go to Göttingen to sit at his feet. Chance came to her aid: the wife of a cousin of hers who was lecturer in mathematics at Göttingen complained in a letter that she had so few women friends there, could not Edith and her sister Erna come to join them. Erna was prevented from doing so, but the next day Edith surprised her family by announcing her intention to go. Her mother was sad to lose her favourite daughter who seemed to become more and more immersed in her abstract studies, and so were her friends. On New Year's Eve 1912 they had a small celebration, as is customary in Germany. On this occasion they sang a poem of many verses, one of which dealt with Edith. It said that, whereas other girls were dreaming of *busserl*,[1] Edith only thought of Husserl. They also produced their own magazine which contained a tale of a little blue stone, with a pun on her name, symbolizing her total submersion in scholarship, and expressing the sense of loss felt by her relatives and friends. Both

[1] Austrian patois for 'kiss'.

these teasing little pieces pointed to the same thing: for Edith, philosophy had become such an overpowering interest that it threatened to absorb her completely: she was in danger of becoming a veritable blue stocking, deaf to the needs of her own feminine nature. In those days, when the German universities had just begun to admit women as students, this danger was greater than it is today, and for a very abstract mind such as Edith Stein's it was doubly so. Her friends saw it and sounded a warning.

It would, however, be a mistake to imagine that she was by now so wrapped up in her studies that the needs of others failed to penetrate into her consciousness. Besides her great love for children she had inherited from her mother a deep sympathy with poverty, and was quick to sense what would give joy to her neighbour. When she had made up her mind to go to Göttingen it occurred to her that her friend Rose Guttmann, who studied mathematics, would enjoy a change of university as much as herself. Rose was overworking at Breslau, earning part of her livelihood by coaching private pupils, and Edith was worried about her health. She went to her mother to ask her to finance her friend's study at Göttingen; and though this generous offer could be dispensed with in the end, it shows that Edith was by no means selfishly devoted to her studies, but had a deep sense of friendship and its obligations.

Her professors as well as her fellow-students at Breslau were amazed to learn that she was going to leave them. She herself wrote that she had shared in the life of this university so fully that 'it might seem that I had become one with it to such an extent that I would not leave it of my own free will. Yet now, as was often to happen in later life, I could, with a slight movement, slip off the seemingly strongest bonds, and fly away like a bird that has escaped its snare.' This remark shows up the natural foundations on which grace was to build later on. For Edith Stein's decision to leave Breslau for Göttingen was more than a mere change of university; 'atheist' though she still was, she desired ardently to discover the truth, and Husserl seemed to her 'the philosopher of our time'.

Though she knew in her heart of hearts that she would not return to Breslau to finish her studies, she thought it safer not to bar her way back to this university, and asked one of her professors to give her a subject for her doctor's thesis on a psychological subject. Characteristically, her choice of a professor was determined by his readiness to give her a free hand. But for once she had misjudged her man: the professor she had chosen wanted her to work on the development of child-thought, which she was to investigate by means of experiments involving the constant use of questionnaires and photographs. But this was the last thing she wanted to do, as such experimental methods were quite foreign to her mentality. She soon realized that it had been a mistake from the beginning to think of a psychological thesis. 'All my psychology study,' she writes, 'had only made me realize that this science was still in its infancy, that it was lacking the necessary foundation of clear principles, and that in itself it was incapable of working out these principles. And what I had so far got to know of phenomenology delighted me precisely because it really consisted in this work of clarification, and because one forged for oneself all the intellectual armour one needed.'

The whole intellectual personality of Edith Stein is in this. On the one hand her thirst for clarity and precision; not for her the obscurity so often deliberately cultivated by philosophers, or the slipshod superficialities of a half-baked science; on the other hand the delight to work things out for herself, to take nothing for granted, to get down to principles of thought rather than to experiment with psychological data. Phenomenology, she hoped, would give her what she sought, and so, at Easter 1913, she left her home and her beloved mother to continue her quest for Truth.

*   *   *

Having spent a short holiday with her sister at Hamburg, she arrived at Göttingen on 17 April, and the very next day began to go 'exploring'—something she had always liked doing. With her open eyes and unprejudiced mind she would look at things and people, taking in new impressions and enjoying beauty wherever she found it. She was not the typical 'idealist' thinker, for whose self-sufficiency the outside world holds no interest; she was the 'phenomenologist', for whom the phenomena, that is to say, the things that appear, are of the highest importance. And so, when later in life she looked back on that happy first term at Göttingen, she remembered not only the professors and their lectures, but also the old town with its churches and its Gothic town hall, the red geraniums against its grey walls, the old inn with its panelwork or the famous café where the best cakes were to be had.

It is true, she had not come for all this—she had come for Husserl. In German universities the way to a famous professor usually leads through an antechamber that is occupied by the celebrity's assistant, very often a distinguished disciple who is still *Privatdozent*.[1] So it was also with Husserl. Before going to Göttingen, Edith had been instructed to call on Adolf Reinach, who acted as the link between the 'Master' and the newcomers. Reinach was himself a personality and thinker of no mean quality. Like so many of the phenomenological circle he, too, was a Jew—and he, too, was led to Christ before his premature death in battle, in 1917. At the time when Edith got to know him he was thirty, newly married, and radiantly happy with his young wife. Edith was delighted to find a man so open and cordial in his manner, whose only concern seemed to be to help others and make them feel at ease.

After he had arranged the necessary formalities, the great day arrived when she was to see the famous philosopher in person, who was then just fifty-four years old. The first meeting took place at a preliminary discussion between the professor and those students who intended to take part in his seminar. When Edith introduced herself he asked her whether she had read any of his works. She confessed to having perused the whole second volume of his *Logical Investigations*. He told her that this was a truly heroic feat, and required no other credentials for her admission.

From the first Edith took her place as an equal among the distinguished philosophers of Göttingen, and the strange thing was that hardly anyone looked askance at this natural self-assurance. There was just one good lady, also a member of the 'Philosophical Society' to which Edith had immediately been introduced, who

[1] i.e. a scholar who, having written a successful thesis, is accorded the right to hold public lectures and to accept a professorship if one is offered to him.

did not like her. Her description of this student is delightful and shows that, charitable though she usually was even then, she could be quite sarcastic where she sensed stupidity and insincerity. 'Fräulein Ortmann,' she writes, 'was a short, thin little person, yet she always walked about so heavily that her coat was usually bespattered all over with the mud of the Göttingen streets. She also used to speak very emphatically, but the content of her sentences, which sounded like solemn pronouncements, often seemed very trivial to me. She did not speak often, however, but listened in the seminar and in the Philosophical Society with an expression of rapt devotion in her large blue eyes. In her that seemed comic to me.'

The dislike was mutual, and Fräulein Ortmann did not hide her antipathy to the newcomer, but expressed it quite openly by being sufficiently unpleasant for Dr. Reinach to notice it. When he asked her what was the matter, why was she so unkind to Fräulein Stein who, he said, was such a nice person, she answered: 'She always joins in the discussions with ease; yet these things are so difficult.' This reply shows clearly how very naturally the young philosopher took her place among her fellow-students, who, as she says herself, were very friendly to her and took her contributions to the discussions seriously. It is understandable that a person very much her senior, but her inferior in intellect, should have been nettled by this easy superiority of the born thinker, who at once agreed to be responsible for the minutes and generally behaved as if this select circle was her natural sphere—as indeed it was.

This situation in which she found herself is very typical. For though all who knew her stress again and again her unassuming manner, which increased later on, though it was present even in these early years, yet she never showed any sign of that false humility that dare not speak its opinion or show its knowledge, when necessary. In fact she was not at all self-conscious. Her outstanding intelligence was a gift she simply possessed and used, and that it could rouse jealousy in others never occurred to her. This simplicity, which caused her to carry her knowledge lightly, is probably responsible for the fact that this early jealousy in one of her colleagues remained an isolated case. Even the unfortunate Fräulein Ortmann later became so thoroughly reconciled to her that she herself told Edith the conversation that had taken place on the subject between herself and Adolf Reinach.

* * *

Towards the end of the term another influence entered Edith's life, which was one of the factors that would lead, many years later, to her conversion. This influence was the philosopher Max Scheler.

Scheler was the son of a Jewish mother and a non-Jewish father, who had adopted Judaism for the sake of his wife. While at school at Munich he met a priest who opened his eyes to the beauty of Catholicism, and he decided to be baptized. His early fervour, however, did not last; he married a divorced woman and so cut himself off from the Church. By 1913, when Edith Stein first came into contact with him, he had separated from her and was on his way back into the Church, to which he was to submit once more in 1916. Strangely enough, the place where he was received back was the Benedictine Abbey of Beuron, which came to play so large a part in Edith's later life. Though his unstable temperament led him to break away again six years later, during the time he was a Catholic his thought moved decidedly on Catholic lines, notwithstanding certain exaggerations and misunderstandings, especially of Thomist philosophy, which he never fully grasped.

Scheler's impulsive and in many ways superficial character was not congenial to Edith's steadiness and depth, yet he did something for her that had far-reaching consequences.

This was the time [she writes] when he was quite full of Catholic ideas, which he knew how to propagate with all the brilliance of his mind and the power of his oratory. It was my first contact with this world, which till then had remained completely unknown to me. It did not yet lead me towards the faith. But it opened up to me a realm of 'phenomena' which I could no longer by-pass with closed eyes. Not for nothing had it been constantly impressed on us that we ought to view all things without prejudice and to discard any 'blinkers'. Without knowing it I had grown up within the barriers of rationalistic prejudices, which now broke down so that the world of faith suddenly rose before my eyes. It was inhabited by people with whom I was in daily contact, to whom I looked up with admiration. At least it must be worth pondering seriously.

Thus, at the end of her first term at Göttingen, when Edith had met Scheler, the 'phenomenon' of the Catholic Church had entered her mind. It was still but a 'phenomenon' to be investigated, and she did not embark on its examination, as she says herself: 'I was as yet too much preoccupied with other things. I contented myself with absorbing without resistance suggestions from those around me, and thus was transformed almost imperceptibly.' But the 'phenomenon' was there, and it had come to stay.

She was indeed extremely busy in this first term at Göttingen. Not only did she attend all the necessary lectures and tutorials on philosophy and psychology; she also read for her third subject, which was history, and undertook to do a very complicated essay for the famous professor Max Lehmann. Lehmann was a rare type among German professors of history: he was a European in the best sense of the word, and, which was even more rare, he did not like Prussianism, but was decidedly Anglophile. English liberty, the English Parliament, the English way of life were his ideals. This is less surprising than it might seem, seeing that he was a native of Hanover, which, from the days of George I to Queen Victoria, had very close links with Britain through the family relationships between the two royal houses. Hence his lectures on Bismarck showed considerably less admiration of this Father of modern Germany than was customary at Prussian universities. Edith herself had a very European outlook; but she thought Lehmann one-sided and suddenly found herself an ardent defender of the Prussian virtues. This was a somewhat paradoxical situation; for if there is one trait sadly undeveloped in the Prusso-German character it is the ability to see the other side and the good there is in other peoples and institutions. She writes herself: 'Since one-sided views always led me to doing justice to the opposing standpoint, it was here more than at home that I became conscious of the good sides of the Prussian character, and was confirmed in my Prussianism.'

A Jewess who admits being proud of her Prussian origin seems at first sight an odd phenomenon. Yet it must be remembered that the great majority of German Jews were ardent patriots, and under William II enjoyed perfect freedom. Indeed, the impoverished Prussian nobility liked to improve both their blood and, especially, their finances by marrying Jewish heiresses. William II himself placed great confidence in Jewish bankers and business-men. The remark just quoted makes it quite plain that for Edith Stein there was no question of divided loyalties between her own Jewish people whom she loved though she no longer shared their religion, and her German Fatherland. She was equally devoted to both and felt no contradiction between the two.

What were the positive qualities of the Prussian character that Edith valued so much as opposed to Professor Lehmann's prefer-ence for English ways? There are some characteristics in herself which, though of course found all over the world, are generally associated with Prussians in a special way. There is, first, her intense devotion to duty and her astounding capacity for work. There is sometimes also, as will emerge later, a certain rigidity in her views, a passion for tidiness, externally as well as internally, an almost military punctuality and even punctiliousness charac-teristic of the Prussian civil service. It was probably these qualities which she appreciated in Prussianism and which, in her own case, were not only mitigated by a very kind and sympathetic nature, but were later transformed by a fervent spiritual life.

This divergence of political views, however, did not diminish the mutual esteem between her and her professor, and his regard for the intellectual qualities of his student soon appeared in a way she had not at all expected. At a visit she paid him in his home he told her that her essay for his seminar had been so excellent that he was prepared to accept it more or less as it stood as a thesis for her *Staatsexamen*.[1]

It had been understood at first that Edith was only to stay in Göttingen for one term.[2] Soon, however, it had become her secret desire not to return to Breslau, and when she was now presented with the offer from Professor Lehmann, she thought

---

[1] An examination more or less corresponding to the one required for a B.A. at British universities, though the standard is higher as a rule, the minimum time of study being four years, with another year for preparing the theses. As distinct from the doctorate, it opens the way into State appointments.

[2] i.e. about three and a half months, as the German university year is divided into two, not into three terms.

it the best thing that could happen to reconcile her family with her plan to finish her studies at Göttingen; and she soon had the satisfaction of securing their consent.

Now it is the most usual thing for German students to take their doctorate first and then their *Staatsexamen*. Husserl, however, did not approve of this arrangement where his own students were concerned. He thought that one ought not to concentrate on philosophy from the start; it was much better first to establish a solid basis for it by making oneself familiar with the subjects and methods of some other branches of study. Edith was a little disappointed, but asserted her readiness to fall in with his views. He then agreed that she might choose a subject at once, and, very significantly, she asked him whether she might work on the problem of empathy (German *Einfuehlung*). Edith herself gives us the reason why she chose this subject, together with an explanation:

> In his lectures on 'Nature and Spirit' Husserl had stated that an objective outside world could be experienced only inter-subjectively, that is through a plurality of knowing individuals who are in mutual exchange of experience. Hence it (i.e. the outside world) pre-supposes the experience of other individuals. Husserl, following the use of Theodor Lipps, called this experience 'empathy', but he did not say in what it consists. Hence there was a gap here, which ought to be filled: I would examine what empathy was.

It was characteristic that she should have chosen this particular subject. For her, philosophy was not just a matter of abstract reasoning. After all, she was a woman, and she approached the problem of knowledge from the point of view of the experience of her own mind and the interrelation of several minds and their experiences through empathy—and the gift of empathy is a specially feminine one.

One would have thought that her intense intellectual work in her first term at Göttingen could leave her practically no time to cultivate human relationships. But the story of the little blue stone that had been read at the New Year's Eve party had not been without its effect. She had taken care not to immerse herself too exclusively in books and ideas. Like most Germans, she loved hiking and the surroundings of Göttingen offered ample scope for it. She, Rose, and often also a young man, a shy assistant at the Chemical Institute, went into the Harz Mountains or to Thuringia; to Eisenach and the Wartburg with reminiscences of Luther who had spent a year there before setting half Europe aflame with his 'Reformation', Weimar with the shrines of Goethe and Schiller, and Jena with more Schiller and memories of the Napoleonic Wars. All these places were—and still are—favourite haunts of educated Germans, nurtured in the eighteenth-century tradition, to which they go on pilgrimage almost as Catholics go to Compostella or Lourdes.

These hiking expeditions were a very necessary relaxation, and so were the occasional parties. One of her circle was a thirty-five-year-old budding lecturer, of whom Edith writes that he had formed a deep affection for her friend Rose, whereas he was attached to herself by a cordial friendship and their common philosophical interests. This remark throws some light on her relations with the other sex. She seems never to have been in love with a man, nor do we hear that she had any suitors. But there seems to have existed a certain emotional relationship with Reinach, and she had an intense devotion for Husserl which remained with her all her life. It seems probable that this devotion, combined with her scholarly ambition, prevented her from becoming entangled in any 'affair of the heart'; in later years she confided to one of her sisters in religion: 'Academical life imposes obligations; I have always lived like a nun.'

This, however, did not prevent her from being an excellent friend and having as friends many men who greatly valued her intellect and her character. Her newly married cousin, the same whose young wife had complained that she had so few women friends in Göttingen, poured out his heart to her about his various plans and worries. She was obviously even then a good listener whose advice could be trusted, for she adds that he discussed his affairs with her in the same way as he had formerly done with her mother. Her headmaster had been right when he had said of her: 'Strike the stone, and wisdom will leap forth.'

*   *   *

Edith's first term at Göttingen had set the tone for those that were to follow. She had resolved to do her *Staatsexamen* as quickly as possible, hence her working day came to be even fuller than before. Moreover, as a coming light of the Husserl school her position in the university had been established, and she was accepted by everybody. In her twenty-second year Edith Stein was already assured of a brilliant future. Her family were proud of her, her professors respected her, her friends admired her, and her unassuming manner prevented any real hostility on the part of those less favoured with success.

The First World War did not at first interrupt her studies. In January 1915 she passed her *Staatsexamen* with an excellent result; but in April of the same year she felt obliged to offer her services to her country and became a temporary Red Cross nurse. In September she was back at Göttingen, where she took an additional examination in Greek, in preparation for her doctor's degree. She completed her thesis in the following winter, but Husserl, who was, as always, full of his own ideas, could not find time to read it. As there was nothing more for her to do at Göttingen, she went back to Breslau, where she took the place of a sick teacher at her old school. In the meantime Frau Husserl persuaded her husband to get down to Edith's work; he read it with approval, and her oral examination, the *Rigorosum*, was fixed for 3 August 1916 at Freiburg University, where Husserl had just accepted a professorship. She passed the examination with the highest honours, *summa cum laude*, and her happiness was complete when her revered teacher now asked her to become his assistant in the place of Reinach, who was at the Front. All the world seemed to smile on her when, in October 1916, she returned to Freiburg to take up her new duties.

CHAPTER THREE

THE APPEARANCE OF THE CROSS

EDITH entered with high hopes on this work as assistant to one of Germany's most famous philosophers, which seemed to hold out great prospects for her future career. Eagerly she began to give introductory courses for the freshmen at Freiburg, to whom phenomenology was as yet a closed book, in order to prepare them for the lectures of the 'Master' himself. She facetiously called them 'philosophical kindergarten'.

Another of her duties was to put his papers in order. This was a most exacting task; it meant finding her way through thousands of slips covered with shorthand of the old German system called 'Gabelsberger', which she carefully transcribed and systematized. This work of hers is still preserved at the Husserl Archives at Louvain. The piles of folio sheets alone, covered with her regular handwriting, are imposing, and they become even more so when one reflects on the hours of patient deciphering and arranging which she must have put into it before each sheet could be written out.

It is clear that these tasks left her hardly any time to pursue her own work. Moreover, she soon found that much of what she did for Husserl seemed quite useless. He was in the habit of evolving his thoughts while writing them down—he thought with his pen, so to speak. Thus a good deal of his notes contained ideas almost immediately discarded; and when Edith had spent her time puzzling them out and transcribing them, he just brushed them aside never to look at them again. One day, when she had secretly taken a bundle of them with her to Breslau and worked them out beautifully during the vacation, he gave them one look and said: 'Burn them.' No wonder that she felt hurt. It was certainly a state of affairs far from satisfactory to an ambitious young woman of twenty-five, the more so as her efforts were truly a labour of love for the man she venerated.

23

The situation was further aggravated by the attitude of Frau Husserl, who knew nothing of philosophy and was always a little jealous of her husband's pupils. So on the comparatively rare occasions when Edith had at last secured a time for discussion with him, his wife would come in pretending she wanted to say how do you do to her. She still remembered it many years later, when she told a priest that thus 'the most beautiful conversations would suddenly be rudely interrupted'.

Edith was frankly disappointed. In November 1917 Reinach was killed in the war. Husserl wanted Edith to go to his funeral, which was to take place at Göttingen in December, and to help in arranging his papers, not without Frau Husserl objecting that this did not come within the scope of her work as her husband's assistant. Edith herself dreaded the journey. The idea that, instead of the happy *jeune ménage* she had known, she would now find a despairing widow in a house poignantly empty of the presence of its master was weighing her down. But things turned out very differently.

Frau Reinach, it is true, had for a short time been disconsolate, while the first stunning pain lasted. But both she and her husband had been baptized a year ago (as Protestants, because he thought that he was not yet ready to become a Catholic, which his widow did a few years later), and she soon came to realize that the man she loved was in the peace of God, that his life had reached its goal, and that it fell upon her to bear her loss as her share in the Cross of Christ. Together with this realization a deep peace came over her, which was so strong that it communicated itself to those who had come to console her. Edith, too, experienced it. The impression of this truly Christian attitude of Frau Reinach was so deep that she still spoke about it to a priest a short time before her own death. He writes that she was quite shaken by the fact that Frau Reinach, 'through her utter faith in a loving God, became a consolation to her husband's friends rather than needing herself to be consoled'.[1]

Edith Stein, in her quest for 'phenomena', had encountered the greatest of them, the one with whose sign her whole subsequent life and her death itself was to be marked.

From that time the slow process of conversion began in

[1] Rev. Dr. J. Nota, S.J., article in *De Linie*, Amsterdam, 1 August 1947.

earnest. It is clear that for a mind like hers, used to thinking out things and following lines of argument to their logical conclusions, conversion had to be first of all a matter of the mind, a real conversion of all her intellectual habits towards the central doctrines of Christianity, the Trinity, the Incarnation, the Redemption. As she was sorting out the papers of Dr. Reinach she found many notes which indicated clearly that he had been well on his road into the Church. For example: 'First and foremost, we must leave intact the meaning of religious experience! Even though it leads to enigmas. Perhaps it is just these enigmas that are of the highest value to knowledge. . . . Through prayer, I am in contact with this ultimate background of the world.' Or: 'Doubtless one can point out historic and national limitations in every man; not so in Jesus.' And again: 'It is hard to say what one feels before the whole Christ: in Him God's Being, outside of time and beyond the world, seems to unfold itself in time and before the world.'[1]

After Max Scheler had opened her eyes to the fact that one can be a philosopher of rank and a believing Christian at the same time, here now was Reinach, a deeper and more secure personality than Scheler, whom she profoundly respected, acknowledging Christ as God and prayer as the way to ultimate reality. When she returned to Freiburg it was clear that she could no longer shelve the vital question: 'What think ye of Christ? Whose son is He?'

While this question began to occupy her, she continued her strenuous work, interrupted by occasional hiking tours. One of her favourite forms of recreation was still to take long walks with her friends, especially with her sister Erna and Rose Guttmann, and to explore the lovely surroundings of Freiburg, the Black Forest or, farther afield, the Lake of Constance. On these tours she would discuss the books she had read; Stefan George, a poet whose work inspired both uncritical devotion and violent opposition, was one of the recurring subjects. He was a Catholic who had lost the faith but whose poetry was still not entirely without its inspiration, and who cultivated an exaggerated austerity of form in deliberate contrast to the formlessness of contemporary German expressionism. But her favourites were

[1] John M. Oesterreicher, *Walls Are Crumbling*, pp. 131 ff.

Goethe and Gottfried Keller, in whom she found the simplicity
and the unreflecting love of nature and beauty which corresponded
so well to her own leanings.

There was one subject, however, which was never broached
in these discussions; the subject of religion. Her own mind was
in ferment, and she knew that her friends would not understand
if she told them about what was moving her so deeply. Yet
every now and again there would be a reminder of that strange
'phenomenon' which had survived so many philosophical
systems, the Catholic religion. A friend who sometimes took
part in their excursions tells of a night spent at a farm in the
mountains. 'It made a deep impression on us,' she reports, 'that
the Catholic head of the household had family prayers with his
farmhands in the morning and shook hands with them all, before
they went out to the haymaking.'[1]

Then came the fateful autumn of 1918. In October Husserl
had a grave attack of 'flu; Edith helped to nurse him, and he told
her to read to him from the Bible, especially Isaias, Jeremias, and
the Beatitudes. By now she had realized that being Husserl's
assistant was not the right kind of work for her; moreover, the
financial side of the matter had proved also very unsatisfactory.
Thus, after he had recovered, she decided to leave him. The war
had ended with the Armistice of 11 November; Germany was
swept by a revolution—she felt that she ought to play her part
in rebuilding her country. She would try to be accepted as
Privatdozent at Göttingen. So she went home to Breslau with
this aim in view. Her relations with Husserl remained very
friendly; on 6 February 1919 he wrote her the following
testimonial:

Dr. Edith Stein, for many years my pupil at the Universities of
Göttingen and Freiburg, took her doctorate of philosophy *summa
cum laude* at Freiburg, in the summer term of 1916. She had written
an excellent thesis on empathy, which roused the interest of experts
immediately after its appearance. Later she was my assistant for
more than eighteen months. She gave me her valuable co-operation
not only by putting my manuscripts into shape for publication, but
also in my work as academic teacher. For this purpose she used to give
philosophical courses which were attended not only by beginners

[1] *Life*, p. 65; 61.

but also by more advanced students. The achievements of my students in my own courses as well as their personal testimony assured me of the excellent results of this co-operation. Dr. Stein has gained a far-reaching as well as profound philosophical knowledge, and is unquestionably well qualified for independent scholarly research and teaching. If the academic career should be made available for ladies, I could most warmly recommend her in the very first place for admission.

Husserl's influence, however, counted little at Göttingen, and Edith did not succeed. So she returned to Freiburg. She continued her work on Husserl's manuscript which she prepared for the press, and also pursued her own philosophical work. The first fruits of this were published in Husserl's *Jahrbuch für Philosophie und phänomenologische Forschung* and deal with the philosophical foundations of psychology.[1]

It is a work of transition. It employs faithfully the phenomenological method of painstaking analyses of the various 'phenomena' in relation to the human psyche. The phenomenological time, in which experiences take place, as well as the duration and interaction of these experiences themselves and their relation to the Ego, are described with meticulous accuracy. She deals with states of consciousness, such as fatigue, freshness, feverishness and the like, which she examines in detail. She discusses the various theories of modern philosophers who have dealt with these problems before her, such as Bergson and the German psychologist-philosopher Theodor Lipps; and it becomes increasingly evident that she is turning away from all irrationality and subjectivity, looking for objective standards by which to judge reality and its 'phenomena'.

And then, now and again, one comes across a passage which shows what is preoccupying her beneath all these analyses. While discussing the problems of taking up an attitude (*Stellungnahme*) she suddenly gives this example: 'I may long for religious faith, and yet it need not be given me.' And, shortly afterwards: 'Supposing a convinced atheist realizes the existence of God in a religious experience. He cannot, indeed, escape belief, but he does not enter into its sphere; he does not make it effective in

[1] Beiträge zur philosophischen Begründung der Psychologie und der Geisteswissenschaften, *Jahrbuch*, 5. vol. 1922.

himself, but clings to his "scientific *Weltanschauung*", which would have been overturned by unqualified belief.'[1]

When Edith Stein first embarked on her philosophical career she described herself as an atheist; her first meeting with Christianity had been through reading the Our Father in the Gothic translation in the course of her philological studies. She had next met Scheler, and after that had come her experience with Frau Reinach. It is just possible that the passage alludes to this latter, for it was evidently a strong experience which she still remembered at the end of her life. It looks almost as if she was here describing her own temptation: to put aside the implications of this experience, to stay outside its 'sphere'; for if she accepted it her whole existence as a philosopher might be jeopardized.

This may seem exaggerated. But Edith Stein was a person who did nothing by halves; she knew only too well that for her there could be no easy compromise between the religion of the Cross and the comfortable life of a philosopher professing some odd mixture of systems of thought. She knew that if she accepted God and His Christ her whole intellectual life would have to be refashioned. She would have to enter into an entirely new sphere—for what could Christianity mean to her, unless it became really 'effective' in herself?

While she was fighting her own battle between faith and unbelief, Germany went through the aftermath of a lost war. She was not without interest in politics; as a convinced feminist she had been an ardent partisan of women's suffrage; and after 1918 she gave her allegiance, like most of her friends, to the *Deutsche Demokratische Partei*, a party of liberal views, equally free from the ardent nationalism of the Right and the socialism of the Left, and precisely for this reason never very popular. She canvassed for it before the elections, which took place so frequently in post-Versailles Germany, and interested herself particularly in the nature and functions of the State, on which she later wrote a treatise which was also published in the *Jahrbuch*.

But even the political passions which at that time were rending Germany could not prevent her mind from returning again and

[1] op. cit., p. 43.

again to the most vital question, compared with which everything else was really only 'philosophical kindergarten', the
only question of a true philosopher: 'Where do I find the
truth?' And there was Someone who had said: 'I am the
Truth.'

CHAPTER FOUR

CONVERSION

EDITH STEIN regarded her conversion as a matter only between herself and her God and was reluctant to speak about it. She is reported to have replied to someone asking her what had led her to take this step: *Secretum meum mihi*—my secret to myself.[1] Yet, even if we would not presume to lift the veil that hides the mystery of grace from prying eyes, we may well attempt to trace as far as possible the influences that led to the final surrender of this chosen soul to her Lord.

It is unfortunate that there are few witnesses for the time before her baptism; but there can be little doubt that she must have come across many Catholic writers in her extensive reading. While she was Husserl's assistant she became an intimate friend of one of his most gifted pupils, Hedwig Conrad-Martius, herself a 'liberal' Protestant, but very open to the beauties of Catholic mysticism. It looks as if even before her actual conversion Edith had been no stranger to a certain kind of experience of the presence of God.

There is a curious passage in her work on the philosophical foundations of psychology from which we have cited before.[2] While analysing the phenomenon of vitality (*Lebenskraft*) and its fluctuations, she suddenly gives this example from the life of prayer:

> There is a state of resting in God, of a complete relaxation of all mental effort, when one no longer makes any plans or decisions, where one no longer acts, but abandons all the future to the Divine Will. . . . Perhaps I have been granted this state after an experience that was too much for my powers, so that it completely absorbed my spiritual vitality and deprived me of all energy. Compared with the failure of energy for lack of vitality, resting in God is something

[1] Isaias 24: 16; cited by Oesterreicher, op. cit., p. 335.
[2] *Beiträge zur philosophischen Begründung der Psychologie und der Geisteswissenschaften, Jahrbuch*, 5. vol. 1922.

entirely new and peculiar. The former was the stillness of death. This is now replaced by the feeling of being in safe keeping, of being delivered from all worry, responsibility and need for action. And while I am giving in to this feeling, I am gradually beginning to be filled with new life and the desire for activity without any voluntary effort. This life-giving influence seems to be the result of an activity and a power not my own, which become effective in me without making any demands on my energy. The only condition of such a spiritual re-birth seems to be a certain receptivity, that has its foundation in the very structure of the person which is removed from all psychic mechanism.[1]

It seems very clear from this detailed description that Edith Stein is here speaking of a state of soul that she has experienced herself, and her explanation is even more remarkable. If she were describing it merely as a psychological phenomenon, the revitalizing of the exhausted psyche by a state of interior repose, there would be nothing extraordinary in it. But her presentation of this experience in the context of a philosophical work may almost be called mystical in a larger sense. For here we have all the components of a mystical experience: abandonment to the divine will, involving passivity of both discursive reason and will, the experimental knowledge of being in the safe keeping of God, and the felt influence of a mysterious power clearly known as being distinct from the ego, and as acting without its voluntary co-operation. Lastly, the effects are wholly salutary: not a nervous exhaustion, such as frequently follows pseudo-mystical experiences, but a revitalizing of the whole personality. Even more, she attributes the possibility of such an experience to the very structure of the person—almost in the way mystic theologians find the possibility of mystical union with God in the fact that the soul is made in His image.

The only point that might be held against the interpretation of the experience as mystical is that, according to the narrative, it seems to have occurred after a certain strain that sapped the recipient's nervous resistance. It seems, however, not intrinsically improbable that God should give a genuinely mystical experience, even in such a state, to a chosen soul soon to be called to the contemplative life, in order to reveal Himself as the source of

[1] p. 76.

strength and peace. This, in fact, would seem to be borne out
by the whole of her later life, in which prayer played such a
decisive part precisely also as the spring from which she constantly fed her intellectual activities. If, as we believe, she
described here in the cold 'phenomenological' way something
that had been her own experience, then we shall also understand
much better why God used for her final conversion the means
He did.

For at first glance one would have thought that a philosopher
of Edith Stein's standing would be converted by reading a
theological treatise, one would have expected her to reach the
faith by the way of the intellect with, say, St. Thomas as her
guide. But God led her by a different path. During her years
at Freiburg, after her failure to secure a lectureship at Göttingen,
she spent much of her vacation time at Bergzabern in the
Palatinate, where her friend Hedwig Conrad-Martius and her
husband were running a farm. During one of these holidays, in
the summer of 1921, she was left alone one night, and went to
her hosts' bookshelves to choose something to read before going
to sleep. The first book she picked up was the *Life* of St. Teresa,
written by the Saint herself.

Edith did not sleep very much that night. For as soon as she
had begun the book she was so fascinated that she read on and
on, until, in the small hours of the morning, she had finished it.
What the experience with Frau Reinach had begun, the 'Mother
of Carmel' perfected. When she finally laid down the book she
said to herself: 'This is the Truth.'[1]

At first glance it would seem hard to find two more different
types of women than St. Teresa and Edith Stein. The saint
vivacious, very feminine, with a naturally gifted, but quite
untrained mind, who learned her wisdom chiefly by prayer,
aided by her innate common sense, and who had never known
life in the storm and stress of the world. Edith Stein, on the
other hand, was a highly cultivated woman, silent and retiring
by nature, with a 'masculine' mind given to philosophizing,
whose life was spent in libraries and on the rostrum of lecture
rooms. What was it that the one had to give to the other, what
was it that the other was so eager to receive?

[1] *Life*, p. 68; 64.

Frau Stein

Edmund Husserl

Edith Stein herself has not told us what it was precisely that
'bowled her over' when she read the *Life* of St. Teresa. Yet,
apart from the mysterious workings of divine grace, there is in
every conversion also a human factor, and this factor is open to
investigation. It may well have been that there was in the young
and brilliant disciple of Husserl a side that had so far been left
unsatisfied. She was searching life for the Truth that lay behind
it; in this search she had met a man whom she revered with all
the ardour of an idealistic young mind. But Husserl had been a
disappointment; the collaboration for which she had hoped had
not been forthcoming; much of her labour for him went
unacknowledged, or, worse, was even cast aside. She was for
him a valuable amanuensis, but he, immersed in his own thoughts,
failed to take her seriously. He gave her a very good testimonial,
it is true, but he did not treat her as an intellectual equal. For
all the friendship and recognition she enjoyed there was an
unsatisfied longing in her heart: a longing for someone to whom
she could give that self-sacrificing devotion which woman was
created to give.

The whole *Life* of St. Teresa is a description of Christ drawing
a soul to prayer, and through prayer to perfect union with Him.
As we believe, Edith had already sometimes experienced a certain
communion with God in prayer; she had also met the Cross and
the power it gave to those who embraced it. St. Teresa showed
her the perfect fulfilment of love in union with Him who had
died on it, the same who had also said: 'I am the Truth'—surely
here was the goal of all Edith's philosophy, not only to know,
but to live the Truth in the union of love with Love.

It seems that in these hours of grace, when she decided once
and for all to become a Christian, she also realized that, to live
her ideal of the Christian life to the full, she would have to be
a Carmelite, and her whole story from the moment of her conversion shows that, together with the gift of faith, she had also
received a distinctly contemplative vocation. We are told that
after she had finally made up her mind to become a Catholic,
she went the very next morning to buy a catechism and a missal—
the two essential books of Catholic teaching and worship. Of
course, she knew already from her other reading what Catholics
believe; but it was characteristic of her that, once her decision

had been made, she did not go to the heavier theological works, which would have seemed to be so much more suited to her highly trained mind, but to the simplicity of the catechism. We shall find again and again in her later Catholic life this childlike docility, devoid of all pretensions, that accepts the teaching of her Holy Mother the Church whole-heartedly and without question, in the authentic spirit of St. Teresa, who once said that she was ready to give her life for the smallest rubrics enjoined by the Church. And so she made herself familiar with all she was required to believe, as well as with the actions and ceremonies of the Mass. When her eager mind had assimilated it all, she went to the parish church at Bergzabern, and, after having attended Mass, followed the priest into the presbytery and asked to be baptized.

Naturally he asked her how long she had been instructed. She could only answer: 'Please, Father, examine me.'[1] It did not take the priest long to discover that here was a soul not only well versed in Catholic doctrine, but full of supernatural faith and the desire to live the Christian life in its integrity. There was really not much more to be done than to arrange formalities. Whom was she to take as her sponsor? It was in the house of her friend, Hedwig Conrad-Martius, that she had found the faith, and so she desired her to be the witness of her baptism. As she was a Protestant, special permission from the Bishop of Speyer had to be requested; and when this had been given, the date was fixed, very appropriately for New Year's Day, 1922. For this day is the Feast of the Circumcision, when, with the first shedding of the Precious Blood, Christ is beginning His great fulfilment of the Law that was to be completed on Calvary. And so, with a symbolism the whole meaning of which could only be seen after her death, Edith, too, began to fulfil the Law of her people by giving herself to Christ, a self-giving that was to be finally sealed in a concentration camp, twenty years later.

For her conversion was a self-giving from the very first moment. The night before her baptism, while all over the world the New Year was being welcomed with dancing and drinking, she kept vigil in prayer, like the catechumens of the first centuries. Early next morning she made her profession of faith in the parish church

[1] *Life*, p. 69; 65.

of Bergzabern, and received the two greatest sacraments of the
Church, Holy Baptism and the Eucharist. Hedwig Conrad-
Martius tells us that she made her profession of faith in Latin,
with ardent determination, and that she was filled with a childlike
happiness that was most beautiful.[1]

Baptism was soon followed by Confirmation, which took place
on 2 February, in the private chapel of the Bishop of Speyer.
Here in Speyer she made the acquaintance of Canon Schwind, a
learned old priest, who soon recognized the outstanding gifts and
personality of the new convert and became her close friend and
spiritual adviser. He encouraged her love of liturgical prayer by
teaching her the Breviary, which from that time she recited every
day, and he introduced her to a number of congenial people, so
that she was spared the loneliness which so often is the fate of
the new convert.

[1] Oesterreicher, op. cit., p. 337.

CHAPTER FIVE

THE CHURCH AND THE SYNAGOGUE

Edith had at last found the truth, the whole truth, that nourishes both mind and heart. This is the pearl of great price, of which our Lord speaks in the gospel, for which a man should sell all his possessions, if this be needed to acquire it. And so it is that almost every true conversion is accompanied by a sacrifice that costs dear. For Edith this was the suffering which her baptism must necessarily bring to her mother, to whom she was united by an extraordinary affection. Even rather lax Jewish families are normally profoundly shocked when one member becomes a Christian. It does not mean merely a 'change of religion', it is for them an act of utter disloyalty to the faith for which time and again their fathers had suffered persecution and ignominy, and to their whole race. Frau Stein was not lax—quite the contrary. She was a most fervent Jewish woman, who practised her religion with the deepest conviction, and whose great grief had been that her favourite daughter was totally uninterested in it. And now this same daughter calmly forsook the faith of her fathers in order to embrace what appeared to her as an incomprehensible superstition, involving all manner of queer practices she had had occasion to observe among the Silesian peasants with whom she came into contact.

Edith realized only too well that, what for herself was perfect loyalty to the true meaning of Judaism, must appear to her mother as the exact opposite. How could she possibly explain? But she had been baptized; and at baptism not only are sins wiped out, but also the great theological virtues and the gifts of the Holy Ghost are infused into the soul, which are further strengthened in Confirmation. We certainly cannot see these gifts, and in most of us they are so much obscured by the consequences of original sin, faults of character and other weaknesses, that we hardly know they are there at all. But from time to time God raises up a soul in which they shine forth with such splendour that it is impossible not to recognize them. Such was the case of Edith Stein. She, who had once trembled with apprehension when she was asked to visit Frau Reinach after the death of her husband, now resolved to face a far greater ordeal in person. It would indeed have been easier for her to break the shattering news by letter, but all the more cruel to her mother. Edith spurned this way, which a worldly prudence might have chosen; and, leaving the outcome to God, went to Breslau to face the storm.

There are moments in human life which are fraught with symbolism; meetings when two people confront each other, not just as individuals, but as representatives of two epochs, two nations, two religions. Where such meetings occur, tragedy is never far away, and when the persons who thus meet are bound by the strong ties of blood or friendship it is indeed inevitable. In Edith Stein and her mother, Church and Synagogue met each other, for the Church is the daughter of the Synagogue. The scene between the two women was as simple as the issue between them; the Holy Ghost gave Edith the fortitude and the wisdom to do no more than state the fact. Kneeling before old Frau Stein, she said: 'Mother, I am a Catholic.'

The effect of this little sentence was shattering. Edith had expected a scene, harsh angry words, even to disowning her daughter who had betrayed her race. Nothing of this happened, but something that was much harder to bear: the strong, capable woman who had never allowed emotion to overcome her, and who had hitherto been equal to every situation, silently bowed her head and wept.

Edith mingled her tears with those of her mother; for both women suffered cruelly. There was then re-enacted in their souls the old history of the incomprehension of the Synagogue who believed her faith in the One God betrayed by the Incarnation, and the pain of the Church, so poignantly felt by St. Paul, of being unable to make her see the new light of this God made Man.

To Edith's family her conversion was utterly inexplicable. They sought in vain for an explanation, and finally suspected that an unhappy love affair must be at the bottom of it, an idea which shows how far they were from understanding. For though her disappointment in Freiburg may have made her more receptive to the Call of Christ when it came, she was the last person merely to seek refuge in the Church from some emotional upheaval. Her writings are enough to make one realize how deeply thought out was her faith, and her whole subsequent apostolic and sacrificial life could never have been built on any but the firmest and most secure foundation of complete conviction.

How deep was her grief at the incomprehension of her family is shown by a remark she once made to one of her pupils: 'If you have not yet experienced it, you will realize it later: it is one of the greatest sorrows in life to be interiorly separated from those one loves, because they can no longer follow one. But such sorrow is also very fruitful.' And on another occasion, when she was troubled about her mother: 'If one realizes what that means, to be excluded from the Church.'

Therefore she did everything she could to soften the blow she had to inflict on those dearest to her, and to conceal the gulf between them as much as possible. After her conversion she stayed at Breslau for several months; she even used to accompany her mother to the synagogue and followed the Hebrew Psalms in her Latin Breviary, so that Frau Stein was much impressed by the deep recollection of her daughter's prayer. She made a point of taking part in all the family's interests, of playing with the children and sharing their amusements, so as to make them feel that her love for them was undiminished, despite the inevitable interior separation.

Besides devoting herself to her family and finding God in prayer, Edith carried on a certain amount of literary work, making the *Philosophical Foundations of Psychology* ready for the Press, and began to think about arranging her life more in keeping with her ever-increasing desire for prayer and mortification.

CHAPTER SIX

FROM LECTURER TO
CONVENT SCHOOL TEACHER

FROM the moment of Edith's conversion her one desire had been to give herself entirely to God in Carmel. But the shattering effect her conversion had had on her mother showed her that she could not think of following her vocation for the time being. As she herself expressed it: 'She would not die of it, but it would fill her with a bitterness for which I could not be responsible.'[1] Moreover, Canon Schwind was against it, because in his view her vocation lay elsewhere; her outstanding philosophical gifts made it imperative that she should stay in the world in order to imbue German philosophy with the Catholic spirit. He understood, however, that she desired to live in a more Christian atmosphere than was possible at Freiburg University; that the most important thing for her at the moment was to settle down in the Church, to adjust her thought to the *philosophia perennis*, and to familiarize herself with daily Catholic life.

It was providential that just as Canon Schwind was casting about for a suitable post for her, the Dominican Third Order Sisters at Speyer were looking for a graduate teacher of German language and literature for the upper forms of their girls' school. They had made a new foundation elsewhere and so were short of staff. When they spoke to Canon Schwind about their difficulty he saw at once that this was the right place for the new convert. At Speyer, this charming medieval city on the Rhine, a little off the beaten track of tourists, she would be in the peaceful atmosphere of a religious house. There she would soon accustom herself to all the externals of Catholic life, and, more important still, she would come

---

[1] *Life*, p. 120. If only one page number is given, pages are identical in the German and English editions unless otherwise stated.

to know also the inner springs of this life as lived in the vowed
dedication to God.

There was the further consideration that, with her brilliant
intellectual gifts, her educational duties would not demand an
inordinate amount of time, and that she would there find sufficient
leisure to study Catholic philosophy. When she discussed matters
with the Prioress, she asked to be allowed to live in the convent.
She was given a small, simple room, containing only the bare
necessities: a bed, an old-fashioned washstand and wardrobe, a
writing-table, a bookshelf, a few chairs—none of the amenities
of modern life. She was served her meals on a tray from the
convent kitchen, and even her clothes came to be made by the
nuns. Once she was delighted when she could present herself in
a clumsy cream-coloured blouse and black skirt which had been
produced from cloth used for the nuns' habits.

Thus her life was to all intents and purposes like that of the
religious, only much more austere. She mortified herself severely,
especially with regard to food and sleep; she was always first
in church in the morning. In the beginning she took her place
in chapel with the other secular staff behind the girls; but her
desire for recollection and for being near the altar led her to make
the request to be given another seat. So she was assigned a
special, velvet-covered kneeling bench within the sanctuary in
front of the nuns, which she did not even have to leave for
receiving Holy Communion—a fact commented on by some of
her pupils. There she would spend every day long hours in
prayer, kneeling upright and motionless like a statue.

This posture in prayer again and again struck those who saw
her. A priest who knew her well once compared it to the old
representations of the Orante, except for the hands, which were,
of course, not stretched out. It was almost rigid, 'unloosened',
as it were, and perhaps may be taken as symbolic of her spiritual
life in these early years. For it should never be forgotten that
Edith Stein was the daughter of a deeply religious Jewish mother,
whom she greatly admired, and who represented to perfection
the unbending austerity of the Old Law.

Old Frau Stein's severe religious pattern remained her example
for many years; hence her way of praying in this tense physical
attitude was the fitting expression of the spirituality of the new

Christian, who had met Christ the Lord—*Christus der Herr*, as she loved to call Him—in His Church, but who had not yet fully fathomed the mystery of the glorious freedom of the children of God. This lack of perfect freedom may also partly account for the complaint made by not a few of her pupils of those years, that she was somewhat unapproachable. One of them, who felt drawn to the religious life, wanted to discuss the matter with her; but when she was actually before her door she was so nervous that she turned back without having asked her. Another one writes of her: 'Fräulein Doktor was somewhat unapproachable— she was too far above us. Indeed, she was too clever and too great a personality. Thus we all were peculiarly shy of her.'[1]

This great intellectual superiority, which made itself felt despite her extremely simple and unassuming manner, might have been counterbalanced if she had been gay and lively. Indeed, she could be light-hearted at times; but this side of her nature was seldom allowed to come to the fore, and in these first years after her conversion, when she was still spiritually strained, it was practically unnoticeable. Her very attitude in the schoolroom was expressive of this calm, unruffled, and at the same time tense concentration that marked both the philosopher and the contemplative, but that would often put up a barrier between her and her pupils. She always taught standing motion- less, below the platform that carried the desk, one arm resting lightly on the latter or against the blackboard; she would never sit down or allow herself to take up another, more comfortable position. Perhaps this attitude was a reflexion of an incident in the life of the great St. Teresa, which had made a deep impression on her. When the saint became Prioress of the Convent of the Incarnation at Avila, she placed a statue of our Lady in the seat of the Prioress and sat down at her feet. It would be in keeping with Edith's love of symbolism if she imitated her patron saint in this way. She used to speak in a low voice, which was practi- cally never raised, and held the attention of the girls solely through her way of presenting the subject-matter, and especially through the deep impression her personality made on her pupils. For though they were a little afraid of her, they had great confi- dence in her justice and discretion; she would never allow any

[1] *Life*, p. 77; 74.

personal likes or dislikes to influence her judgement, nor would she hurt their feelings by ridiculing their work or their opinions.

If she thought it necessary she could, however, be severe. Both her intellectual genius and her immense will-power made it sometimes a little difficult for her to show forbearance to those less gifted, and her remarks could occasionally be scathing. One of her pupils, a very industrious and ambitious young girl, had injured her right wrist just the day before they were to write an essay. Naturally she thought the accident would be sufficient excuse for her. When she told Edith Stein about it she calmly looked at her and simply said: 'Well, then you will try with your left hand.' The unfortunate girl was dumbfounded—but she later said herself that if Edith Stein had been in her place she would never have thought of holding herself excused and would have used her other hand as a matter of course. Another time the same girl had followed the advice given them by a previous mistress and adorned her essay with many citations. Edith Stein wrote underneath: 'The use of quotations proves that *other people* are clever.' Certainly true—but one can understand that the cool sarcasm of a remark like this would put off some girls and make them feel that they could never live up to her standards.

For we must never forget that these standards were really university standards. Even as a child Edith herself had always been far more mature than most of her school friends, and having been used to teaching undergraduates—and often finding even them very childish—she simply could not adapt herself to the mentality of very ordinary young girls. She treated them like grown-ups, and though they did their best to live up to her ideas, they found it a bit of a strain and could not behave quite naturally with her. Thus they all respected and admired her, but some of them, at least, found her difficult. Hence the admiration she inspired was sometimes not without criticism. Her very perfection was too much for some of the girls—if they could only have detected a flaw in her they would have liked her much better. This total absence of flaws extended also to her dress. However unfashionable it might be, she never tolerated the slightest spot or speck of dust on it. Girls who were themselves exuberant and full of mischief were naturally somewhat exasperated by this

almost superhuman perfection and would have preferred her to
have lost her temper—or at least a hairpin—occasionally.

Nor was this irritation, which her quiet, somewhat self-
contained impeccability could inspire, confined to her pupils.
One day a director of education came to inspect the school and
assisted at one of her lessons. He gave as his opinion: 'She knows
much, but she cannot teach.' This criticism was not wholly
without foundation. It was just the time when, in the twenties,
the German educational system was reformed by the introduction
of the new methods of *Arbeitsunterricht*, the chief feature of which
was that the teacher was supposed to contribute as little as possible
by lecturing himself, and to content himself with something like
the role of the chairman of a discussion, i.e. guiding the conversation of the pupils so that they would find the desired results themselves. Edith Stein had not only never been trained in this
method, but also was by temperament and profession a lecturer
rather than a school teacher, so that this new form of teaching was
quite foreign to her.

The verdict of the inspector upset her very much. Up to this
time she had never come face to face with any serious criticism
of her work; she had been almost universally admired, and
though this admiration had never made her conceited, yet it had
given her an unobtrusive self-assurance, very natural to such an
outstanding intellect, but which may have presented an obstacle
to the full development of the life of grace. However, she took the
criticism quietly and bore no resentment.

Though she struck some of her pupils as unapproachable, she
entered as far as possible into their joys and interests. The very
subjects she would give them for composition showed that she
tried to make work as attractive to them as she could. 'In the
Cinema,' is one of the titles, 'A Woman's Life in the Middle
Ages' another. The themes she set the girls in the upper school,
who were preparing to become teachers, sometimes reflect her
own views and aspirations; for example: 'Everyone who Thirsts
for Truth finds its Source in all his Ways' or 'If One Desires to
Direct Others Well, One Must be Capable of Giving up Many
Things.' She herself would work out each subject carefully
beforehand.

Outside school hours, too, she was always at the disposal of both pupils and nuns. She was ever ready to listen to them when they wanted advice or sympathy, though the frequent knocks on her door meant constant interruption of her work, so that her only undisturbed hours were late at night. She never showed impatience, but always received callers with the same peaceful kindness. Yet she rarely dropped her innate reserve. *Secretum meum mihi*—she had given herself wholly to God, but she had not yet reached the fullness of charity where every strain is released. She was still the virgin who keeps herself for the Lord; she had not yet attained to the summit where the virgin becomes the mother who can freely give herself to others, and by thus giving becomes herself more and more enriched.

Her natural reserve and dignity ensured perfect discipline among her pupils, who were all the more delighted when it was sometimes slightly relaxed. Once the girls had acted a play, and at the end there was an improvised procession through the hall; all the actresses except one were walking in pairs, but the one without a partner did not know what to do. So Edith, the only secular teacher present, quickly joined in, quite unself-conscious, to the great delight of both girls and nuns. One afternoon she had arranged to read a play of the Antichrist, not, as usual, in the classroom, but in a park near the Rhine. This play contained an often recited verse: 'People of destruction, I will destroy thee.' Now, as they were reading, they were molested by a pest of mosquitoes. At last, as it was becoming unbearable, Edith drew herself up and shouted at them with comic pathos: 'People of destruction, I will destroy thee.' Needless to say the reading ended in uproarious mirth.

This combination of intellectual superiority with austerity, recollection, and occasional flashes of humour gave her a lasting influence not only on the pupils, but also on the sisters, especially the younger ones. In fact, it can be said without exaggeration that she became something almost like an unofficial novice mistress to the latter. It says much for her natural tact as well as for her supernatural endowment that she slipped into this extraordinary position almost without attracting any attention to the strangeness of the situation. On the contrary—and this is also a great credit to the enlightened outlook of the community at Speyer and of its Prioress in particular—she was allowed not only to teach the young sisters Latin, but also to give them conferences on spiritual matters. Only once did she overshoot the mark, when she suggested in an address given to the community that it would be a good idea to let the pupils participate more in the religious life of the convent by allowing them to attend the Offices. Though perhaps justified in itself, this suggestion was resented, especially by the older nuns, as an interference with the customs of the house on the part of a member of the secular staff. But the very fact that she could venture such a suggestion without any serious consequences for her position shows how greatly she must have been esteemed by the community.

The nuns were well aware that this exceptional position was not due to any desire on her part to put herself in the foreground or to teach others their business. Quite the contrary. All who knew her in these years invariably stress her silence, which went so far that she often let people talk on for a long time, even if they were talking nonsense and she could easily have put them right. This silence could sometimes even be a source of irritation; her friends were puzzled and did not know what to make of it. She realized, however, that in order to get to know people one must let them talk on and voice their opinions, however mistaken they may be. And then it would happen that, after the other speakers had exhausted their arguments, she would sum up the discussion and give her own opinion simply and lucidly. Thus, frequently both pupils and nuns, who had at first been put off by her remoteness, found that, when they came to know her better, she lost her inaccessibility and could be a kind, reliable friend.

It appears already in these early years after her baptism that the Holy Ghost must have infused into her, together with His gift of Wisdom, also that of Counsel in rich measure. Grace builds on nature—her calm, detached philosopher's mind was certainly an ideal natural soil in which to plant the more contemplative of the seven gifts. In her long hours of prayer, when she was kneeling motionless before the tabernacle, these baptismal gifts grew in the contemplation of the mysteries of the faith. For though she was very reticent about her prayer, it is clear from her own writings that it was nourished by scripture and

the teaching of the Church. 'Little devotions' were foreign to
her large and penetrating mind; as her later director, Archabbot
Walzer of Beuron, expresses it in a letter to the present author:
'Her spiritual food consisted of pure theology.'

CHAPTER SEVEN

PUPIL OF ST. THOMAS

URING her first years at Speyer Edith had practically ceased to do systematic philosophical work. As she herself says in the Foreword to *Endliches und Ewiges Sein*, in these early days after her conversion 'nothing was further from my mind than the thought of a public career. I had found the way to Christ and His Church, and was occupied with drawing the practical consequences.' But she continues that 'the desire soon made itself felt to come to know the intellectual foundations of this [Catholic] world'.[1]

At this point another influence entered her life, which played an important part in her intellectual development during the next years. Through Canon Schwind she was brought into touch with the well-known Jesuit theologian, Father Erich Przywara, himself a highly original thinker, with whom she remained in constant exchange of ideas from 1925 to 1931. Father Przywara, with his mind always wide open to new interests, was not slow to throw out suggestions to her that were to bear much fruit. He was at the time planning to bring out a German translation of Cardinal Newman's works, together with the Benedictine, Dom Daniel Feuling, and so he asked her to contribute some volumes. At the same time he stated his ideal of a translation: 'not a so-called "translation according to sense", but a severely objective one according to the letter, even aiming at preserving the rhythm of the sentences and the order of words. . . . Edith Stein knew at once what I wanted, because it was her own idea.'[2]

The translation she produced, of Newman's *Letters and Journals* from 1801 to his conversion in 1845, is indeed a fine piece of work, precise and readable, with only an occasional flaw here and there. It fully comes up to Fr. Przywara's requirements in that it even

[1] p. viii.   [2] *Die Besinnung*, Glock and Lutz, Nürnberg, 1952, pp. 238 f.

preserves some Anglicisms, and on the whole a less strict adherence to English word-order and idioms might have improved it. The translation must have been a labour of love for her, as it showed the way into the Church of one who was to become one of her greatest sons in recent times, and the workings of grace in a soul as generous as her own, though otherwise very different. It was later followed by another volume, *The Idea of a University*.

While she was engaged on this work, Fr. Przywara came to Speyer to discuss details. He himself describes their meeting:

> So we had our first conversation in Speyer, under the auspices of the unforgettable, wise and kindly Vicar-General Dr. Schwind. Dr. Schwind told me at once that I was going to have a surprise: for he had never met anyone whose looks betrayed her race as little as those of Edith Stein. He was right; for the woman who met us might rather be compared to the statue of Uta in Naumburg Cathedral.[1] . . . This was indeed a very special trait of Edith Stein— she came from absolutely pure Jewish blood and was yet a true German woman. . . . From this sprang the really great style of Edith Stein: classical, philosophical austerity (of which her intellectual union of Husserl with Thomas was the principal symbol), and deeply artistic feeling, for which Bach, Reger, and the classical plain chant of the Church were the great signs.[2]

This first meeting between the future Carmelite and the brilliant Jesuit, who immediately conceived a great admiration for her, was to have very important consequences. For Edith consulted him on her future philosophical work and on the best way to make herself acquainted with scholastic thought. He told her not to go to manuals and interpreters, but straight to St. Thomas himself. In his view this course would be the most profitable not only for herself, but also for contemporary philosophy in general. It was bound to show the immediate effect of Thomist thought on a mind steeped in modern philosophy; at the same time it might very probably result in a work that would present the mind of scholasticism in a form both intelligible and acceptable to contemporary thinkers. He therefore suggested that she should translate St. Thomas's *Quaestiones disputatae de Veritate*, of which there existed no German version.

[1] A famous statue of a German medieval lady.   [2] *Die Besinnung*, 1952, pp. 239f.

Beuron

*Two photographs of
Edith Stein at Speyer*

When she went to one of the priests at Speyer to borrow a copy of the work there was an outcry. She came back from her expedition very much amused by the attitude of the theologian in question. She, a recent convert from Judaism, and, worse, a phenomenologist and disciple of Husserl, translate St. Thomas? Such a thing was unheard of and could only end in heresy! But Edith, in her quiet way, prevailed. She got the copy out of the priest and set herself to work.

She herself describes how profoundly disconcerting was this first meeting between the Prince of the Schoolmen and the young exponent of phenomenology.

> When I began to study the works of Aquinas I was constantly troubled by the question: according to which method does he proceed? I had been accustomed to the phenomenological method, which uses no traditional teaching but examines everything that is needed for the solution of a question *ab ovo*. I was baffled by a procedure that adduces sometimes Scriptural passages, sometimes citations from the Fathers, or again sayings of the old philosophers in order to deduce results from them. Yet one gets the impression that this procedure is by no means 'unmethodical'.... Its reliability is proved by the wealth of results achieved in this way.[1]

After being a teacher and holding 'philosophical kindergarten', she had once more become a pupil, patiently and reverently following a master very different from those who had been her masters before, and in no way more so than in that he himself acknowledged an authority above him. Against the *Sed hoc est contra fidem*—'but this is against faith'—there is no further argument, however cleverly thought out. All Edith Stein's prayer before her conversion had been for truth; in the *Life* of St. Teresa she had ultimately become convinced of where Truth was to be found; now, in the great work of the *Doctor Communis Ecclesiae* she was led to its metaphysical foundations.

There is a humility of behaviour, expressed especially in the taking of the last place, as Christ teaches in the Gospel; there is also a humility of the mind, willing to be taught and accepting correction even in things that one believed one knew quite well. It was this latter humility that must have been the most difficult to achieve for a woman like Edith Stein; it sounds like the echo

[1] *Endliches und Ewiges Sein*, p. 489.

of an interior struggle when she writes in her Foreword to her
later work on Being: 'At an age when others can dare to call
themselves teacher, the author was compelled to start again from
the beginning.' But a few lines further on she can write with
conviction: 'St. Thomas found a reverent and willing disciple.'[1]
She continues, however, 'my intellect was no *tabula rasa*, it had
already received a definite formation that could not deny itself.
The two philosophical worlds that met in me demanded to be
confronted and discussed.'[2]

This confrontation she undertook in a very interesting essay
she contributed to a symposium presented to Husserl on his
seventieth birthday in 1929.[3] She had originally written it as a
dialogue between the Prince of the Schoolmen and the father of
the Phenomenologists, but complied with the wish of Martin
Heidegger to change it into a straightforward article. We will
give the introduction of the original 'Dialogue'[4] because it shows
her sense of humour.

> Time: 8 April 1929, late at night. Husserl (alone). 'The good people
> really did mean well with their kind wishes—certainly I should not
> have liked to miss anyone. But after such a day it is difficult to find
> rest, and I have always insisted on a good night's sleep. Indeed, after
> all this small talk I wish I could now enjoy a really good philosophical
> discussion so that my brain would get straightened out.' (A knock
> at the door.) 'What, so late? Come in, please!' (A religious in a
> white habit and black mantle enters): 'Please excuse the nocturnal
> disturbance, professor. But I heard your last words, and so thought I
> might still venture to come.'

Then the two philosophers begin their discussion.

She starts with the difficulty of finding a way from the intellectual world of Husserl to that of St. Thomas, a difficulty which
she herself had experienced to the full. Yet there is a *philosophia
perennis* not only in the sense of the Aristotelian-Thomist system,
but in the sense of 'the spirit of genuine philosophizing which is
alive in every true philosopher, that is to say in everyone who,
by an interior necessity, is irresistibly drawn to investigate the

---

[1] p. viii.   [2] ibid.
[3] *Husserls Phänomenologie und die Philosophie des hl. Thomas von Aquino*. Versuch einer
Gegenüberstellung. 1929.
[4] With kind permission of the Husserl Archives at Louvain where the MS. is preserved.

logos or the *ratio* (as St. Thomas translated it) of this world'.[1] Both St. Thomas and Edmund Husserl were impelled by this interior necessity; but the great difference between them was that 'for Husserl *ratio* meant never anything but *natural reason*, whereas Thomas distinguishes between natural and *supernatural reason*'.

By excluding the supernatural factor from their thought, modern philosophers have intolerably limited their field of knowledge. For there is a knowledge that apprehends the whole truth, and this is the Divine knowledge. From the fullness of His knowledge God can impart to created spirits according to their capacity; and He can do that not only by the way of natural knowledge, but also by the way of faith. Edith Stein has to admit that this way of seeing things is totally foreign to modern philosophy, for which faith could never be a way of apprehending truth. With great perspicacity she traces this refusal to make a place for faith in the system of knowledge to the Protestant conception of faith as a feeling or something similarly 'irrational', which goes back to Luther. 'If faith had meant that for St. Thomas,' she writes, 'he, too, would not have given it a voice in philosophical discussions.'[2] But, she continues, 'a rational understanding of the world, that is to say a metaphysics . . . can be obtained only through the co-operation between natural and supernatural reason. The fact that this was no longer understood is responsible for the abstruse character of all modern metaphysics and, consequently, for the rejection of metaphysics by modern thinkers.' And, conversely, we may add that the comparative lucidity of Edith Stein's own metaphysics is due precisely to her acceptance of the supernatural knowledge of faith as indispensable for approaching the problem of being in all its ramifications.

She herself is fully conscious of this advantage of the Catholic philosopher when she writes: 'The philosopher whose foundation is the faith *possesses* from the very beginning the absolute certitude which one needs in order to build with safety; whereas the others have first to look for a point of departure; and so it is quite natural that in modern philosophy the theory of knowledge (rather than metaphysics) became the fundamental discipline. . . . This happened also to Husserl.'[3]

[1] p. 316.   [2] p. 319.   [3] p. 322.

And so the disciple has to part company with her old master. For, as she writes at the end of the treatise: 'Husserl seeks the "absolute" point of departure in the immanence of consciousness, for Thomas it is the faith.'[1]

The original 'dialogue', however, had ended on a different note. 'We shall see each other again,' says St. Thomas, 'and then we shall understand each other perfectly.'

Because the two worlds of modern and medieval philosophy were so foreign to each other, she could not approach her translation of St. Thomas's *De Veritate* simply as a translator rendering the text in another medium, but she had to act also as a philosopher interpreting it to her colleagues. She saw that modern readers would be puzzled by the medieval form which first states a series of objections, then a counter-argument, after this the master's own exposition, and lastly a detailed refutation of the objections. As the late Professor Grabmann, one of the most authoritative modern Thomist scholars, points out in his Foreword to the translation, this method 'does not appeal to the modern mind which is only interested in the objective contents, and it is more congenial to Latin than to German'. He therefore considered that she had been well advised to begin each 'article' with the fundamental solution of the problem and to reproduce only the most important objections with their answers.

It would have been almost miraculous if by this procedure she had really achieved a perfectly faithful translation, as Fr. Przywara claimed when he wrote in *Stimmen der Zeit*: 'It is everywhere Thomas, and only Thomas.' Thomist scholars have pointed out not a few serious mistranslations, though she had been assured by some of them, as she writes in her Preface, that the translation as a whole was faithful. However, Josef Piper says in discussing one of her mistakes: 'This shows how difficult it is for a mind trained in modern philosophy to grasp the fundamental ideas of the old ontology.'[2]

This difficulty was aggravated by the fact that she had never before studied scholasticism at all; in omitting to do so she only

[1] p. 338.
[2] *Wahrheit der Dinge* (Truth of Things), note 48, p. 126. 'The reader without knowledge of the original who looks at the only German translation of *Quaestiones Disputatae de Veritate* is at a disadvantage, since the translator, Edith Stein, the disciple of Husserl, has completely missed the mark of the fundamental First Article not only in her explanations but in the translation itself.'

followed Fr. Przywara's advice, but it is at least doubtful whether this counsel was wise. Nevertheless the work was no mean achievement and was hailed as such on its appearance. For even though it did not come up to the standards of the specialists, it formed a very valuable introduction to scholastic thought for those modern scholars who were unacquainted with medieval philosophy. By translating the language of the schools into their own idiom and supplying a short commentary to most articles, in which she confronts St. Thomas with Husserl, Heidegger, and other contemporary thinkers, Edith Stein made the classic Christian philosophy available to many who would otherwise have remained ignorant of it, and so combined her vocation of a scholar with that of an apostle.

CHAPTER EIGHT

SPIRITUAL LIFE AND INFLUENCE

S o far we have spoken of Edith Stein only as a teacher and philosopher; but it is quite possible that these sides of her, though the most noticeable in the eyes of the world, weighed but lightly in the sight of God. For there was another Edith Stein beneath the *Fräulein Doktor*, the one destined one day to be called Teresa Benedicta of the Cross. The woman who spent long hours every day before the tabernacle knew that at the heart of the Christian life there is not learning, however exalted, but love. It is sometimes difficult to realize that this fine intellect that grappled with the most intricate problems of being belonged to a woman capable of deep tenderness and sympathy. Fr. Przywara calls it: 'The double nature of her spiritual being: large feminine receptivity and companionship coupled with severe masculine objectivity.'[1]

This struck everyone who knew her well. One of the nuns at Speyer, to whom she had been a tutor and later a close friend, writes of her:

> In the philosophical works she is often of an almost uncanny lucidity and depth; but the most fundamental trait of her character was surely a warm love that could penetrate into another's mind, suffering with him, and helping him as only a Christ-centred saint is able to do. You ought to have seen the crowds of those who came to her for help, the poor and the sick, and specially those who sought advice in spiritual anxieties. Many priests regarded her as an 'oracle', for she was a refuge of despairing souls, and never was anything too much or too difficult for her when it was a case of helping someone. And she was often able to help where even priests and spiritual directors had given up all hope.

Even if we allow for some exaggeration in this glowing account,

[1] *Die Besinnung*, p. 239.

due to the unbounded admiration she inspired in some of her friends, enough is left to show the picture of a very remarkable apostolic soul.

Her readiness to help others found many opportunities. On 17 September 1927 the priest who had been her director ever since her conversion died suddenly in the confessional of a heart attack. Canon Schwind had been a much beloved priest with a large correspondence. Edith, far from giving in to her own grief, realized that owing to the unexpectedness of his death, there would probably be a great number of confidential letters lying about in his desk which might easily be tampered with by some indiscreet person. As she had been given the run of his flat during his lifetime, she at once went there and returned all the letters that had remained unanswered to their senders, accompanied, where necessary, by a short note. It was the last personal service she could do for this trusted friend and guide, for whom she wrote a beautiful obituary notice in the *Innsbruck Clerical Review*. The death of her director was certainly a great loss to her; but she took it in a thoroughly Christian spirit and a few weeks later could write to a friend: 'Please do not imagine the sorrows too great and the joys too small. Heaven takes away nothing without making up for it immeasurably.' Little though she would divulge of her spiritual life, it is clear from this that she enjoyed great consolations.

Naturally she helped the poor of Speyer as much as possible; she used to give away whatever she could, not only clothes but also books; and her friends were often astonished when she came to church once more with a different missal because she had just given away the one she possessed. She had made the three vows of religion privately, and her vow of poverty enabled her to give to others what she would not use for herself. Indeed, she needed extremely little for herself; therefore her modest salary left her sufficient for almsgiving. She also knew how to give in the case of those who were not poor. She never forgot anyone's birthday or feast, and before Christmas there used to be great excitement in her room: no end of parcels were being neatly packed up, after long and loving deliberation as to what present would give most joy to its recipient.

It might seem almost as if these were years of uninterrupted effort, of continual exhausting educational and intellectual work at high pressure, without any relaxation. But unrelaxed strain must always result in a breakdown in one form or another—and there has never been any trace of such in her life. She knew that even she needed a holiday from time to time, and she took it as naturally as she took her work.

In the long summer vacation she almost always went home to Breslau to her family. There she did everything she could to heal the wound which her conversion had necessarily left in the heart of her mother, to whom she never omitted to write her weekly letter despite her crushing load of work. When she came home she showed a lively interest in her business; for Frau Stein never abandoned her position as head of the firm despite her years. Edith's magnificent memory helped her here; she remembered the names of all her mother's customers and their relations with the firm, and never failed to ask the right questions, so that her mother could talk about all her affairs with her and be sure that her daughter gave as much attention to them as to a philosophical discussion. During these holidays she used to see her friends, both old and new; but it was one of her great sorrows that her beloved Rose, now Mrs. Bluhm, the companion of her first term at Göttingen, could not follow her into the Church. As Mrs. Bluhm herself writes: 'We spent many hours talking about religion; it would have been a great joy to her, had I been able to become a convert; she was (since she loved me dearly) sorry that I could not find my way there.'[1]

Though at Breslau she would rest, at least part of the time, from her intellectual labours, the very fact that her family and her dearest friends were poles apart from what had now become the most absorbing interest and love of her life must have put an emotional strain on her that did not allow of complete repose of the whole person. But there was one place where she could find recreation in the truest sense of the term, a re-creation of both mind and emotions, and this place was the Benedictine Abbey of Beuron, one of the liturgical centres of Germany.

It was again Fr. Przywara who suggested this monastery, whose abbot, the young and brilliant Dom Walzer, was his friend, when she asked him for a convent where she could retire for a private

[1] Letter to the present writer.

retreat from time to time. She went there for the first time in Holy Week, 1928.

Beuron is an enchanting place and she loved it as soon as she got there. When the traveller leaves the train at the small station a wonderful peace seems to descend on him. The abbey stands in the green valley of the Danube, at this point a stream of modest size with a peculiar charm of its own; it is surrounded by mountains covered with dark forests, which are interrupted by shining white rocks—a perfect setting, in its natural loveliness, for the majestic liturgy celebrated within. As one walks along the walls of the monastery in the shadow of the old trees towards the door of the abbey church, the noise and cares of the world slip away. One can imagine Edith Stein, after the last exhausting weeks of Easter reports and conferences, slowly walking along, ascending the stone steps, and thankfully falling on her knees before the tabernacle in the large Baroque church, drinking in the *Pax Benedictina* which so palpably fills the whole place.

For long hours she used to pray before the austere Pietà, the miraculous old image, as if she knew that one day she would be allowed to share the grief of the Mother of Sorrows, Rachel weeping for her children. And, strangely enough, on the walls there were pictures not only of Christian saints, but also of the great heroines of her own people: Esther, the queen for whom she had a particular devotion, and Judith, who triumphed over Israel's enemies.

There was more than this. For the first time in her life she was able to follow the central events on which our faith rests in the way the Church herself follows them in her liturgy. The singing of the Passion by monks whose principal work in life is the celebration of the liturgy is a very different thing in its presentation, though not in its essence, from the same service performed in an ordinary parish church. For the first time she was allowed to attend the long Tenebrae services with their atmosphere of approaching tragedy, when one by one the fifteen candles are extinguished; the plaintive chanting of the Lamentations, the penetrating cry *Mortem autem Crucis* at the end, and the *Miserere* murmured in complete darkness, which are the incomparable setting for the Masses of Maundy Thursday and Good Friday. These gave to her mind, which was so exceptionally receptive to the beauty of austerity, spiritual food that satisfied her perfectly.

During the night from Maundy Thursday to Good Friday she would watch immovable before the Altar of Repose, lost in contemplation of the mystery of the death of God made man. In these days of the mourning Church she kept perfect silence, as well as a strict fast, and she reduced her sleep to a minimum, rising at three in the morning, if she did not spend the whole night in prayer. On Good Friday she would remain the entire day, without any interruption, in the abbey church. The mere physical exertion would seem almost an impossibility; but it must be remembered that such was also the practice of devout Jews on the Day of Atonement. She had seen her mother do the same—should not she herself do it for Christ on the day when He worked the Redemption of the world?

But when Good Friday was past and the Lord had risen, when the first Alleluias of Easter had been chanted, Edith Stein, too, would emerge from the sorrows of Holy Week into the radiant joy of the Resurrection. Her whole being seemed to be lit up by the wonder of this glorious mystery, the centre of the faith, which she must have lived the more deeply, as it was precisely this that had ultimately separated the Church from the Synagogue, the Apostles, witnesses of the Resurrection, from the unbelieving Jews for whom His life ended with the Crucifixion. This was the glory of the Messias, sung by the Prophets and misunderstood by the people; this was the seal of the Redemption—not from foreign oppressors and captivity, but from the oppression and captivity of sin.

Immediately after this first visit to Beuron she had to give an address to the Catholic women teachers of Bavaria on the specific function of woman in the national life, the opening words of which reflect the deep impression these days of Retreat had left in her.

Permit me [she said] to begin with a few personal words. Two days ago I left Beuron, where I was privileged to spend Holy Week and Easter, and came here to Ludwigshafen straight into the preparations for this Congress. A greater contrast could hardly be imagined: there the silent valley of peace, where the praise of the

Lord is chanted regardless of anything that happens in the world out-side—and this assembly which has met to discuss the burning ques-tions of our time. That was almost like a plunge from heaven to earth. But just this contrast is perhaps a symbol of the task that has been laid upon us all. . . . Passiontide and Easter are not meant to express simply a transitory festive mood quickly submerged in the daily humdrum; no, they are the Divine power living in us, which we take with us into our professional life so that it may be leavened by it.

With this leaven of Paschal joy something else was given her at Beuron. Canon Schwind's death had left her without a director; she found another in Abbot Walzer, who became a real spiritual father to her, so that her saying 'Beuron is my home' was true in more senses than one. Abbot Walzer recog-nized not only her deep spirituality, but also her great maturity. Between them there could be no question of a relationship such as sometimes exists between director and spiritual daughter, of the one laying down the law to the other, inventing trials and tests and demanding unquestioning obedience. He knew that he had before him a soul who had found her way under the guidance of the Holy Ghost, who needed no more than to be encouraged in this way. The only matter on which he gave her definite guidance in opposition to her own desires was her attraction to the religious life. Here he took the same line as Canon Schwind before him: her work in the world was too important to be given up; this was the apostolate to which the Lord had called her, and which she ought not to leave even for the heights of Carmel.

One of Edith's most remarkable characteristics was her perfect docility to the Church and whoever represented its authority; so she did not demur, though she found obedience difficult. For the effort to combine exacting intellectual and teaching work with an intense spiritual life did place a great strain on her; and this probably also accounts for some of the unapproachableness and remoteness of these years. However, she was quite willing to continue carrying the burden, if such was the will of God. But at Beuron, at least, she was free from this strain, in an atmosphere of prayer and the company of contemplatives. It is therefore not surprising that those who saw her at Beuron emphasize how different she seemed there from her everyday self at Speyer. Except for the intense days of prayer and penance during Holy Week, she was much gayer, much freer in this congenial monastic atmosphere; and when their strictly spiritual conversations were over, she and Abbot Walzer would sometimes rag each other like children, and the serious *Fräulein Doktor* of Speyer would be transformed into a merry, light-hearted woman, whose interior joy was for once allowed to express itself in unrestrained playfulness. Here, at Beuron, she would recuperate spiritually, so that she could emerge once more into the daily round of activities with fresh energy and endurance.

But this lighter side of her was reserved for only the very few. Even at Beuron her austerity and remoteness caused comment among the other ladies who spent Holy Week at the abbey. They resented it that Edith was always the first in church, that she ate less than anyone else, and hence was also the first to rise from table. Her very intensity caused her to be regarded as singular. Nor was this impression confined to lay people. For she occasionally allowed herself to judge others by her own standards. One incident that happened in the presence of two young religious is characteristic. Many years later one of them still remembered it and gave a lively description.

Praying [she writes] was no effort for her, and I had the impression that it was not difficult for her to remain in a motionless position. Once her somewhat inhuman manner annoyed me. She visited Sr. C. and myself when she was travelling through Würzburg, in the middle of July. We decided to celebrate the Feast of Our Lady of Mount Carmel (16 July) with the Carmelites of Himmelspforten, near Würzburg. After our midday meal we walked in very hot weather to the Carmelite convent, which was three quarters of an hour's distance. We arrived soaked in perspiration and went at once into the church where there was Exposition of the Blessed Sacrament. The Carmelites were just saying None in choir, then the Rosary, then Vespers and Compline. After that we paid a short visit to the Mother Prioress, then there were devotions at four and Matins and Lauds were said at five.[1] On account of the many candles the air in the church was so thick you could have cut it with a knife. When, after the devotions, Dr. Stein still remained motionless, I

---

[1] A very unusual *horarium*, if the Sister remembers rightly.

went out to have a little fresh air, though even outside it was hot enough. Dr. Stein and Sr. C. followed me, but I realized that the former did not like it. At first we walked several times up and down in the shadow of a wall, then Dr. Stein said: 'I cannot understand how prayer can make one tired.' She sounded somewhat irritated, and I answered in the same tone: 'Perhaps one may already have been tired because of one's work before one started to pray.' After a few words intended to smooth things over she said she also could not understand how one could meditate sitting down. I took that to be a criticism of the customs of our convent, and so I kept an unpleasant impression of this afternoon—the only one, by the way. On our way back I secretly envied her her 'Jewish toughness' as I angrily called it, which permitted her to kneel before God for hours without getting tired.[1]

Most of us would probably have shared the irritation of Edith Stein's companion. She shows here the same lack of understanding for physical weakness as in the case of her pupil with the injured wrist; only here her conduct is even more surprising, since the nuns were not her pupils. Moreover, she permitted herself to criticize not only them, but also their customs, approved by the Church, because they did not happen to come up to her exaggerated standards. These were undoubtedly due to her education, to the formalism of her ancestral religion which she had not yet completely overcome. She would be shocked to the depths by any even slightly familiar behaviour in church. She was horrified, for example, when once a nun lifted the curtain of a tabernacle to look at the workmanship underneath. It was perhaps in the merciful providence of God that she never went to Italy; her religious sensibility would have been outraged by the ease bordering sometimes on irreverence with which southern Catholics behave in the house of God. She had a sense of the 'sacred' that still betrayed its Old Testament origins; she had not yet found the fullness of the freedom of the children of God.

[1] Letter to the present writer.

CHAPTER NINE

GROWING REPUTATION

URING her first years at Speyer Edith Stein's life had been
rather hidden. Through the school and through her
translation work she was in contact with a good many
people, apart from the old friendships of her university years.
But her name was known only to a comparatively small circle.

Her light, however, was not to remain under a bushel for long.
She was soon asked to lecture on Thomism to priests, and she
also spoke on the same subject to larger audiences, but her
reputation as a lecturer was really established when she began
to talk on questions connected with the position of women in
modern society and in the Church. The suggestion that she
should occupy herself with this subject had once more come
from Fr. Przywara, and it found a ready response in her own
mind. Since she had been a feminist in her youth, the task of
thinking out the problem of the position of women in modern
society in the light of the principles derived from Scripture and
the teaching of the Doctors of the Church was very congenial to
her. After the address, already mentioned, on the function of
woman in the national life (1928), she came to be increasingly
in demand. Her hidden life was at an end, at least for the present;
once more she had to take her place in the midst of the intellectual
world. A letter of hers to one of the nuns at Speyer (dated
12 February 1928) gives an insight into her own attitude to this
change.

> Of course religion is not just something for a quiet corner and a few
> hours of leisure; it must be the root and ground of all life, and this
> not only for a few chosen ones, but for every true Christian (of
> whom, indeed, there is always only a small number). It was through
> St. Thomas that I first came to realize that it is possible to regard
> scholarly work as a service of God. Immediately before, and a long

time after my conversion, I thought living a religious life meant to abandon all earthly things and to live only in the thought of the heavenly realities. Gradually I have learned to understand that in this world something else is demanded of us, and that even in the contemplative life the connexion with this world must not be cut off. Only then did I make up my mind to take up scholarly work again. I even think that the more deeply a soul is drawn into God, the more it must also go out of itself in this sense, that is to say into the world, in order to carry the Divine life into it.

But how, her correspondent had asked, was she able to do this work and yet make sufficient time for prayer?

I do not use any special means [she answers] to prolong my working time. I do as much as I am able. Evidently the ability increases with the number of things that are necessary; if there is nothing urgent it ceases much earlier. Heaven evidently knows all about economy. That in practice things do not work out precisely according to the laws of reason is due to the fact that we are not pure spirits. No use rebelling against it; the chief thing is first to have a quiet corner where one can converse with God as if nothing else existed, and this every day. The early morning seems to me the best time for this, before the daily work begins. Further, I think, this is where one receives one's mission, preferably for each day, without choosing anything oneself. Lastly, one should regard oneself entirely as an instrument, especially those powers with which one has to work, for example in our case one's reason—I mean as an instrument which we do not use ourselves, but God in us. . . . My life begins every morning anew and ends every night; beyond that I have neither plans nor intentions; except that, of course, thinking ahead can be part of one's day's work; work in a school would be impossible without it. But it should never mean being 'solicitous for tomorrow'. Now you will understand that I cannot accept it if you say: 'You have become somebody.' It seems as if the volume of my day's work is going to be enlarged. But this, I think, makes no change in myself. It has been asked of me, and so I have accepted it, though it is not yet clear to me what it will include and what will be the practical means to carry it out.

Her whole character is in these last words. She did what she had been asked to do, without any false humility of not feeling herself equal to the task. The work was given her, God would show her the way to do it, just as she was sure that He would give her the time and the strength necessary for it. She was an instrument in His hands to be used at His good pleasure.

The most important of her lectures was given before an illustrious audience at the Congress of the German Association of Catholic Graduates (*Deutscher Katholischer Akademikerverband*) at Salzburg in 1930, and had as its subject *The Ethos of Women's Vocations*.[1] It was unanimously acclaimed as the highlight of the Congress, and to herself as well as to Abbot Walzer it now became increasingly clear that the classrooms of the convent at Speyer were no longer the sphere where the Lord wanted her. During the Christmas vacation of the same year (1930) she went to Beuron to discuss matters with her director, and at the same time to assist at the baptism of a Jewish friend, for whose conversion she was herself partly responsible. At Beuron it was decided that she should give up her post at Speyer at the end of the school year at Easter 1931, and apply for acceptance as a lecturer (*Privatdozent*) at Freiburg University.

After her return to Speyer she gave notice, much to the regret of the Prioress, and immediately set to work to procure a post at Freiburg. She went there in January 1931, and discussed the matter with various professors, Martin Heidegger among them. The prospects seemed favourable, and so she used her last months at Speyer for working on a great philosophical project which had been in her mind for a long time, a treatise on the relationship between potency and act, which subject had been suggested to her by her Thomist studies.

Parting from Speyer, where she had spent these first formative years of her Catholic life, was a wrench, though perhaps less for herself, who had by now completely outgrown the limitations of a school job, than for the nuns, to many of whom she had become their trusted spiritual guide. Her departure had been kept secret till the very last day. After the girls had sung their traditional farewell song to the form that left school at Easter, Edith Stein got up and told them that this time they had sung it also for herself, because she, too, was leaving St. Magdalena's. There was great consternation and distress among

---

[1] *Das Ethos der Frauenberufe*. The term *Beruf*, which has been translated by vocation, means in German also profession, and both are treated in the lecture.

the girls and those of the nuns who had not known before that she was leaving. For herself things were made easier, because immediately after the school had broken up she fled to Beuron for a few days' recollection, to share once more in the Passion of Christ, in the desolation of Good Friday and the glory of Easter. The time was short, for on Easter Tuesday she had to leave to take part in a teachers' conference at Munich. So she began her total silence sooner than usual, on Palm Sunday, writing to a friend immediately beforehand: 'I enclose in my letter for you even from these first two days (I have been here since Thursday night) a wealth of peace, quiet and love.' After Munich she went home to Breslau, where she intended to stay for some time, with the double purpose of working quietly on her philosophical treatise and of helping her sister Rosa, who had lately been feeling drawn to the Church.

Her mother, whom she loved so deeply and whose favourite child she had always been, had not yet got over Edith's conversion—and now another daughter was contemplating the same step. Edith's presence was badly needed to make things easier; her gift of counsel, which she had so often used in her work for souls, especially for those of her race for whom she had smoothed the way into the Church, was at last needed for one of her own family. God alone knows how many ardent prayers had constantly risen from her heart to obtain the grace of conversion for those nearest to her. Once, as she was paying a visit to the Blessed Sacrament with a friend, she whispered to her: 'Will you now say one decade of the Rosary with me?' and, after a pause, in an even lower voice and very tenderly: 'For my mother.'

Edith desired deeply that her mother should find the wonderful happiness she herself had found in Jesus, the Messias of her people—and now old Frau Stein might be further estranged when she saw yet another daughter give up the faith of her fathers. Was it possible to inflict this second blow on her? In Edith's case her constant absence from Breslau had made things easier; but for Rosa, who was living at home, the situation would be intolerable. Therefore it was decided to delay her baptism until after her mother's death.

This decision, however, often became a source of scruples. Had it really been right to sacrifice the call of Christ to her

6

filial affection? There was no one to whom she could turn in these doubts but Edith, whose calm, spiritual prudence quietened her conscience and soothed her pains. Her influence was especially necessary as just at this time a niece who was living with the Steins adopted an increasingly militant Jewish attitude, so that Rosa found the atmosphere at home almost unbearable. Edith herself could do nothing except to pray both for and with Rosa, and to make some opportunities for her to visit a church and draw strength from the tabernacle, while she herself stayed at home to entertain their mother.

Edith spent almost all this summer at Breslau, apart from a visit to Vienna at the end of May, where she had to lecture on St. Elizabeth of Thuringia. While there she stayed at the house of Professor Rudolf Allers, and it is characteristic of the very retired life she was leading even then, that she refused to take part in any social activities there, except for a visit to the president of the society who had arranged the lectures. Though she had never been in Vienna before, she also refused to do any sightseeing, pleading work. 'Only the very last day,' writes Professor Allers, 'she suddenly admitted that it had been a mistake on her part not to learn something about Vienna (she had claimed that she needed all her time for working), and so Mrs. Allers took her on a rapid tour through the city.'[1]

It is difficult to determine what were the reasons for her missing this opportunity of seeing one of the loveliest cities of Europe. Work can hardly have been the only one. But it would be quite in keeping with her austerity if she had deliberately denied herself the pleasure of carefree roaming about the *Prater*, though she might have excepted the famous cathedral and the art galleries. In any case, she herself admitted that she had made a mistake; perhaps she had just given in to a sudden craving for quiet and solitude, understandable enough if we remember that she had to lecture on a religious subject needing concentration and recollection.

After her return to Breslau, while she was working on her great treatise on potency and act, negotiations were going on for a new post. Besides Freiburg, another possibility had opened up at Münster in Westphalia, where the director of the German

---

[1] Letter to the present writer.

Institute for Educational Theory, Professor Steffes, wanted to secure her as a lecturer on topics of women's education, since there were many women students, but no woman lecturer. The high degree of detachment to which she had already attained at this period of her life is revealed in a characteristic letter.

> I should prefer to come to Freiburg [she writes], when the work [i.e. Potency and Act] is finished. I do not know when that will be. And if the call to the Educational Institute came before, I should perhaps give up the lectureship altogether. After I had started on the work this became immediately much more important to me than any purpose it might ultimately serve. God knows what He has in store for me, I need not worry about it.[1]

A true scholar, her heart was in her work rather than in any advantage this work might bring her. For her philosophizing was a necessity of her very being, and once she had set out to deal with a problem this problem occupied her wholly, regardless of any practical results. While she was quietly working away yet another opening presented itself: a Catholic theologian at Breslau had heard in Rome very favourable judgements on her translation of St. Thomas and thought it might be a good idea if she applied for a lectureship at the university of her native city.

The sequel of this suggestion reveals poignantly the depth and tenderness of the relationship between Edith and her mother, for her first reaction after hearing of the project was to ask Frau Stein whether she would have any objection to her daughter taking a prominent part in public Catholic activities in her home town. To her surprise her mother replied that she would not mind anything if only Edith would stay.[2] For she knew quite well what it meant to a devout Jewish mother to have her daughter living in her house, publicly teaching Catholic philosophy and most probably carrying out an active apostolate while doing so. What she did not know was that her own personality, whose natural charm had only been increased by her intense spiritual life, had become a source of strength and consolation with which her mother would not willingly part.

[1] *Life*, p. 94; 93.　　　　[2] ibid.

During the quiet summer her work on potency and act began to assume enormous proportions. At this time she also carried on an ever-increasing correspondence, all written in her even energetic hand, a large part of it being addressed to people who came to her for advice. She generally heads her letters with the Benedictine motto PAX. In the troubled years of the Third Reich and the Second World War much of this precious correspondence was lost or deliberately destroyed for fear of the Gestapo; however, a few letters still extant, written during this period to one of her former pupils shed a good deal of light on her way of guiding young souls. They are addressed to a girl who had trouble with her school career and show a rare combination of factual teaching, spiritual guidance, and personal affection.

'9 June 1931. Dear A. Only a short greeting. . . . "Universal human characteristics" are such as are common to all men, in contrast to individual ones and those of a special type, e.g. the feminine type. Don't lose courage even if externally everything goes wrong. Most affectionately yours, Edith Stein.'

Things had indeed gone wrong, for soon Edith had to write another letter, this time very much longer. It is dated from Breslau, 4 July 1931.

My dear A. You must indeed soon have a reply to your question. It would be a good thing if you could even now give your parents in a letter a clear picture of the situation. Of course it would have been even better if you had kept them informed of everything in the past. . . . If your parents should decide that you ought to leave school, then you must tell them that you would like once more to have some regular work, and if possible some that will result in an independent professional position. . . . It would be best to let your parents advise you what to do. Possibilities are: domestic science, commercial subjects, nursing, kindergarten—any of these would be a step further towards the goal. But even if this should not be realized, I think you definitely need work. And your parents will probably realize, too, that you require a living.

When I hear of your misfortunes I must always think of the verse from Psalm 118: *Bonum mihi quia humiliasti me*—it is good for me that you have humbled me. The Lord must have some special design for you, because He makes you pass through so hard a school. Would you not like to place yourself under the special protection of your Patroness, St. Elizabeth? A lecture on her which I have given at Vienna has been published in *Das Neue Reich* of 13 and 20 June. Sr. A. will probably be able to get it for you. . . . In affectionate remembrance.

These letters were written while she was constantly occupied with heavy philosophical work. It is one of the most remarkable characteristics of this remarkable woman that she seemed to combine without effort the capacity for the most abstruse speculations with the ability of giving shrewd advice on quite practical matters while, at the same time, viewing everything from the supernatural point of view. Her allusion to Psalm 118 is revealing: her own spiritual life was nourished on the Liturgy, and the words of the Psalms come quite naturally to her. Her next letter makes the importance she attaches to the Psalms even more clear. It was written on 17 August of the same year, after A. had returned home. She writes:

Dear A. God guides each one of us by His own paths, and one reaches his goal more easily and quickly than another. In proportion to what is done to us that which we ourselves can do is little indeed. But this little we have to do. This is before all: to pray persistently that we may follow the right way and the attraction of grace as soon as it makes itself felt.

Is there no Old Testament, or at least a translation of the Psalms, either in your own home or elsewhere within reach? . . . I think you will be able to get the Psalms in every Catholic bookshop. . . . The 118th Psalm is said every Sunday in the Office of the Church (Prime to None). It is the longest of all, but very rich and beautiful.

Of course it will not be easy for you to return to Speyer. But so it has now been decided for you, and you have no responsibility in the matter. Do as much as you can, and keep your parents informed of your progress, so that there will be no surprise if there should be a catastrophe at Easter. Have you got Andersen's *Fairy Tales* among your children's books? Then you ought to read once more the story of the ugly duckling. I believe in your swan's future. Only don't blame the others if they cannot discover anything of that at the moment, and don't become bitter about it. You are not the only one to make mistakes every day—we all do that. But the Lord is patient and of great mercy. In His household of grace He can make use even of our mistakes, if we place them on His altar. *Cor contritum*

et humiliatum Deus non despicies—a contrite and humbled heart, O
God, thou wilt not despise (Ps. 50). This is one of my favourite
verses. With affectionate greetings in faithful remembrance, Yours,
Edith Stein.

Edith Stein's spirituality, as this letter clearly shows, was
nourished on the Psalms, and she found in them not only consolation for herself, but guidance and help for others. She herself
had said the Divine Office almost from the day she had been
baptized; the songs of the official prayers of the Church came
quite naturally to her, for they were the songs by which generation
after generation of her ancestors had worshipped God. When
she accompanied her mother to the synagogue the old lady was
astounded to see with what intense devotion her Catholic daughter
followed the Psalms from her Breviary. For her Christ had
indeed come to fulfil the Law and the Prophets, and it is significant
that she advised her former pupil to get an Old Testament, where
one would have expected that the Gospels would have been more
helpful, especially for a young girl without sufficient intellectual
and spiritual equipment to penetrate into the deeper meaning of
the books of the Old Covenant. Edith's great intellectual and
spiritual superiority made it difficult for her to gauge always
correctly how much—or how little—those with whom she had
to deal could take in, and so she sometimes could not but talk
above their heads. But then, as if she had realized herself that
something more simple was needed, she suddenly changes into
a lower key. Let the poor troubled girl read a fairy story—at
the moment she seems to be no more than a little ugly duckling,
doing all the wrong things and being the despair of her teachers.
With deep tenderness and perfectly naturally, Edith, who had
rarely made mistakes and always been admired, places herself on
the same level: 'Don't worry, we all make mistakes, cheer up,
you will be a swan one day—I have this confidence, even if no
one else has.' She certainly knew how to guide and encourage
souls.

After the quiet summer at Breslau, in the autumn she once
more went on lecture tours. She had already lectured on St.
Elizabeth in Vienna, now she was asked to give the address for
the seventh centenary of the saint's death for the Catholics of

Heidelberg. She herself evidently attached some importance to her interpretation of this young medieval saint, or she would not have recommended her pupil to read what she had said about her.

In order to keep up this ceaseless activity which was so much at variance with her deepest spiritual aspirations, she needed the background of a religious house, with the Presence of the Lord in the tabernacle and the peaceful regularity of monastic life. This had become an urgent necessity to her. A few months after her return to Breslau she writes:

> Here the silent Liturgy is my share. Of course, in this way, too, one can amply receive what one requires. But only if I can then live in fullness again for a time, do I realize how much I have missed it. When I decided to leave Speyer I knew that it would be very difficult not to live in a convent. But I never imagined that it could be so difficult as it actually was during the first months.[1]

Thus she was probably not sorry when the lectureship at Breslau came to nothing, since such a post in her home town would have completely ruled out the possibility of living in a religious house. In the late autumn of 1931 she therefore went to Freiburg, where she could more easily remain in contact with developments about her lectureship either at that university or at the Educational Institute at Münster.

At Freiburg she once more had the happiness of living in a convent, a little outside the city, which belonged to the modern Benedictine congregation of St. Lioba. Here she could take part in the Divine Office which she loved so dearly, and read the proofs of her translation of De Veritate. It had not been easy to find a publisher for this work. In her essay on Husserl and St. Thomas, in the Husserl Festschrift of 1929, she had mentioned that it would be published by Herder in that same year. But there had evidently been a hitch somewhere, for it was only brought out two years later, and not by Herder, but by the small Breslau publisher O. Borgmeyer, for whom she had a special word of thanks in her foreword 'for the courage and confidence with which he offered his publishing house for the work and undertook the printing at a financially most difficult time'.

She had not succeeded in obtaining a university lectureship

[1] *Life*, pp. 98f.

either at Freiburg or at Breslau. We do not know what exactly were the reasons for this failure; probably both her sex and her religion were against her. Thus she accepted the position as lecturer at the Educational Institute at Münster, which she took up in the spring of 1932. Professor Steffes wanted her to help building up a Catholic science of education with a special view to the needs of women, but she was also entrusted with philosophical lectures. He had a great admiration for her, which came out in the description he gave of her to the present author: 'She was extremely simple and modest, and looked like a Madonna. She was always dressed in dark colours, and her way of speaking was very quiet and reserved. She never spoke about her interior life, but it was a great experience to watch her praying at Mass with the deepest recollection. She had the persistency of her race: when she wanted something she was sure to get it.'

At first Edith had some misgivings when she resumed her scholarly career which had been interrupted by her conversion just about ten years ago. She was afraid that, owing to her extremely retired life and her growing desire for solitude and contemplation, she might not succeed in making contact with the new generation. But these fears proved to be unfounded. She was soon able to write to her friends that she was in close touch with both students and professors, and was holding animated discussion groups on women's problems. In fact, her quiet and reserved manner proved very attractive to many students who came to be almost fanatically devoted to her, though there were also others who disliked her; she hardly ever left people indifferent.

As it was the 'Goethe-Year', the first centenary of the poet's death (1832), she was entrusted with the address in his honour. She chose as her subject: 'Nature and Supernature in Goethe's *Faust*,' treating it, as became a lecturer of the Educational Institute, from the educational angle, fearlessly pointing out the deficiencies, from the Christian point of view, of Goethe's purely humanist conceptions. Though she was a fine speaker when she had a small, well-trained audience, she was less successful before a wider public, because she hardly ever raised her voice and made no gestures, but spoke rather meditatively, as if turning things over in her mind. So after the address a colleague came up to Professor

Steffes and said jokingly: 'Listen, if you put her up for such an address again, you'd better give her a good glass of something strong first to put a little more temperament into her.'

Nevertheless she could be very lively, especially at parties, where she was often the centre, though without in the least aiming at that. She would dominate simply by her intellect and her dynamic personality.

From Münster, too, she continued to go on lecture tours. In July she spoke at a Conference of Catholic Young Girls on 'The Task of Woman as a Guide to the Church', and in September she went to a Conference of the Société Thomiste on *Phenomenology and Thomism* at Juvisy. There she herself did not lecture, but played a prominent part in the discussions, and the scholars present were particularly struck by the clarity with which she developed her ideas, not only in her native tongue, but also in French if necessary.[1]

The late Dom Daniel Feuling, O.S.B., one of the members of the conference, has preserved a story which throws a vivid light on the close ties by which she still felt herself bound to her race. One day he went with her and Professor Koyré, a former assistant of Husserl, up to Montmartre, and on the way she and Koyré discussed other philosophers; whenever they mentioned one of Jewish extraction, they referred to him as 'one of our people'.

I was a little amused [writes Dom Feuling] by the way in which Koyré and Edith Stein simply said 'we' as soon as they spoke of Jews or anything Jewish. I realized very vividly the bonds of blood which were so strong also in Edith, as once in St. Paul, who said with such pride and emphasis: '*Hebraei sunt: et ego.*' 'They are Hebrews: so am I.' So now I became a little malicious and asked quite seriously: 'Well—and where are the two of you going to place me?' Then they looked at me with consternation and asked: 'Good Heavens—are you one of *us?*' Whereupon I reassured them that I was not.[2]

This strong attachment to her race is very characteristic of her and in striking contrast to the not infrequent attitude of converts from Judaism, who wish to forget as quickly as possible their

[1] *Life*, p. 109; 110.   [2] ibid., p. 112; 111.

own origin in order to amalgamate completely with the 'Gentiles' among whom they live. But Edith Stein was proud to belong to the race that had produced such 'strong women' as Judith and Esther, as well as the crown of all women, our Lady herself.

In October she went to Aachen for a Conference of the Catholic Women's League on 'The Spiritual Attitude of the Younger Generation'. Here she was conscious of a fundamental lack of inner contact with the other members of the conference. She writes in a letter from there: 'I understand now very well that I must have seemed very strange to people leading active lives in the world. For I realize only now, when I am myself in the same position, how utterly alien the world had become to me, and how much it costs me to make contact with it. I do not think I can ever quite succeed in doing so again.'[1]

This was the position as she herself felt it to be. Nevertheless she had succeeded in making contact with the students, and her work was greatly appreciated. She soon acquired the reputation of being the lecturer who represented the Catholic point of view without any compromise—and this uncompromising attitude seemed to some to betray an other-worldliness not very profitable in those troubled days. Yet, despite her own uncertainty, her teaching is very practical indeed and in close touch with modern trends.

[1] *Life*, p. 131; 112f.

CHAPTER TEN

EDUCATIONAL LECTURES AND ADDRESSES

EDITH STEIN's reputation as an expert on women's questions had been established by her address at the Congress of Catholic German Graduates at Salzburg in 1930, though she herself had by no means been satisfied with it. A year later, in August 1931, she wrote to a friend:

> I believe that since then I have learned a good deal and have to learn yet more. At school and as a young student I was a radical feminist; then I lost interest in the whole question. Now, being obliged to do so, I am looking for purely objective solutions. Perhaps the Father [Przywara] is too one-sidedly interested in curbing exaggerations. These are indeed present, and among Catholic feminists perhaps more than among the others, because the former are now troubled with those 'children's diseases' which the others got over twenty to thirty years ago. From the truly Catholic . . . standpoint, much more is possible than is generally thought. . . . It would be more effective to let the facts speak for themselves and to give up an unobjective fighting attitude. That the sex difference is due merely to the body[1] is a statement suspect on several grounds. 1. If *anima forma corporis*, then the physical difference is the indication of the difference of soul. 2. Matter exists for form, not vice versa. This makes it probable that the difference of soul is the primary one. Of course it must be thoroughly examined how far growth into the supernatural can and should be an outgrowing of the natural differences.

Much of her own writing touched on these questions.

The Salzburg lecture on *The Ethos of Women's Vocations* was later published in extended form. It contains a wealth of her most fundamental thought on the whole problem. Here Edith Stein speaks to us not as the philosopher—though her whole argumentation betrays her philosophical mind and training—but as a woman of her time in the best sense of the word, aware of

[1] The view of a Catholic feminist to whose ideas this whole letter refers.

contemporary needs, clear-sighted and wise, and steeped not only in the teaching but in the prayer of the Church. She is well aware of the special gifts no less than of the limitations of her sex. She does not fear to stress the difference between man and woman which she deduces from St. Thomas's principle that the soul is the form of the body—and where the bodies are so different, she argues, the souls must necessarily be different too.

Woman [she writes] tends towards the living and personal, she wants the whole. To cherish, to keep and protect, this is her natural, her authentically maternal desire. The dead thing, the 'object', interests her in the first place in so far as it serves the living and the personal rather than for its own sake. This is connected with another feature: every kind of abstraction is foreign to her nature. The living and personal which is the object of her care, is a concrete whole and must be cared for and encouraged as a whole, not one part at the expense of the others . . . this she tolerates neither in herself nor in others. And to this practical attitude corresponds her theoretical endowment: her natural way of knowledge is not so much notional and analytical, but envisaging and sensing the concrete.

Perhaps it might be objected that in thus describing the nature of woman she actually excludes her own. Is she herself not really interested in things for their own sake, is she not a philosopher coolly analysing 'phenomena', living in a world of abstractions?
This would be a very erroneous conception. All her male friends, a Father Przywara and an Abbot Walzer, stress her tender femininity; and though she had a philosophical mind, she had a typically feminine one in that she did not philosophize by deduction from principles. The phenomenological way is in fact singularly adapted to a feminine mind, since it is concerned with 'phenomena' as they surround and affect us, regarding everything as much as possible as a whole, finding what it really is by the intuitive glance of a mind that loves and reverences reality as it is. Such a philosophizing is not foreign to the feminine mind as she describes it, though of course the gift of any form of philosophical mind is rarer in women even than it is in men.
After describing woman as a mother, she goes on to the other essential feminine quality: that of companion. 'To share in another's life,' she writes, 'to take part in all that concerns him,

in the greatest as well as in the smallest things, in joy and sorrow, but also in his work and problems, that is her special gift and her happiness.' This she herself had done time and again—as Husserl's assistant, as the friend of Canon Schwind, of Father Przywara, of Abbot Walzer, and, not least, of other women. She was, indeed, herself an ideal companion, sympathetic, discreet, and self-sacrificing. But this did not prevent her from realizing that the very qualities that God had given to woman in order to make her the perfect helpmate of man could be turned into something evil unless properly balanced.

The picture she draws of feminine virtues turned into vices reveals not only her clear-sightedness, but also her own experience of the less perfect specimens of her sex. After giving her portrait of the ideal woman, created to be the mother and companion of man, she admits that woman's nature is only very rarely developed in its purity. She marshals a formidable array of faults to which women are only too prone.

> The personal tendency is usually unwholesomely exaggerated; on the one hand woman is inclined to be extravagantly concerned with her own person and to expect the same interest from others; this expresses itself in vanity, desire for praise and recognition and an unrestrained urge for self expression and communication. On the other hand we shall find an unmeasured interest in others which shows itself as curiosity, gossip, and an indiscreet longing to penetrate into the intimate life of other people. The tendency towards wholeness easily leads her to frittering away her energy, it makes her disinclined to discipline her individual talents properly and leads to superficial nibbling in all directions. In her attitude to others it shows itself in a possessiveness far exceeding what is required by her maternal functions. Thus the sympathetic companion becomes the interfering busybody that cannot tolerate silent growth and thus does not foster development, but hinders it.

A grim and gloomy picture—but who could say it was unduly exaggerated? Over and against woman as she only too often is, Edith Stein sets up the picture of the Immaculate Mother, whose life is centred in her Son, whom she loves and serves without thought of herself in obedience and trust, the great example of all Christian women.

Edith Stein strongly opposes the view that women are incapable of having any other professions than those of wife and mother, which, she says, can only be accounted for by blind prejudice. Taught by the experience of the First World War, she holds that 'if need be, every normal and healthy woman can fill a post; and there is no post that could not be filled by a woman'. However, she makes an important distinction. She distinguishes between professions which are really 'feminine', because they are suited to the special natural gifts of woman, and those which are not so suited, but for which individual women may be fitted by strong personal inclination and talent. In the first category she counts all those professions which offer scope to the feminine gift of sympathetic understanding and care, such as that of doctor and nurse, of teacher and governess, of everything connected with social service and, of course, with help in the homes of others. In the sphere of scholarship she singles out activities such as translating and editing; in short, every kind of work that tends towards assisting others rather than being strictly creative. But this, she argues, does not mean that other professions, less suited to the feminine character, cannot also be filled in the true womanly and maternal spirit. It is here that her suggestions are particularly valuable; for the majority of women 'with a job' are in employment that is even more foreign to their nature than it is to man's because it is totally soulless.

How can a woman exercise her God-given function in a factory or a business office, in some municipal institute or in a chemical laboratory? Edith Stein gives valuable advice on how to retain and make fruitful feminine qualities even in such unpromising surroundings.

In most cases [she says] the work will involve being together with others at least in the same room, often also in division of labour. And with this we have at once an opportunity for developing all the feminine virtues. One may even say that precisely here, where everyone is in danger of becoming a piece of the machine, the development of the specifically feminine can become a beneficial counter-influence. In the soul of a man who knows that help and sympathy are awaiting him at his place of work, much will be kept alive or aroused that would otherwise be dwarfed. This is one way of feminine individuality forming professional life in a way different from the average man's.

She also traces another way: owing to the feminine gift of seeing the whole, a woman who remains faithful to the special characteristic of her sex will retain her vision of the end even in the midst of abstract occupations, and will thus contribute to a better adaptation of the means to the end.

Here again Edith Stein holds up the Mother of God as an example for women.

> Mary at the wedding of Cana: her quietly observing eyes see everything and discover where something is missing. And before anyone else notices anything, before there is any embarrassment, she has already remedied the situation. She finds ways and means, she gives the necessary directions, everything quietly and without attracting attention. Let this be the example of woman in the professional life. Wherever she is placed, let her do her work quietly and efficiently, without demanding attention or recognition. And at the same time she should keep a vigilant eye on the situation, sensing where there is something lacking, where somebody needs her help, and rectify things as far as possible without being noticed.

Perhaps this picture of the perfect woman may be a trifle academic, and at the same time a little too much the reflection of her own very quiet, disciplined nature. After all, there are women of very vivacious temperament, who do things in a different and not always unobtrusive and quiet way—who may even be very great saints, as were St. Catherine of Siena, St. Joan of Arc, or St. Teresa of Avila. There is always a danger for the philosopher of taking too little account of the varieties of the real living world; and here it seems Edith Stein has not altogether escaped the danger. Of one thing, however, she is fully conscious: of the frightening gulf between the ideal of a woman, which, whether vivacious or otherwise, will always have to be unselfish and loving, and the reality of what woman actually is. She describes the state of German women after the First World War; but her picture is only too similar to what may be seen today all over the civilized world.

Many of the best are almost crushed by the double burden of professional and family duties; they are always on the go, worn out,
nervy and irritable. Where are they to find the interior calm and
serenity in order to be a support and guide for others? In consequence
there are daily little frictions with husband and children despite real
mutual love and recognition of the other's merits, hence unpleasantness in the home and the loosening of family ties. In addition
there are the many superficial and unstable women who want only
amusement in order to fill the interior void, who marry and are
divorced, and leave their children either to themselves or to servants
no more conscientious than the mothers. If they have to take a job
they regard it only as a means to earn their living and to get as much
enjoyment out of life as possible. In their case one can talk neither of
vocation nor of ethos. They are like dry leaves blown about by the
wind. The breaking up of the family and the decline of morals is
essentially connected with this group and can only be stemmed if
we succeed in diminishing its number through suitable educational
methods.

Here she lays her finger on the root of the trouble. What
are the proper education methods capable of stemming the tide
of selfishness and worldliness that has invaded the lives of modern
women? She finds the answer in restoring the proper balance
by a sound spiritual life, at the centre of which must be the
Eucharist. She realizes that no external devices, however cleverly
thought out, can lead women to fulfil their true vocation of mother
and companion, whether in the physical or in the spiritual sphere.

Only through the power of grace [she says] can nature be freed
from the off-scourings of sin ... and receive the Divine life. And
this Divine life is itself the fountain from which spring the works of
love. If we want to preserve it, we must nourish it constantly from
the sources whence it flows unceasingly, that is from the holy
Sacraments, above all from the Sacrament of Love. A woman's life
for which the Divine Love is to be its inner form, will have to be an
eucharistic life. To forget oneself, to be delivered from all one's own
desires and pretensions, to open one's heart to all the pressing needs
of others—this is possible only through the daily intimacy with our
Lord in the tabernacle.

We know that Edith Stein practised what she was teaching.

For her the hours before the tabernacle were the times of re-creation, the times that gave her the strength to carry on her professional work as well as her hidden work for souls.

In *Problems of the Education of Women* she deals with kindred matters. She demands a thorough study of the whole complex of sex education, pathology and psychology, on the part of Catholics, who ought to study it

> critically—that is to say not simply negatively, but so as to separate, after serious investigation, what we can accept and what we must reject. For we can, indeed, learn a lot from these forms of modern research. The traditional Catholic treatment—or non-treatment—of these questions is capable, and even in need, of a renewal, if it would satisfy the demands of our time. It is a most urgent task of the education of our youth, including of course the girls, to build up the Catholic theory of sex and marriage on a grand scale, together with the educational principles derived from it.

What Edith Stein demanded more than twenty years ago has not yet become reality, but the urgent need to approach these questions is at least being widely recognized.

Next she turns once more to the question of women's professions other than that of wife and mother. She does not think that after the 'emancipation of women' has become an accomplished fact one can turn back the clock, though (she is evidently thinking of National Socialism) 'such efforts are being made'. Dealing with the position of women within the Church, she demands that a distinction should be made between the teachings of dogmatic theology, canon law, the human representatives of the Church and the Lord Himself. Christ Himself, she holds, made no distinction between men and women in His attitude towards them except in barring the latter from the priesthood, neither is there any dogmatic definition on the question. But in her view canon law and the official representatives of the Church are not impartial in this respect. She cites the Encyclical on Marriage of Pius XI, in which he declares that the primary task of woman is to be wife and mother, significantly without any comment of her own. She openly disapproves of the present canon law, according to which there can be no question of equality between the sexes, since women are excluded from all sacred offices. This, she holds, is a deterioration in the position, since in the early times of the Church there were deaconesses, ordained for their office by the bishop. 'The fact,' writes Edith Stein, 'that there has been a gradual transformation in the matter, shows that it is possible for the development to go once more in the opposite direction. And the life of the Church in the present age suggests that we may expect such a development, since we see women being drawn increasingly into Church activities, whether in the field of charity, of pastoral care or of teaching.'

This was, and still is, the case particularly in Germany, where the shortage of priests after two world wars makes it imperative that women should play a far more active part in the Church than they do as yet in most other countries. This problem of the position of women in the Church was so widely and eagerly discussed that Edith Stein could even seriously raise the question of the priesthood of women. In the Germany of those days it was quite definitely a subject of controversy, and the way in which she treats it shows her sense of balance.

She deals with it explicitly in an essay on 'The Vocation of Man and Woman according to the Orders of Nature and of Grace':

If we look at the attitude of our Lord Himself in this matter [she writes], we see that He accepts from women the free services of love for Himself and His disciples, and that women are among His closest friends—but He did not give them the priesthood, not even to His Mother, the Queen of Apostles. . . . The primitive Church shows manifold charitable activities of women in the parishes, an intensive apostolate of the women martyrs and confessors, she has the liturgical consecration of virgins and the ordination of deaconesses . . . but she has not introduced the priesthood of women. . . . Dogmatically it seems to me that nothing could prevent the Church from introducing such an unheard-of novelty. Whether it could be recommended from a practical point of view would admit of many pros and cons. Against it would be the entire tradition from primitive times to the present moment, but even more than this the mysterious fact . . . that Christ appeared on earth as the *Son* of Man, that therefore the first Creature on earth that was created in an eminent sense after the image of God was a Man. This seems to me to point to the fact that He wanted to appoint only men to be His official representatives on earth.

She joins issue with St. Paul, however, on his teaching on woman's position in the Church. Whenever a woman dares to raise her voice to express her opinion on any religious matter, there is usually somebody or other to be found who thunders at her the famous Pauline *Mulier taceat in Ecclesia*. Edith Stein could not let this attitude go unchallenged. She subjects the crucial passages of the Pauline Epistles to a searching exegesis, especially the famous verses of 1 Corinthians xi. 3–16.

'We do not think that we offend the Apostle,' she writes, 'if we say that in this instruction to the Corinthians divine and human, temporal and eternal things are mixed up. Hair styles and clothes are matters of custom. . . . If his decision as to the appearance of the Corinthian women in church was binding for the Church he had founded, this does not mean that it should be valid for all times.' We may note in passing that the custom of women having their heads covered in church does not exist in Germany, nor in Austria, which gives to this passage more force than it would have in other countries, where the Pauline injunction is observed.

She then goes on to distinguish in the passage from 1 Corinthians between what is divine law and what is a merely temporary enactment. 'What he says about the fundamental relationship between man and woman must be judged in a different light, for it claims to be an interpretation of the Divine order of creation and redemption: man and woman are destined to lead together *one* life as if they were a single being. To the man, as to the one who was created first, is due the direction in this community of life.' But here she is not quite satisfied with the Apostle either. For she comments: 'One has the impression that the interpretation does not reproduce the original and the redemptive orders in their integrity. In stressing the relationship of subjection and even more in assuming a mediatorship of man between the Redeemer and woman he is still influenced by the order of fallen nature. Neither the account of the creation nor the Gospel knows such a mediatorship in the relation with God. On the other hand it is known both to the Mosaic and to Roman law.'

She finds this attitude even more explicit in the First Letter to Timothy, and

has the impression that the original order and the order of Redemption are made to disappear by the order of fallen nature, and that the Apostle still speaks as the Jew who is guided by the spirit of the Law. The evangelical conception of virginity seems entirely forgotten. What is said here, and may have been suitable in view of certain abuses in the Greek Churches, is not to be considered as of obligation for the fundamental teaching on the relationship between the sexes. It is too much opposed to the words and practice of the Saviour, who had women among His most intimate friends and proved everywhere in His redemptive work that the soul of woman was as much His concern as the soul of man. It also contradicts the words of St. Paul himself, which express the spirit of the Gospel perhaps most purely: 'Wherefore the Law was our pedagogue in Christ: that we might be justified by faith. But after the faith is come, we are no longer under the pedagogue. . . . There is neither Jew nor Greek; there is neither bond nor free: there is neither male nor female. For you are all one in Christ Jesus.'

This passage is revealing in many ways. It seems almost paradoxical that Edith Stein, herself a convert from Judaism, should so misunderstand St. Paul; but on this point she has evidently allowed her feminist tendencies to carry her away. In other contexts, however, it is obvious that she does in fact recognize the fundamental differences between the sexes, which shows that here she has failed to distinguish sufficiently clearly between the principles underlying the injunctions of the Apostle and the particular applications he made.

It is evident from errors such as this that Edith Stein, far advanced though she was on the way of perfection, had not yet reached her full stature. In her very critical mind—a common heritage of her race—there were still harshnesses which had not yet been smoothed out. She herself, however, was well aware of the dangers of a one-sided intellectualism, which she points out in an article, 'The Intellect and the Intellectuals', published in a small periodical, *Das heilige Feuer*, in 1931. There she writes:

All of us who live in the universities absorb a little of the 'type of

the intellectual'. . . . But we must be quite clear that this attitude
separates us from the crowds. Outside people battle with the daily
needs of life in their manifold forms. As soon as we go out they
confront us. . . . We are placed among people whom we are meant
to help in their needs. They ought not to think of us as strange
beings living in an inaccessible ivory tower. We must be able to
think, feel, and speak like them, if they are expected to have confidence in us. . . . The intellectual can find the way to the people—
and without finding it he cannot guide them—only if, in a certain
sense, he frees himself from the intellect.

There was one influence in her life which helped her more
effectively than any other to overcome her own intellectualism,
and that was the influence of our Lady. In all her utterances on
the vocation of woman, Edith Stein returns again and again to
the figure of Mary, the Mother of God and our Mother. Like
all the other components of her spiritual life, her devotion to
our Lady is based on the doctrines of the Church, without any
'frills', but all the more profound. She brings out very forcibly
the intimate relationship between Mary and the Church, so dear
to the Fathers, and which is again being increasingly stressed in
the works of modern theologians. She writes in an essay on
'Woman's Place in the Corpus Christi Mysticum':

Mary is the most perfect symbol, because type and origin, of the
Church. She is also a unique organ of the Church, for she is the
organ from which was formed not only the whole mystical Body,
but the Head itself. In order to denote her position as the central
and essential organ she is frequently called the Heart of the Church.
Certainly such terms as Body, Head, and Heart are images. But
they express a reality. And in the same way as head and heart
play a prominent part in the human body, whose other organs and
members depend on them for their being and working, so also
Mary, because of her unique relationship with Christ, must have
a real, that is to say a mystical, relationship with the other members
of the Church. This relationship is superior to that between the
other members in degree, manner and importance, in a way
analogous to the relationship between a Mother and her children,
which is also superior to that between the children themselves. If
we call Mary our Mother it is not only a figure of speech. Mary is
our Mother in the most real and eminent sense, surpassing earthly

motherhood. She has born us into our life of grace, by casting her whole being, body and soul, into the Divine Maternity. Therefore she is intimately united to us: she loves us, she knows us, she is anxious to make everyone of us what he ought to be, especially to bring each of us into as close a relationship as possible to the Lord. This is so for all men; but it must have a special significance for women. For in their maternity, whether natural or supernatural, and in their vocation to be brides of God, the maternity and Divine Bridehood of the Virgin Mother are, as it were, continued. And . . . so we may believe in the co-operation of Mary wherever a woman fulfils her womanly vocation, as well as in all the work of the Church. But just as grace cannot accomplish its work in souls, unless they freely open themselves to its influence, so also Mary cannot fully realize her maternity unless men freely entrust themselves to her. If women want to fulfil their vocation in the various ways open to them, they will most safely reach their goal if, besides forming themselves after the pattern of the Virgin Mother, they entrust themselves to her guidance and place themselves entirely under her direction. For those who belong to her she can form in her own image.

We have here, in a nutshell as it were, the teaching of St. Grignion of Montfort on the place of Mary in the life of Christians, applied in a special way to Christian women. We have met Edith Stein before, and we shall meet her again, as the philosopher, fearlessly probing the depths of knowledge. Here we meet the other side of this richly gifted nature, what Father Przywara calls 'her tender femininity', the daughter of Mary, who has placed herself entirely in the hands of the one who became our Mother under the Cross. This fullness of Mary's maternity, with which she had been endowed on Calvary, Edith had realized in her long hours of prayer before the Mater Dolorosa at Beuron, a realization which grew in her together with the deepening of her own interior life.

This side of her found beautiful expression in another of her papers, called 'Living in the Spirit of St. Elizabeth'. It is not the well-known story of this saintly Hungarian princess that interests Edith Stein most deeply. 'We would like to penetrate,' she writes, 'to what lies behind these external facts, we would wish to feel the beating of this heart that bore such destiny and did such

deeds, and to make our own the spirit acting in it.' She finds
the motive force of the saint's life in her all-embracing love with
which she loved first her husband in the Lord, and then the Lord
alone. This love, in its turn, is the source of a deep joy that
overflows to others and brings them happiness, at the same time
rebelling against the arbitrary social conventions of her time and
position which would hem in her charity and prevent this joy
from spreading itself.

Yet to follow the desire of one's heart, however holy, is not
without its dangers. If we would form our lives according to
the spirit of St. Elizabeth, we have to discipline ourselves. 'Even
in her last years Elizabeth asked the Lord for three things: to
despise all earthly riches, to bear humiliations with joy, and to
be freed from her inordinate love for her children. She was able
to tell her maids that all her requests had been granted. But the
very fact that she had to pray for them shows that they were
against her nature and that she probably had long had to struggle
for them in vain.' Then follows a discussion, marked by great
insight, of the relationship between St. Elizabeth and her austere
director, Conrad of Marburg, to whom she vowed obedience,
and under whose direction she remained till her death.

This [she writes] was probably the most effective breaking of her own
will, to subject herself to him and to remain always subjected to him,
for not only did he take up the merciless struggle against her lower
nature, which was what she herself desired, but he also directed her
love of God and her neighbour into ways different from those she
would have preferred. He never permitted her to give up all her
property, neither before nor after the death of her husband; he
objected to her indiscriminate almsgiving which he gradually
restricted and at last forbade altogether; he sought to prevent her
from nursing contagious diseases—the only point in which Elizabeth
did not completely obey.

Is it fanciful to perceive in these words an echo of Edith's own
experience? She, too, had desired to do things for God that were
contrary to the ideas of her directors. From the moment of her
conversion she had felt the call to a wholly contemplative and
sacrificial life in Carmel, but neither Canon Schwind nor Abbot
Walzer had allowed her to follow it. Years later, when she

herself had at last been able to follow the call, she wrote about the poetess Gertrud von le Fort: 'When Gertrud von le Fort visited us in November, I realized even more clearly than before how outrageous the appearance in public and the travelling about must be for this delicate being, and I asked myself whether the results were worth the sacrifice. Her account of the effects of these evening recitals was a "Yes" to this question.'[1]

She, too, must have felt her lecture tours a great strain, for she disliked the limelight, and we have seen how anxiously she avoided any but the most essential social contacts on these occasions. In accepting the many invitations to speak in public, she obeyed her directors who saw in this apostolate God's will for her—nevertheless her heart was not on the speaker's platform but before the tabernacle. That this was so is shown clearly by the reply she made to a criticism that was sometimes voiced with regard to her lectures. People had been remarking on her persistent stress of the supernatural. To this she could only answer: 'If I should not speak about that, I should hardly ascend a speaker's platform at all. . . . In fact it is always one small, simple truth about which I speak: what one can do to live close to the Lord. But if people want something quite different from me and give me highbrow subjects which are quite outside my scope, I can only take them as a point of departure from which to proceed to my *Ceterum Censeo*.'[2]

[1] *Life*, p. 166.
[2] Reference to Cato's famous words which he reiterated time and again in the Roman Senate when Carthage was the principal rival to the supremacy of Rome: *Ceterum censeo Carthaginem esse delendam*—As for the rest, my opinion is that Carthage ought to be destroyed. Letter cited in *Life*, p. 104; 103.

CHAPTER ELEVEN

IN THE SHADOW OF CARMEL . . .

D ESPITE her absorbing intellectual work Edith Stein continued to intensify her life of prayer and asceticism. She
had always been very moderate in her food and drink,
and a severe attack of gastric influenza in 1925 or 1926, five or
six years previously, had left her stomach permanently weakened,
so that her diet became even more meagre than before.

At St. Lioba her austerity aroused the admiration of all who
came into contact with her. In accordance with her vow of
poverty her clothes were mended again and again and mostly
quite out of fashion. In fact, she sometimes looked so dowdy
that her friends had to criticize her for her complete disregard
of her appearance; only when she had to make a really important
speech would she put on something less old-fashioned. For Carmel
had by now begun to cast its shadow over her whole life. Indeed,
she had once more asked her director to be allowed to enter, but
again he refused to give his permission for the same reasons as
before: the distress it would cause to her mother and her important apostolate. So she had to content herself with remaining in
the world, but living as far as possible in the spirit of Carmel.

A friend who helped her with reading the proofs of her translation of St. Thomas noticed the loving glances she often cast at
the carved wooden crucifix lying on her table. In those days she
read and discussed Father Przywara's collection of poems entitled
Karmel, and Gertrud von le Fort's stirring novel *Die Letzte am
Schafott*, the story of the sixteen Carmelites of Compiègne who
were killed in the French Revolution. At this time, too, she
wrote a short essay, 'Ways to Interior Silence', which already
breathes the spirit of Carmel, though it is meant for people
living busy lives in the world. In it she sounds the notes of St.
John of the Cross: 'We must open ourselves to grace. This means:
we must completely renounce our own will and surrender

ourselves as prisoners to the will of God, placing our souls in
His hands ready to receive Him and be formed by Him.' And
again: 'When I begin my working day after the morning's Mass,
I shall be filled with solemn silence, and my soul will be empty
of all that threatened to attack and burden it.' Silence, emptiness,
renunciation of self—she teaches it for the world as St. John
taught it for the cloister, well knowing that these are not special
features of convent life, but the essentials of all true Christian
living, though the manner in which they are practised must
necessarily vary according to one's station in life. So she counsels
some intervals of rest, if possible a few minutes of prayerful
recollection before the tabernacle, but if that is impossible, at
least 'a period of breathtaking in one's own room. And where
there is no possibility of getting some external rest, because there
is no place where to retire . . . at least a moment to shut out
everything else and be with the Lord. For He is there, and can
give us in a single moment what we need.'

She preached what she herself had practised for many years.
School and lectures, philosophical studies and extensive reading,
giving help to others and piles of correspondence—all this had
been her lot, and all who knew her are unanimous that they
had never seen her flustered. No doubt this was partly due to
her exceptionally calm temperament and her capacity for working
according to a rigid time-table. But there was also in her a supernatural peace that did not fail to strike those who came into
contact with her. As one of those who met her at St. Lioba
expressed it: 'She was so incredibly modest that one hardly
noticed her presence. . . . And yet, from the very first moment
one felt as if under the spell of a great sanctity that emanated
from her silent personality.'[1]

It was the same at Münster, where she was staying at the
Collegium Marianum, a student's hostel run by the Sisters of
Notre Dame. In accordance with her vow of poverty, she contented herself with one bed-sitting-room, much to the surprise
of the students, who expected different standards from a lecturer.
They watched her at meal-times, for she dined with them, not
like the other lecturers in her room, and found out that she never
ate meat and was also very abstemious in other ways. It was

[1] *Life*, p. 99; 98.

evident that she was already trying as far as possible to lead the
life of a religious; she rarely went out, not even into the garden.
She had become even stricter in this matter than at Speyer, where,
according to her own remark, 'theoretically I go for a walk along
the Rhine every day—though practically I usually end up at the
Municipal Library'.

At Münster her days consisted quite literally of nothing but
prayer and work. As was her habit, she went to the chapel every
morning early, long before the sisters; she never allowed herself
to sit down, even if she assisted at two or three Masses, as she
loved to do if at all possible. During the day, too, she would
give as much time as she could to visits to the Blessed Sacrament,
since she attached great importance to time spent in prayer in
the Eucharistic Presence. It was here, before the altar, that she
learned to see the deep and distressing problems of her time in
the light of eternity. Profoundly concerned, and yet calmly
detached, she saw the dangers, the approaching dissolution which
so many of her contemporaries were desperately trying to brush
aside or to hide behind a smoke-screen of wishful thinking. Not
that she thought out the problems which confronted her during
her time of prayer. No. But she emptied herself of all these
cares and preoccupations, just as she had always advised others
to do, and delivered herself over into the keeping of the
Lord. It was a simple 'being there', in the beloved Presence of
her Christ, peaceful and without any human contribution to
this *tête-à-tête*, or rather *cœur-à-cœur*, other than the openness of
the loving soul, desiring to be filled with the good things of the
Lord. In such a state of peaceful waiting on the Lord, God would
fill her soul, not with her own ideas, but with His infinite peace
and wisdom, so that, returning to her everyday activities and
preoccupations, she found herself able to read clearly the signs of
the times, and to give the counsel that was needed.

Prayer simply did not tire her; a fact probably due partly to
a certain physical toughness, but partly also, it would seem, to
the consolations she received. An Ursuline nun at whose convent
she spent Christmas in 1932 remembers this typical incident.
'On Christmas Eve we sang Matins, at which she assisted. Then
we went to rest for some hours till midnight. As I came into
the church a little early, she was still kneeling motionless in the

same place as in the evening, and assisted at Mass and Lauds. When I later asked her whether she was not tired she answered with shining eyes: "How could this night make one tired?"[1] Her attitude had remained unchanged since the little unpleasantness with the two nuns unable to stand hours of prayer in a hot Carmelite chapel. She still could not understand that even with the best will in the world a person may be overcome by natural weakness and exhaustion of mind and body—paradoxically enough, it needed the austere Carmel to teach her that. For her, Christ was even now the Lord, *Christus der Herr*—He had not yet become the Lover, nor had she quite become the child, like a St. Teresa of Lisieux, who when fatigue overpowered her even during prayer-time, would go to sleep without scruple, knowing that parents—and how much more God—love their children as much when they are asleep as when they are awake. This is not a form of laxity—the 'little' St. Teresa was a most austere Carmelite—but it is a certain freedom which grows with perfection. Despite her deep insight into the spiritual life and her great modesty, Edith had not yet found the secret of 'treating with God as with a lover', as the great St. Teresa expresses it, nor of hiding anything that might appear extraordinary. As a student at the Marianum, who knew her well, said of her: 'She was too rigid; she was not yet a fully free person.' The Jewish Law, personified as it were by her mother, was still holding part of her captive.

[1] *Life*, p. 114.

CHAPTER TWELVE

. . . AND OF THE CROOKED CROSS

A T the end of 1932 Edith once more writes to her former
pupil A: 'Above all I want to answer your question.
There is a vocation to suffer with Christ and thereby to
co-operate in His redemptive work. If we are united to the
Lord, we are members of the Mystical Body of Christ; Christ
continues to live and to suffer in His members, and the suffering
borne in union with Him is His suffering, integrated and made
fruitful in His great redemptive work. This is a fundamental
idea of all religious life, above all of the life of Carmel through
voluntary and joyful suffering to intercede for sinners and to
co-operate in the redemption of mankind.'

In the days when these words were written, Germany was in
ferment. For several years now brown-shirted young men had
been marching along the roads and through the streets of the
great cities, shouting their slogan *Deutschland erwache*, often followed by the horrible, brutal threat *Juda verrecke*, and singing
their aggressive Horst Wessel song, *Die Fahne hoch, die Reihen
dicht geschlossen*. The fanaticism that was sweeping Germany
penetrated even into the peaceful atmosphere of the Collegium
Marianum at Münster. One of the students there was an
ardent Nazi, who would extol Hitler and his book *Mein Kampf*
to the skies. Edith Stein used to treat all people with unfailing
kindness and equanimity, but when it was a case of hearing the
arch-enemy of her people praised her patience gave way. It was
generally noticed that she could not hide her disgust, and on
one occasion she vented it sarcastically by remarking that this
Nazi student's addiction to chain-smoking must certainly be a
sign of disloyalty, seeing that Goebbels was everywhere propa-
gating the slogan: The German woman does not smoke.

Nazism was making headway everywhere among German
students. One incident was typical. The Catholic women

students had called a meeting to counteract the influence of the organization of their Nazi fellows. The discussion was lively, and Nazi elements were making a good deal of noise. Then Edith Stein wanted to speak. She had been listened to with great respect by assemblies of scholars of world-wide reputation—but this was a different kind of meeting. Though they were Catholic students, the methods of Nazism had already had their effect; if one wanted a hearing in Germany at that time, one had to shout. But shouting is foreign to dispassionate argument—and Edith Stein had a clear-thinking mind and a low voice. She had to tell the students things of importance, for she never spoke unless she really had something to say. But this no longer mattered. Because she was so quiet and spoke without gesture and noise, hardly anyone listened, so she sat down after a few sentences, and it was as if she had never spoken at all. Only a few friends who knew her were appalled by the change. The speaker who had held so many audiences spellbound by her lucid exposition of vital problems was now simply brushed aside. All over Germany the 'still small voice' of wisdom was being silenced, and the shouting of slogans filled the air. *Deutschland, erwache!*

Only once more was Edith Stein invited to speak to Catholic students, this time about National Socialism and racial problems. This last public lecture made an immense impression, precisely on account of her quiet objective way, because she was speaking on the question that most deeply affected her own existence. She was always serious when she lectured, and hardly allowed a flicker of humour to lighten the subject—but now she struck the note of tragedy, tragedy simply accepted, without false pathos or self-pity. She spoke about the curse that lay on the Jewish people—her own people—and the necessity of expiation, of an expiation that must come from the race, because the race had rejected Christ, their Messiah. For her it was the judgement of God on her people, which she loved so much that she herself wanted to be a victim for it, though her way towards that goal had not yet become clear.

*   *   *

On 30 January 1933 Hitler took over full powers in Germany

by becoming *Reichskanzler*, and he immediately began to enact
anti-Jewish laws. Edith Stein knew that her days at the Institute
were numbered. In Passion Week she once more went to Beuron,
both to make her customary Easter Retreat and to ask advice
from Abbot Walzer.

During the last weeks, when the persecution of the Jews in
Germany had started in earnest, she had constantly been delibera-
ting with herself whether there was nothing she could do about
it. As she had for some years now been used to a public career
she conceived the plan of going to Rome and, in a private
audience, asking the Holy Father, Pope Pius XI, for an encyclical
on the Jewish question. There was a certain *naïveté* in this idea
of a lay woman going to Rome to ask the Pope for an encyclical
on a subject that did not even affect the Church immediately,
and on which he certainly would be sufficiently well informed
already. So it is not very surprising that, when she made inquiries
in Rome, she was told that in view of the great pressure of
visitors she could not hope for a private audience; the most that
would be granted would be a 'special' one, where she would be
included in a small group of people. This was not what she had
desired, so she contented herself with writing a letter to the
Pope. In an account of these days, which she wrote for her
Prioress in the Cologne Carmel almost five years later, she says:
'I know that my letter was delivered to the Holy Father sealed,
and I received his blessing for myself and my family some time
afterwards. But nothing else happened. Later I have often been
wondering whether he may not sometimes have remembered
this letter. For in the following years everything has taken place
precisely as I had predicted it for the future of Catholics in
Germany.'[1]

This letter of Edith Stein's had been handed to the Pope in
April 1933, and soon afterwards a new concordat was signed
between the Holy See and the German Government. The last
words of the passage just quoted sound almost as if she meant to
say: If the Holy Father had only listened to my predictions he
would have acted differently. But the Church has an experience
of about two thousand years' standing to guide her in her dealings

---

[1] My description of the time before her entering Carmel closely follows this account,
which is printed, pp. 115–132 of the *Life*.

with dictators. In those days it cannot have been very difficult for Roman politicians to foresee that a new wave of persecutions of Catholics—and indeed of other believing Christians, too—was about to be launched by Hitler. In such cases the Church goes to the utmost limits to safeguard the lives and conscience of her children; to fulminate encyclicals at this stage, when there was still hope of finding a *modus vivendi* however unsatisfactory, would have been very unwise. The Lord soon made it clear to Edith that it was not her vocation, like a St. Catherine of Siena, to play a role in the public affairs of the Church—hers was to be a different task.

On her way to Beuron to see the Abbot she broke her journey at Cologne, where she attended the Holy Hour before the First Friday, together with a woman friend about to enter the Church. She herself describes her experience there. 'I spoke to our Lord and told Him that I knew it was His Cross that was being laid on the Jewish people. Most of them did not know that; but those who did, ought to embrace it willingly in the name of all. This I desired to do. He should only show me in what way. When the devotions were finished I had the interior certainty that my prayer had been answered. But in what manner I was to bear the Cross, this I did not yet know.'

In these few simple words is the clue to all her later life. Once more, as on that first Good Friday morning on Golgotha, the Cross was planted in the sight of the Jewish people, but those who had turned away from it outside the gates of Jerusalem had now to bear it themselves. The Cross has not lost its saving power, but it must be accepted willingly. In the name of her people who knew not the Cross of Christ, she offered herself to accept of her own free choice what the others were compelled to bear against their will.

In Beuron she discussed not only her letter to the Pope, which was approved by the Abbot, but also her future. What was she to do if she had to give up her post at Münster? It shows how clearly she saw the situation that she wanted to talk over this possibility with her director. He could not believe it possible that this was going to be asked of her—it seemed too incredible that a Catholic institute should not be left free to choose its own staff. But Edith knew better what totalitarianism meant. On her way back to Münster she read in a paper the report of a big National Socialist Teachers' Conference in which the denominational associations had also had to take part. 'It became clear to me,' she writes, 'that least of all in education would influences opposed to the dominating philosophy be tolerated. The Institute for which I was working was purely Catholic . . . so its days were probably numbered. Even more had I to reckon with the end of my own short-lived career as a lecturer.'

If there was one weakness completely foreign to Edith's nature it was wishful thinking. She had once confided to a friend her way of dealing with difficult situations, at least as far as the natural side of it was concerned. 'If I have reason to be afraid of something, I consider all the possible calamities that may happen, especially the worst. I prepare myself to face that—and then things usually turn out better than I had anticipated.' It is the attitude of a strong nature that looks evil in the face rather than, ostrich-like, bury its head in the sand. There is something of the Old Testament Prophets about her in the way she refuses to cry 'Peace, peace' where there is no peace. But grafted on to this natural courage and clear-sightedness was something else: the Christian's supernatural prudence and fortitude that recognizes the Cross of Christ when it sees it and is ready to embrace it.

When she had read the report of the Teachers' Conference and realized what it meant, she lost no time but went to the Institute immediately after her return. The director, Professor Steffes, was abroad, so she discussed the situation with the manager, a Catholic teacher. He told her that someone had already been to ask him whether she was still going to continue her lectures—in the circumstances it would be better if she would give them up for the summer term and carry on with her private work at the Marianum. By the autumn the situation would no doubt have been clarified; the Institute would possibly have been taken over by the Church, and she would then be able to resume her activities. But Edith knew better. 'If it is impossible here,' she said, 'then nowhere in Germany will there be an opening for me.' Whereupon the manager expressed his admiration for her clear-sightedness, the more so as she was living in such retirement, and unconcerned with the things of this world.

She then discussed matters with the President of the Catholic

8

Women Teachers' Association. She, too, advised her to stay on at the Marianum and continue her private work, while at the same time looking out for possibilities abroad. In fact, she soon received an offer from a school in South America. But by that time another way had been shown to her.

From the moment of her conversion her one desire had been to enter Carmel—but both her apostolate in the world, and the despair such a step would cause her mother, had so far prevented her from following the call.

The waiting had at last become very hard for me [she writes]. I had become a stranger in the world. Before taking up my work at Münster, and again after the first term, I had urgently asked to be allowed to enter the Order, but was refused. . . . I had given way. But now the walls that had kept me out had broken down. My apostolate had come to an end. And would not my mother rather have me in a convent in Germany than in a school in South America? On 30 April 1933, which was the Sunday of the Good Shepherd, the Church of St. Ludger celebrated its patronal feast with thirteen hours of prayer. I went there in the late afternoon and said to myself: I will not go from here until I know for certain whether I may now enter Carmel. When the final benediction had been given I had the consent of the Good Shepherd.

CHAPTER THIRTEEN

PREPARING TO ENTER

THE Good Shepherd had given His consent. It is not quite clear what these words imply—but we may well assume that they do not refer to any 'sensible' experience, such as a vision or words heard interiorly, but to a deep inner conviction that it was God's will that she should now go to Carmel. But however deep this conviction, Edith Stein was a true daughter of the Church in that she would not take such a step without the full consent of her spiritual guide, who for her represented the authority of Christ on earth. A delay was caused by Abbot Walzer's absence in Rome (where he gave her letter to the Pope), and the interference of the Nazi State had already become so all-pervasive in the spring of 1933 that she was afraid to send the letter (in which she explained everything) across the frontier. The Lord was still testing her patience, as He had done for so many years; she did not receive the Abbot's permission to take the preliminary steps until the middle of May.

As soon as she had his answer she made her preparations with the determination and circumspection that are so characteristic of her. She knew a lady in Cologne who had intimate connections with the Carmel there and asked her for an interview. During the ensuing conversation she told her of her desire, adding at the same time the facts that might tell against her: her age—she was forty-two at the time—her Jewish origin and her lack of an adequate dowry. None of these drawbacks, however, was considered very important. She was even told that there might be an opening in Cologne itself, since the Carmelites there were about to make a foundation in Silesia, her own home province.

Her interview with the Carmelites themselves was no less satisfactory. While she was waiting in the chapel, kneeling close to the altar of St. Teresa of Lisieux, she writes that she experienced 'the calm of a person who has reached her goal'. She told the nuns of her early and constant attraction to Carmel: 'I had been eight years a teacher with the Dominican nuns at Speyer, I was deeply united to the whole community, yet I could not enter there. I regarded Beuron as a forecourt of Heaven, yet I never thought of becoming a Benedictine. I always felt as if the Lord had reserved something for me in Carmel, which I could find only there.' This was decisive. There was just one last difficulty: was it right to accept someone who could still accomplish so much outside? This objection was raised to show her that she could not hope to continue her philosophical work in Carmel. Edith was perfectly ready to make the sacrifice: 'Human activity cannot help us, but only the Passion of Christ—my desire is to share in that.'

The nuns were deeply impressed. They did not give a final decision, however, but asked her to come back when the Provincial would be there, which he was to be very shortly. In the meantime they asked the priests who knew her best for testimonials. These are very interesting, as they give an insight into the esteem she enjoyed with her spiritual guides. The Provost of Münster Cathedral wrote on 9 June:

> Fräulein Edith Stein has knocked at the door of Carmel. The Providence of God, which has smoothed her way, now leads her there also. She is a soul filled with grace, rich in the love of God and men, filled with the spirit of the Scriptures and the Liturgy, from which she draws, in which she prays and meditates, and by which she lives.
>
> She has, indeed, done much by word and pen, especially in the Association of Catholic Graduates and the Catholic Women's League. But she would like to give up all such external activity in order to find in Carmel the one pearl, Jesus Christ, after the example of St. Teresa. As a priest and director I can urgently recommend to you this noble and faithful soul. She will be an example to all in deep piety and zeal of prayer, a joy for the community, full of goodness and love of her neighbour, and she will walk among you in silence like a ray from God.

Abbot Walzer expressed himself in no less glowing terms:

> I can, indeed, give you information about the postulant in question. Her extraordinary intellectual gifts are unquestioned. This is well known to a wide German public. It is all the more surprising that

she should be very simple and easily guided. Her spiritual maturity
and depth are such that I need not tell you about them, you will
realize that yourself. The only difficulties as regards her entering are
consideration for her old mother and her position in public life. I
should not like to take the responsibility for this valuable member
to be lost to the Church Militant, and I ask that, should she enter, my
name be not mentioned if there were a complaint.

Carmel has long been her ideal, and I have never attempted to
suggest another one to her when the idea of a convent came up.
Until recently, it is true, I have been against her entering a convent,
because of her vocation to an active life. However, since through
the changed external circumstances the way is practically free, I no
longer oppose her entering.

After her interview with the nuns Edith returned to Münster.
But now, so close to the goal, waiting became harder than ever,
and the Provincial delayed his coming. About the same time,
on 11 June, she wrote to a teaching nun: 'Indeed I consider it the
duty of a teacher to see this time through with the children. This
means, that one seeks oneself to come to a judgement, to measure
the [Nazi] Movement by our standards and to speak to the
children in this sense.' She then told her friend that her work at
Münster had come to an end at Easter and asks for prayers for
her mother. She signs the letter: 'From the deepest security
(*Geborgenheit*) *in tabernaculo Domini*.'

She spent most of Pentecost praying in Münster Cathedral,
and finally decided to write once more to Cologne, pointing out
that the uncertainty of her situation made it imperative that as
soon as possible she should see clearly what was going to happen.
The nuns understood her difficulties and replied that they would
not wait for the Provincial; she should once more come to
Cologne and there see the Ecclesiastical Superior of the convent.

He gave her a strange reception. On her way there she had
been surprised by a thunderstorm and arrived completely
drenched. This did not prevent him from keeping her waiting
for a whole hour. When he finally received her, he pretended
not to remember who she was or what she wanted, and even
went so far as to call her *Du*.[1]   It was evidently a somewhat

[1] English 'thou', a very familiar form of address reserved to relatives and intimate
friends, like the French *tu*, but otherwise only used for children, and sometimes also for
persons considered socially quite inferior.

disconcerting 'trial of humility' which he deemed necessary in the case of a well-known scholar—but Edith took it without turning a hair. Why he should have staged it at all is not quite clear, since he told her at the end of the conversation, after enumerating all the objections he would raise against her, that the nuns generally took little notice of these, and that in the end he always complied with their wishes.

When she returned to the convent all the Chapter nuns came to the grille, and there she had to submit to a custom of the house and to sing them a little song. She found this rather disturbing, and shyly sang a little German Marian hymn, *Segne, Du Maria* (Bless thou Mary). Afterwards she told them that this had been more difficult for her than speaking before a public of a thousand people. The sisters received the remark in silence, since they had no idea to what she referred. It was, indeed, somewhat naïve to imagine that these nuns, most of whom, since they were fully professed, must have entered Carmel at least several years before she had begun to lecture on a wider scale, should have heard of her. She had lived in an intellectual atmosphere all her life, even at Speyer. Lectures, books, and philosophical and other problems had been her daily bread from childhood; it never entered her head that there could be a world where such pursuits were practically unheard-of. But when she sat before the grille of Carmel, asking to become a daughter of St. Teresa, nothing of all her former achievements and qualifications was required. A little song—that was all. And precisely because no one had ever asked such a simple thing of her it was harder than all the lectures and examinations. But, unless you become as little children, you shall not enter the Kingdom of Heaven—and so the philosopher, who had for so long been at home in the regions of metaphysical speculation was gently made to descend from her heights into the sphere of quite ordinary young girls who would never be able to utter a single sentence on a speaker's platform, but could easily sing a ditty before a convent grille.

That evening Edith went back to Münster. Her admission could be put to the vote of the Chapter only next morning; so there was yet one more day to wait. But then came the longed-for telegram: 'Joyful assent. Greetings. Carmel.' She had

reached the goal and went into the chapel to say her 'Thank You'
to the Lord.

★   ★   ★

All the details had already been arranged at the interview
on the previous day. She would have wound up her affairs at
Münster by 15 July, so that she could celebrate the feast of Our
Lady of Mount Carmel (16 July) at Cologne. There she would
stay as a guest in the quarters of the out-sisters for about a month,
then go home to Breslau, and be received as a postulant on the
Feast of the great St. Teresa, 15 October.

At Münster she was busy packing up her books. Six big
boxes of them preceded her to Cologne, and she wrote in the
accompanying letter that she did not think any other Carmelite
had ever brought such a dowry with her. She had arranged
them all very carefully and labelled them 'Theology', 'Philosophy',
'Philology', etc. She might have saved herself the trouble; for
when they were unpacked everything was gaily muddled up,
despite the efforts of the poor sister in charge of them to keep
them in their original order. It was yet another indication of the
fact that the standards of Carmel were not those of the world
of libraries and lecture-rooms to which she had been used, that
she was about to enter an entirely different sphere with totally
different values and ideals.

She now wrote to her relatives with deliberate ambiguity that
she had found a place with nuns at Cologne, which they took
to mean another post. At Münster only few people knew where
she was going. Shortly before she left, the students of the
Marianum arranged a farewell party for her, and on the day of
her departure five of them saw her off at the station. Edith herself was touched by all the marks of affection she received; the
sisters had given her a reliquary cross, and the students had
provided large bouquets of roses. 'Less than eighteen months
ago,' she writes, 'I had come to Münster as a stranger. Apart
from my professional activities I had lived in monastic retirement. Yet now I left a large circle who stood by me in faithful
affection.' She meant these words to be a tribute to her friends,
yet they are really a tribute to her own lovable personality,
which, despite her silence and solitary life, or perhaps rather

because of them, had once again exercised its attraction on all who knew where to look for the true human values.

The roses her friends had given her she laid at the feet of Our Lady of Mount Carmel. The next month was a happy time. She took part in all the offices and prayers of the community, and had many conversations with the Mother Prioress, with whom she found herself in agreement on all the practical questions which she brought to her for decision. After a fortnight she had the great joy of assisting at the baptism and first Communion of one of her Jewish friends, and a little later she went to Trier to see Abbot Walzer and to receive his blessing for the hard task that lay before her: the weeks at Breslau, when she would have to break the news to her mother. At Trier she saw the famous Holy Coat, and before this reputed relic of the Passion she asked for strength to face the coming ordeal. Once again we meet in her that childlike piety which accepts all the practices and traditions of the Church without questioning, which rejoices in her holy places and her relics with no desire to examine or doubt. It is the more surprising, since she does not hesitate to use her critical faculties even on the teaching of St. Paul and St. Thomas. For all her simplicity her personality had two very pronounced sides: the searching, critical intellect and the unquestioning affection of the heart, which strove to be ever more deeply harmonized. One more spiritual enjoyment she allowed herself: together with her newly baptized friend she went to the famous Benedictine liturgical centre, Maria Laach, for the Feast of the Assumption, and then she travelled to Breslau for the last, heart-rending encounter with her mother.

*   *   *

She was met at the station by her sister Rosa, the only member of her family who felt herself drawn to the Church. For this reason Edith thought it right to tell her of her intention, and though Rosa did not show any surprise it was clear that she had never anticipated such a decision. The first two or three weeks were peaceful, for, strangely enough, nobody asked her exactly what she was going to do in Cologne, except a nephew of hers, to whom she told the truth, asking him not to divulge it for the time being. Her mother, of course, suffered greatly because of what was happening in Germany and could not understand how 'people could be so wicked'. Frau Stein's domestic arrangements were being affected by the persecution; her daughter Erna's two children, whom she loved particularly, left the house and moved with their mother to another part of the town. Everyone was depressed in the extreme; the future was looking black, indeed.

When Edith came the old lady brightened up considerably. She knew how to soothe the sorrows of her mother by her calm way of listening and her ready sympathy. Frau Stein, like most old people, loved to speak of the past, and her daughter, who had conceived the idea of writing a history of her family, encouraged her to relate her reminiscences. And so, when she came back from her office where she still went every day, her mother would sit contentedly by her side, knitting away while pouring out her troubles of the present and her memories of the past, while Edith was dreading the day when she would at last have to reveal her secret.

She had a foretaste of what to expect when her sister Erna, whom she helped with her removal, asked her what would be her position at Cologne. Edith's eyes filled with tears as she said: 'It is terrible in this world—what is happiness for one, is the worst that could happen for the other.' A few days later she told Edith that her husband had asked her to tell her that, if her step was due to financial worries, she could live with them as long as they themselves still had any money. But her sister knew her well enough to add that she realized such motives had nothing to do with it.

Edith's only consolation during these difficult days of suspense and apprehension was the presence at Breslau of two Carmelites from Cologne who were there to prepare the new foundation. With them, at least, she could speak unreservedly, and rely on their prayers and affection.

At last the fateful hour came. 'On the first Sunday of September I was alone with my mother at home. She was sitting by the window with her knitting, and I close to her. Then suddenly came the long-expected question: "What are you going to do with the sisters at Cologne?" "Live with them." Now there was a desperate resistance. My mother did not stop working.

Her knitting wool became entangled; with trembling hands she was trying to unravel it. I helped her with it, while the discussion between us was going on.'

When Edith had decided to become a Carmelite, she had consoled herself with the thought that her mother would be sure to prefer her being in a convent in Germany to teaching at a school in South America. It is difficult to decide whether she had really believed that; the scene which now followed must have quickly shown her that this assumption had been wrong.

Probably Frau Stein did not realize exactly the external circumstances of a Carmelite's life at the time; but Edith must have told her enough in answer to her agonized questions for her to realize that the life her daughter was henceforth to lead was totally different from all she had ever known before; more, that all her gifts, her brilliant career, would now count for nothing. It was indeed the end of Dr. Edith Stein, of her own most beloved daughter, who had always been so sympathetic, so clever, so loving and kind to her old mother. But the mother now counted for nothing; her tears, her agony were brushed aside—and why? Why? That was what she simply could not understand. For she could not know that there was Someone in Edith's life who had once said: 'He that loveth father or mother more than me is not worthy of me.' And He alone knows what it costs His disciples to leave father and mother, to seem to break their hearts for His sake, while all their own natural feelings are in revolt from the sacrifice He demands, though outwardly they may seem calm and almost cold. If even Catholic mothers often cannot understand the vocation of their children, how much less a Jewish mother, to whom the consecrated life of religion is totally foreign?

Old Frau Stein was in despair; periods of silence alternated with scenes and arguments. During one of the former Edith wrote: 'I know that my mother has become a little more quiet only because she is still secretly hoping that I shall not, in the end, be capable of doing the most dreadful thing she can imagine.' One of Edith's nieces, a very orthodox Jewess, tried to influence her aunt; whereas the other members of the family knew her well enough to realize that such efforts would be fruitless. Only her sister Else, who had come from Hamburg for their mother's birthday, recounted to her the desperate outbursts of the latter because she imagined Edith did not realize how much her mother was suffering.

God was indeed trying this strong woman to the limits of her endurance; did He not take her beloved daughter from her just at the moment when she needed her most? The business was going from bad to worse; for which carpenter in the Germany of 1933 was still brave enough to buy his timber from a Jewish firm? More, her daughter Erna with her family had left the house, and now nobody was going to rent the flat that had become vacant. There were many who came to see it; but when they heard the proprietors were Jews the negotiations were dropped. At last a Protestant parish was going to take it over. Everything seemed settled when, at the last minute, the pastor drew back. Edith resolved to make one more effort herself and went to see him at his home.

It seemed that there was nothing more to be done. But as I was going to take my leave he said: 'Now you are looking so sad; I am sorry.' I told him that my mother was now burdened with so many cares. He asked sympathetically what these cares were. I told him briefly about my conversion and my intention to enter a convent. This made a deep impression. 'I want you to know before you go there that you have won a heart here.' He called in his wife, and after a short consultation they decided to call another meeting of the parish council and to raise the matter once more. Before my departure the head pastor and his colleague came to our house in order to conclude the business. As he left he said to me under his breath: 'God keep you.'

This story reveals better than anything else the extraordinary influence Edith had on people. Wherever she went she inspired genuine affection; it had been so at Münster and at Speyer; Canon Schwind had loved her as a daughter, Father Przywara was devoted to her, her own family adored her, and now, in half an hour with a Protestant pastor she had made such an impression that he reversed his decision on an important business matter solely in order to please her. The unassuming charm of her manner, which hardly concealed the deep spirituality of an exceptional soul, captivated most people who came into contact with her and caused them to comply with her wishes whenever possible.

The incident with the pastor was one of those slight consolations which the Lord allowed her in these difficult days. For her mother remained inconsolable. One of the Carmelite nuns who had called on Frau Stein before had another *tête-à-tête* with her, but it was of no avail. All her mother wanted the nun to do was to dissuade her daughter from joining them; and this, of course, could not be. On the other hand, she would not have dared to make any attempt to encourage Edith in her resolution; as things were, the responsibility would have been too great for anyone to try to interfere in either direction. As Edith herself wrote: 'The decision was so difficult that no person could say for certain which way was the right one—good reasons could be adduced for either. I had to take the step in the utter darkness of faith. In those weeks I often thought: Which of us will break down, my mother or I? But both of us held out to the last day.'

For her no visions and revelations that might have relieved the bitterness and uncertainty of whether her decision was in accordance with the will of God or not. The old legends of the saints abound with such supernatural interventions, but in everyday life, as most men know it, they are rare indeed. St. John of the Cross teaches that God has given His final Revelation in the New Testament, which, together with reason, should suffice to guide us. No doubt signs are sometimes given, but this is done extremely rarely, and even then there is always the danger of misinterpreting them in accordance with one's own desires. Edith Stein was led by the safe road of dark faith, with all its sufferings, its heart-rending uncertainties, yet at the same time its total abandonment into the hands of God in whose guidance she trusts even though He seems to leave her entirely to her own doubts and difficulties.

One of these was formulated by her little twelve-year-old niece, when she raised the question, which no doubt had often been asked by her parents: 'Why are you doing this *now*?' 'I gave her my reasons as if she were a grown-up. She listened thoughtfully and understood,' writes Edith. Indeed, a child would understand better than an adult when she spoke to her

about her desire to sacrifice herself for her people. The child's
father, who came later to make a last effort to dissuade her, was,
of course, unable to comprehend. 'What I was going to do,'
she writes, 'seemed to him to emphasize even more my separation
from the Jewish people—just now, when it was being so much
oppressed. He could not understand that from my point of view
things looked quite different.'

It was, indeed, not to be expected that a Jewish business-man
should be able to enter into the ideas of suffering and self-
sacrifice of Christian contemplatives. For her, however, the
knowledge that what she was doing out of love for her people
was interpreted by them as an act of desertion, made the step
harder than ever. In her own small sphere there was thus re-
enacted the great drama of precisely nineteen hundred years ago
in one of its aspects: the misunderstanding of the Gospel by
Israel.

*   *   *

Her last day at home had come. It was 12 October, her
birthday, and that year at the same time a Jewish feast day, the
end of the Feast of Tabernacles. She accompanied her mother
to the service in the synagogue. In the tram on the way there
she had tried to console her by remarking that the first months
in the convent were only a time of trial. But Frau Stein knew
her daughter too well to let herself be comforted by that. 'If
you undertake a time of trial, I know that you will go through
with it.' On the way back she insisted on walking, though it took
three-quarters of an hour, despite her eighty-four years; for she
wanted one last uninterrupted talk with Edith.

Once more the Church and the Synagogue seemed to confront
each other in these two women. 'Wasn't the sermon beautiful?'
'Yes.' 'So one can also be devout in the Jewish way?' 'Certainly—
if one has not come to know anything else.' And then the
desperate, infinitely pathetic reply: 'Why did you come to know
it? I won't say anything against Him. He may have been a very
good man. But why did He make Himself God?'

'For I came to set a man at variance against his father, and the
daughter against her mother.' Rarely can these words of Christ
have been so literally fulfilled as in these two women, both

equally noble, generous, deeply devoted to the service of God—divided only by Him, who had planted His Cross at the very centre of their relationship.

After this painful conversation in the morning the tension was relieved in the afternoon by the many visitors who arrived for Edith's birthday. But at night, after all the guests had left, her mother's self-control gave way at last. 'She covered her face with her hands and began to weep. I stood behind her chair and placed her silver-white head against my breast. So we remained for a long time, until she let herself be persuaded to go to bed. I led her upstairs and helped her to undress—for the first time in our lives. Then I continued to sit on her bed till she herself told me to go to sleep. I do not think that either of us had any rest that night.'

The final ordeal came in the morning. As usual, Edith went to Mass at half-past five. The family had breakfast at seven; but Frau Stein pushed away her cup and began to cry. Edith went and held her in her embrace till it was time for her to go. Her mother kissed her good-bye and wept aloud as she kissed her sister Erna, who was to stay with their mother, while Rosa and her other sister Else accompanied her to the station. Else in her despair clung to her sister till the train moved in. Edith noticed that in her grief she looked like an old woman, whereas Rosa was calm and peaceful. Both of them waved till the train was out of sight, and at last Edith, exhausted, could sink back on her seat.

During those past weeks that had seemed endless, she had hardly dared to hope that she would at last reach her goal. In the midst of all the discussions, the despair of her mother, the arguments of her sisters and other relatives, the political situation, she sometimes no longer knew whether what she was going to do was right or wrong. At last the turmoil had ceased—and here she was, in the train to Cologne, to Carmel. 'There could be no rapturous joy. What lay behind me had been too dreadful for that. But I was perfectly at peace—in the harbour of the Divine Will.'

CHAPTER FOURTEEN

THE POSTULANT

MANY of those who knew Edith Stein, even close friends, found it difficult to understand why she should have chosen Carmel, and not the Order of St. Benedict, to which she seemed attached by so many ties, or another religious family like the Dominicans, more akin to her intellectual and liturgical inclinations. Yet her decision is not so difficult to understand. There are souls for whom God intends the religious life to mean using their natural talents in His service. There are also others to whom it must mean the renunciation of these talents and of all their natural self holds dear. In this case, although their gifts are left unused in the natural way, they are made fruitful in a supernatural way. The highly intellectual contemplative, who sweeps the convent floors or mends the linen of the community, will thereby offer to God his most precious possession: his mind; and his time, which seems wasted in the eyes of the world, will bear rich fruit towards eternity.

The vocation of the total sacrifice of the natural self corresponds to a certain type of soul which one might perhaps call the 'all or nothing' type, who bring to all they do the whole of their personality. Edith Stein was of this type. When she began to study philosophy she studied it with her whole being. When she became a Catholic she immediately strove to dedicate her whole life to God, knowing nothing else but prayer and work in His service. It was the logical consequence of this that she should have felt drawn to Carmel throughout her Catholic life, since the programme of Carmel, and especially of St. John of the Cross, is this *Todo y Nada*, the rejection of all that is not God, who is found only in His totality if all His creatures become *Nada*, nothingness.

If this characteristic of the Carmelite vocation made its appeal to her from the moment she had met it in the *Life* of St. Teresa, it was supported by another consideration at the particular time when she at last found herself free to follow the call. When the persecutions of the Jews began she had realized that the Lord had laid His Cross on His people, and she wanted to embrace it willingly. What she desired was to be a victim of expiation in the name of Israel. Once more it was Carmel, with its idea of voluntary suffering for the salvation of others so urgently demanded by St. Teresa of Lisieux, that presented itself as the obvious means to this end.

Therefore the question whether or not she would be allowed to continue her scholarly work in Carmel simply did not arise. She wanted but two things: to give herself totally to God, without reserving to herself anything whatsoever, and, by so doing, to offer herself as a willing victim in expiation of the sins of her people. For she had come to love them as a Catholic even more than before her conversion, because her love had become wholly spiritualized. She had indeed meant what she had told the Prioress at their first interview: 'Human activity cannot help us, but only the Passion of Christ—my desire is to share in that.' This was what she wished for, this was what Carmel could give her.

*   *   *

When she entered the enclosure after the First Vespers of the Feast of the great St. Teresa had been sung, on 14 October 1933, her human activity seemed, indeed, to have come to an end. Dr. Edith Stein, the brilliant philosopher and lecturer, ceased to exist, and instead there emerged a new being, 'the little postulant'. Even before her entry one of the older sisters had asked anxiously: 'Is she a good needle-woman?'[1] Edith was not a good needle-woman, and though she had occasionally lent a hand with domestic jobs, both at home and in the various convents where she had been staying, housework was not her strong point, and the professional way in which the nuns swept the floors and handled the crockery in the refectory bewildered her. Her premonition had been right: the Lord had certainly reserved something for her in Carmel which she could find only there.

[1] *Life*, p. 137.

Convent of St. Magdalena, Speyer

The Carmelite Chapel, Cologne, on the day of her clothing

The Refectory

Throughout her life, one might almost say since the days when she was a small child, she had always been admired and made much of in whatever society she had mixed. Her family adored her, at school she was always among the best if not actually at the top of her form. At the university she immediately became one of the stars of the philosophical faculty. It was the same after her conversion: her directors admired her, to say nothing of the nuns; the audiences to whom she lectured were mostly enthusiastic; her converts and friends treasured her advice. Wherever she went, people were deeply impressed both by her personality and her abilities. If not always literally, at least metaphorically, she had till then been living on a platform, always teaching, always setting an example. None of the pupils or of the nuns at Speyer can remember ever having seen her getting into a temper or behaving in any but the most perfect way, so that her very perfection struck at least some of them as almost inhuman.

At Carmel she was suddenly and completely removed from the platform. As her Prioress puts it: 'Edith Stein's entry into Carmel was, in fact, a descent from the height of a brilliant career into the depths of insignificance.'[1] During the six months of her postulancy she was treated like any other postulant—she had to take part in all the community duties and work, and, for the first time in her life, she was not particularly good at what she had to do. She certainly knew how to handle a pen better than a broom, and though she took the greatest pains to do things well, her needle was not nearly as quick nor her stitches as even as those of the other sisters. After having been accorded the first place throughout her life, now, at the age of forty-two, she had to begin to take the last. Later she wrote to one of her pupils, who met with the same difficulties in the Nazi *Arbeitsdienst*,[2] that no one was of so little use in the kitchen as she, but that it was a good school of humility, after she had been so excessively honoured throughout her life.[3] Evidently she realized only now what an exceptional position she had been enjoying while she was living in the world; for in Carmel there was no question of

---

[1] *Life*, p. 137; 136.
[2] A semi-military organization for training girls in domestic and other work.
[3] *Life*, p. 137.

her being honoured. They all liked her, because she was always friendly and anxious to do her best; but they knew nothing about her intellectual work, and even if they had known about it, they would hardly have understood what it meant. To them she was the 'little postulant', conscientious and willing, but rather exasperatingly slow and devoid of the normal feminine accomplishments.

But this was not the only mortification the Lord had saved up for her in Carmel. Six years later, she writes to a nun who had asked her how one could combine the fulfilment of conventual precepts with Christian liberty. 'I think the answer is: *Fiat voluntas tua*. The holy Rule and Constitutions are for us the expression of the Divine Will. It is our part in the sacrifice of Christ to sacrifice to them our personal inclinations. Moreover, charity demands that we should also adapt ourselves to the customs of the house and the taste of the community. If we do this in order to give joy to the Heart of Jesus, it will not be a restriction, but the highest exercise of liberty, a free gift of bridal love.'

Perfect adaptation to the life of the community—this was perhaps the hardest sacrifice of all; for this, in her interpretation, included both the customs of the house and the taste of her fellow nuns. Now Rule and Constitutions are generally not so difficult to accept, because they are the result of many years of experience and consultations, and aim at devising the best way of attaining the end of the institute for which they are drawn up. It is far otherwise with the customs of the house. These may often be quite arbitrary regulations which were found useful fifty years ago and are still followed scrupulously though they are totally out of date. They may refer to a way of doing things irrelevant in itself, but which is very irksome to newcomers who are used to other ways.

As she mentions especially the taste, this, too, must have been a source of mortification to her. Her own was very austere; she loved the drawings of Rembrandt and Reger's *lieder*, predilections which could hardly be expected to be shared by most of her sisters. The effort to adapt herself to it all, especially to the observance of every little rule and custom, was particularly irksome to the scholar of forty-two, whose memory had been trained to remember very different things. After about two months she frankly admitted to the Prioress, pointing to her forehead: 'This machine here found it very difficult indeed to learn all those little rubrics.' The lack of intellectual work and of the exchange of ideas was another hardship; it seemed that all that had interested her before had to be buried completely.

Yet, if it was difficult in some ways, in others this new life came as a real relief. For all her admirable balance, there had been something strained and exaggeratedly reserved about her, even something a little spinsterish, as the sisters thought. Carmel worked a real transformation. St. Teresa, who loved laughter, could write, 'The Lord preserve us from frowning saints'—in this school Edith learned to laugh as she had never done before. Indeed, she learned it so thoroughly that sometimes the tears ran down her cheeks; her Prioress writes that Edith herself confided to her that she had not laughed so much in her whole life as she laughed at recreation in Carmel,[1] which, to her, became occasions of a re-creation in the most literal sense. Here at last she was no longer the 'Fräulein Doktor', the famous philosopher, educationist and lecturer, here she was simply the little sister postulant—and her soul expanded as the responsibility of being a teacher and a model was lifted from her shoulders, and she could at last be just the same as anybody else. No more singularity of being in church before everybody else, of kneeling rigidly for hours, of being silent when others were talking. At last she had, by virtue of holy obedience, to do what they were all doing: she had to get up at the same time, eat the same food (with the further mortification that she had to accept exceptions made for her on account of her weak stomach), and, best of all, she was anything but outstandingly successful at the work she had to do. Though she suffered a good deal from the cold, which once even made her faint, this new life had an excellent effect on her health; she seemed to be growing younger and more cheerful, despite the increasing seriousness of the situation of her family. This she felt as deeply as ever, and she did not fail to speak of it to her sisters; for as she shared all their little joys and sorrows, so she did not hesitate to let them participate in her own.

She had indeed been given much freedom to keep up her contacts with the world. Even before her entry she had written

[1] *Life*, p. 142; 141.

to a friend: 'Of course you will be able to write to me later. It will, however, depend upon my superiors whether I shall be allowed to answer. I am convinced that I shall always be permitted to do so if this is an act of charity to a soul. For the *major horum caritas* takes precedence of all our other rules.' After she had entered it was chiefly lack of time, not of permission, that compelled her to curtail her correspondence. There was, however, one person for whom she found time every week. This was her mother. Every Friday she had her letter ready for her Prioress to send off—but there was rarely an answer. Shortly after Christmas 1933 she wrote to a friend: 'I still need your prayers for my mother very much. She has not yet become at all reconciled to the thought.' But even this sorrow could not take away her deep joy to be at last in the place where she knew God wanted her to be. She continues in the same letter: 'When I am in our silent choir I cannot be sufficiently grateful for the wholly unmerited grace of having been taken out of all these troubles into this profound peace. For I have never been able to celebrate Advent and Christmas as I did this year.'[1]

Yet once she ventured one of those criticisms which had annoyed her friends from time to time. She said at recreation that she could not understand how a Carmelite could sleep during meditation. The sisters smiled but made no reply, thinking: 'Wait till you are clothed and have to follow the Rule in its entirety.' They were right. There were no more remarks like that after she had been given the habit; in fact she soon learned by experience how easy it is for a Carmelite to go to sleep during prayer-time.

Despite such little incidents her humility was very striking. Once the Novice Mistress said by way of testing it: 'In the world you may have been a clever woman—but here you are getting more stupid every day.' Without a word she blushingly made the prostration prescribed by the rule after committing a fault. Another time a sister about twenty years younger than herself had taken some trouble trying to teach her how to sweep the corridor properly; afterwards she thanked her most touchingly for having taught her so patiently, causing considerable embarrassment to the younger nun. The famous scholar showed a childlike

[1] *Life*, p. 143.

delight when she had at last finished embroidering a cingulum, an achievement she found very difficult indeed. As her Prioress expressed it: 'It almost seemed as if Edith had forgotten her past, all her knowledge and abilities, and had only the one desire to be a child among children.'[1] But of such is the Kingdom of Heaven.

[1] *Life*, p. 140.

CHAPTER FIFTEEN

SISTER TERESA BENEDICTA OF THE CROSS

IT was now the Sunday of the Good Shepherd, 1934, the same feast on which, a year before, she had asked our Lord to allow her to enter Carmel. Today her desire was to be fulfilled; for she was to receive the habit of the Order.

The one great sorrow on this otherwise so joyful day of her clothing was the incomprehension of her mother. In a letter of 4 May she told her sister Erna how sad it made her that her mother had such wrong ideas not only of the Catholic faith and the conventual life in general, but also of her own motives for becoming a nun; and the worst was that she could do nothing to change this attitude: 'I know that every word would be in vain and only upset her unnecessarily.'[1] It was the price she had to pay for the new name with which she signed herself for the first time to one of her family:'With deepest affection, Your sister, Benedicta.'

For weeks before the great event the sisters had been busy with the preparations. There was the dark brown habit to be made, then the alpargas (the old Spanish hemp sandals), the big rosary and, not the least important, the white bridal dress, for which her sister Rosa had given the heavy silk, and the veil. However, 'she could not easily adapt herself to being, in her role of "little bride", the object of particular sisterly love and care.'[2]

One may well believe that she found it difficult, and perhaps a little irritating, as she had to go from one office[3] to another to try on the different garments. She received all the solicitude with marked gratitude; but this essentially feminine atmosphere of fussing over wedding dresses and veils, wimples and tunics must have been foreign to her, who had always accorded only the minimum of time and interest to such unscholarly pursuits. But now she had—by virtue of obedience as well as of charity—to

[1] *Edith Stein*, par une Moniale Française, p. 170.
[2] *Life*, p. 143.
[3] In Carmel the various workrooms are called 'offices', e.g. linen office, bread office, etc.

take part in it all: another step in her initiation into this strangely unknown world, the world of a contemplative convent peopled by very ordinary women with an extraordinary vocation.

For this was one of the surprises that God had reserved for her in Carmel: that the contemplative life does not require spiritual 'athletics' so to speak; that contemplative nuns can take a wholly legitimate interest in their daily domestic duties, and that these belong as much to their way of life as contemplation itself; that even Carmelites are expected to get tired at prayer and need sufficient sleep and food: 'The excess of intellectual work, the physical fast, the arbitrary reduction of sleep, all these austerities which she had undertaken on her own account, gave way to the order of obedience: to eat properly, sleep free from care, and be very gay.'[1] In the company of ordinary women, under the rule of obedience which, while cutting at the roots of self-love, took full account of the limitations of their physical endurance, Edith Stein was gradually freed from a weakness whose very existence she had evidently never suspected when she was still in the world. For she had used to lay on herself excessive burdens, even though she was perhaps better able than most to support them, since she had an extraordinary physical resistance enhanced by a Spartan education and an inclination to austerity natural to many scholars; but she had failed to understand that other people might be led by different paths, that the length of time a person was capable of spending on her knees in prayer was no measure of her holiness.

In the world, with very few exceptions, she had been admired even by her directors for this capacity of hers, which did indeed go with a deep interior life. In Carmel all this would count for nothing. Postulants are not supposed to outdo professed nuns in their austerities, and so here, too, she had to take the lower place. Moreover, she was made to realize that natures are different, and that with the best will in the world most other people were physically incapable of her endurance. She herself was well aware of what she owed Carmel in this respect. Several years later she wrote to a former pupil of hers, who had also entered a Carmelite convent: 'One really only gets to know one's faults when one lives in a convent. If we live alone, we can have very wrong ideas of ourselves. This by itself is an inestimable advantage of

[1] *Life*, p. 140.

community life.' For Edith, who had lived by herself nearly all her adult life, this was indeed true. When, six months after she had entered, the day of her clothing came, she was no longer the famous Dr. Stein, philosopher and educationist. She chose another name, by which she would henceforth be known, a name whose full symbolism was to be worked out during these last eight years of her life: Sister Teresa Benedicta of the Cross.

*   *   *

On the day of her clothing the Prioress realized to the full how famous and well loved her postulant had been in the world. Masses of flowers had been given by her friends for the decoration of the chapel; and when the guests began to arrive it became clear that this was going to be the most illustrious assembly of scholars and other distinguished people that the Cologne Carmel had so far seen. The Lord Abbot of Beuron was to sing the Pontifical High Mass and the Provincial of the Carmelites was to clothe her. There was a whole galaxy of university professors, representatives of the Catholic Women's League, her godmother Dr. Conrad-Martius, and a large number of her former students and pupils, as well as many religious.

An hour before the ceremony she left the enclosure in her convent-made bridal dress of heavy white silk, adorned with a long white veil and a myrtle wreath, according to the German wedding customs. She looked tired, for she had been keeping vigil the night before; and it must have been an ordeal to have to speak a few words to each of the guests immediately before the clothing, which to her, the mature woman who had suffered much, must have meant even more than to most postulants. So she felt relieved when the ringing of the bells announced the beginning of the Mass. A choir of Third Order Dominicans sang, so that the three Orders who had most deeply influenced her Catholic life—Carmelites, Benedictines and Dominicans—all took part in the ceremony by which she now dedicated herself formally to God.

After the Mass Abbot Walzer gave an address in which he asked the congregation to thank God with him for having given them Edith Stein, and after God, to thank her mother, to whom both the Church and the Order were indebted for having reared this daughter. They should pray for this mother, for whom the conversion of her beloved child had been a great grief, and who knew nothing of the significance of this day of her clothing. And what did the world say to this? In normal times it would probably have been indignant that such a talent should be buried in a convent. Yet he felt that even though she was now a nun hidden in Carmel, she was called to place her light, her talent entrusted to her by the Lord, on a lamp-stand, and to exercise her influence in the world through her writing; though now it would be used even more exclusively for God than in her last times at the Institute. Therefore they were now waiting to see her literary work continued. After some personal wishes and counsels, he announced her new name, through which the friendly relations between her and the Abbey of Beuron would receive a new symbolic meaning: Teresa Benedicta of the Cross.

There followed the actual clothing ceremony, beginning with the ancient dialogue between the superior and the postulant, who desired 'the mercy of God, the poverty of the Order and the company of the Sisters'. Then she entered the enclosure and quickly exchanged the white bridal silk for the dark brown penitential tunic of the Order. She reappeared before the now wide-open grille of the choir, and while the Provincial was reciting the words prescribed by the ritual, drawing attention to the symbolic meaning of the belt, the scapular and the white mantle and veil, the Prioress placed these parts of the habit on the novice who was kneeling before her. The Provincial intoned the *Veni Creator*, while Edith prostrated herself in the form of a cross, signifying the mystical death which the 'old man' must die before entering on the higher life for which the reception of the habit destined her. On a sign from the Novice Mistress she rose, kissed the hand of the Prioress and embraced her sisters, who took her in their midst and led her away from the grille into the interior of the convent.

The intellectual *élite* who had watched this clothing were deeply impressed, and there were few who had not been aware of the poignant symbolism of the scene that had been enacted this Sunday morning. Dr. Edith Stein, once a representative of Jewish intellectualism at its best, then a Catholic scholar intent on grasping the philosophical foundations of her new religion and on communicating her knowledge to others—now a contemplative immolating herself for souls in an ever-growing union with her crucified Lord: Teresa Benedicta of the Cross.

Abbot Walzer had been somewhat apprehensive lest the total sacrifice of herself should prove too difficult even for a soul cast in her heroic mould. After the ceremony he had an opportunity to speak to her alone—it was the last time in his life that he saw her—and on this occasion he asked her bluntly how she felt in this community of quite simple women, and so far without facilities to continue her scholarly work. She answered with perfect sincerity and conviction, that she felt completely at home in Carmel.[1]

Christ Himself promised His disciples: 'Amen I say to you, there is no man that hath left home or parents, or brethren or wife or children, for the kingdom of God's sake, who shall not receive much more in this present time, and in the world to come life everlasting.' Sister Benedicta had been willing to give up her beloved plain-chant; but soon she was to have the happiness of seeing it introduced in her Carmel, in accordance with the new regulations from Rome which allowed it where the nuns would prefer it to the customary monotoning of the Office; she herself was one of its most ardent advocates.[2] She had freely given up all thought of continuing her scholarly work, but God was going to give this back to her, too.

After her clothing the Provincial held the canonical visitation, and on this occasion questioned her about her occupations in the convent and her philosophical work. The bulky treatise on Potency and Act, which she had begun several years ago, had remained unfinished, and she felt that it needed to be thoroughly recast. So the Provincial ordered her to be dispensed from all other work (except, of course, the essential duties such as choir office, meditation, recreation, etc.) in order to have sufficient time to continue her writing.

[1] *Life*, p. 154.
[2] The present author had the privilege of hearing the nuns sing the Mass on the Feast of Our Lady of Mount Carmel, and they did it beautifully indeed.

CHAPTER SIXTEEN

SPIRITUAL WRITINGS

BESIDE her continuous work on the philosophical treatise, several minor writings came into existence, occasioned by requests from publishers and Catholic associations. The first of these was her translation of the prayers said at the Clothing and Veiling of a Novice, which was published together with the Latin text; truly a labour of love to make both her sisters and the friends of Carmel better acquainted with the treasures of the Church's ceremonies. This was followed by a booklet on the life of the great St. Teresa, and another on a little known Carmelite saint, Teresa Margaret Redi, on the occasion of her canonization in 1934, neither of them much above the average of the general type of devotional biography.

On an altogether different level is an essay on a subject particularly congenial to her, 'The Prayer of the Church', which formed part of a symposium on 'The Stream of Life in the Church'. It shows how perfectly her Jewish upbringing had been blended with her Catholicism, and, on the other hand, it makes the reader realize how truly the Church is the heir of the Temple and the Synagogue. Its leading idea is that 'The prayer of the Church is the prayer of the still living Christ; its exemplar is the prayer of Christ during His human life.' She applies this thought to the two principal forms of the Church's prayer; to the public prayer of the Liturgy and to private, that is to say meditative and contemplative, prayer. For in her view both are the authentic prayer of the Church; the idea that one should be extolled at the expense of the other, or, worse still, that one might be sacrificed to the other, is entirely foreign to her. She shows from the Gospels that 'Christ prayed as a believing Jew, devoted to the Law, used to pray', and how, through the Institution of the Eucharist He brought to perfection and at the same time transcended the Jewish Liturgy. She shows how, in place of the Temple of Solomon, He erected another: the Temple made of living stones, the Communion of the Saints in His Church.

The second part of the essay is called 'The Solitary Converse with God as the Prayer of the Church.' The title may come as a surprise; for ordinarily only the liturgical prayer is called 'prayer of the Church'. Yet, by using it, Sister Benedicta expresses a much fuller truth. 'The prayer life of Jesus,' she writes, 'should be the key to understanding the prayer of the Church. . . . But Jesus did not only take part in the official public prayer. Perhaps even more frequently the Gospels record His solitary prayer in the stillness of the night, in the freedom of high mountains, in the desert, far from men. . . . And once He has allowed us to look long and deeply into this secret conversation.' She is referring to the High-Priestly Prayer in the seventeenth chapter of St. John's Gospel. She interprets it in relation to the ritual of the Day of Atonement, the only day of the year when the Jewish High Priest was allowed to penetrate into the Holy of Holies, this greatest day of the Old Law that was a type of Good Friday. Did she remember, as she was writing these lines, that she herself had been born on the Day of Atonement, that for her, too, it had been a symbol and a type that was to foreshadow her vocation to be Benedicta of the Cross?

It may be so; for she quickly passes on to relate the High-Priestly Prayer of Christ to the prayer of the contemplatives of the Church in words which betray that what she describes is part of her own experience.

The High-Priestly Prayer of the Saviour [she writes] reveals the mystery of the interior life: the circumincession of the Divine Persons and the Indwelling of God in the soul. In these hidden depths the work of salvation was prepared and accomplished in secrecy and silence; and so it will be continued until, at the end of time, all will have been truly consummated into being One. In the eternal silence of the interior Divine Life the plan of Redemption was decided. In the hiddenness of the quiet chamber of Nazareth the power of the Holy Ghost came upon the Virgin praying in solitude, and brought about the Incarnation of the Saviour. Assembled round the silently praying Virgin, the nascent Church awaited the promised Coming of the Holy Ghost that was to vivify them unto inner enlightenment and fruitful external activity. In the night of blindness that God had laid on his eyes, Saul awaited in solitary prayer the answer of the

Lord to his question: 'What wilt thou have me to do?' In solitary prayer Peter was prepared for his mission to the Gentiles. And so it remains through the centuries. In the solitary conversation of consecrated souls there are prepared those widely visible events of the Church's history that renew the face of the earth. The Virgin, who kept every God-sent word in her heart, is the pattern of those listening souls in whom the High-Priestly Prayer of Jesus is for ever renewed. And women who, like her, forget themselves completely in their contemplation of the Life and Passion of Christ, the Lord has chosen with preference to be His instruments for doing great things in the Church, such as St. Bridget and St. Catherine of Siena. And when St. Teresa, the powerful reformer of her Order in the time of the great apostasy, desired to come to the aid of the Church, she saw the means to that in the renewal of the true interior life. . . . What was it that inspired with the ardent desire to do something for the cause of the Church this nun, who had been living in prayer in her cloistered cell for so many years? What caused her to realize the needs and demands of her time with such penetration? Precisely the fact that she was living a life of prayer, that she let herself be drawn ever more deeply into the inner parts of her 'Interior Castle', even unto that hidden chamber where He could say to her: 'that it was time she took upon her His affairs as if they were her own, and that He would take her affairs upon Himself'. The person who gives herself to the Lord without reserve, He chooses to be His instrument for building His Kingdom. He alone knows how much the prayer of St. Teresa and her daughters has contributed to preserve Spain from the so-called Reformation, and how great has been its power in the violent wars of religion in France, in the Netherlands and in Germany. The official historians are silent about these invisible and unaccountable powers. But they are known to the trust of the faithful and the patiently examining and carefully weighing judgement of the Church. And our own time, seeing that all else fails, finds itself more and more urged to hope for ultimate salvation from these hidden sources.[1]

This passage reveals a little of her interior life otherwise so hidden. It has been noticed before, in the advice she gave to a pupil, how large a part the Old Testament played in her spirituality. Here she cites not only from the Psalms which, of course, have always been part of the prayer of the Church, but from such more recondite books as Leviticus; and she sees our

[1] *Das Gebet der Kirche*, Bonifacius-Druckerei (Paderborn).

Lord, as the Apostle saw Him in the Epistle to the Hebrews, as the true High Priest, superseding the many high priests of the Old Dispensation. Hers is a beautiful defence of the necessity and high importance of solitary prayer not only for the perfection of the individual soul, but for the building up of the Mystical Body, which is worked out in the third part of the short treatise, entitled 'Inner Life and External Form and Action.' In a masterly synthesis she establishes the mutual relation and interdependence between 'public' and 'private' prayer.

The mystical stream [she says], which flows through all the centuries, is no spurious side-current that has strayed from the prayer life of the Church—it is her very life-blood. If it breaks through the traditional forms, it does so because the spirit that blows where it listeth is living in it: He who has fashioned all the traditional forms must ever fashion new ones. Without Him there would be neither Liturgy nor Church. Was not the soul of the royal Psalmist a harp whose strings sounded as they were touched by the gentle breath of the Holy Ghost? From the overflowing heart of the Virgin full of grace comes forth the exultant hymn of the *Magnificat*. The prophetical song *Benedictus* opened the dumb lips of the old priest when the angel's secret word became visible reality. Whatever ascended from the spirit-filled heart and expressed itself in word and song is transmitted from mouth to mouth. It is the *Divinum officium* to see to it that it should continue to sound from generation to generation. Thus is formed the mystical stream of the polyphonous, ever-increasing song of praise to the Triune God, the Creator, Redeemer and Perfecter. Therefore it is inadmissible to oppose, as 'subjective' piety, the interior prayer free from traditional forms, to the Liturgy as the 'objective prayer' of the Church. Every *genuine* prayer is prayer of the Church: *through* every genuine prayer something *happens* in the Church, and it is the Church herself who prays in it, for it is the Holy Ghost living in her, who in every individual soul 'asketh for us with unspeakable groanings'. . . . What is the prayer of the Church if not the self-giving of the great lovers to the God who is Love?[1]

Here is the perfect answer to the exaggerations of so-called, as opposed to the true, liturgical movements, as well as to the aberrations of a quietist or merely 'devotional' individualist piety;

[1] ibid.

an answer in complete accord with that given by Pope Pius XII several years later in his encyclicals, *Mystici Corporis Christi* and *Mediator Dei*.

Despite its objectivity this little treatise reflects her own spiritual life. There is no doubt that all her major decisions were made in solitary prayer, as was, for example, her resolve to enter Carmel. And this prayer was nourished by the Bible, by both the Old and the New Testaments. This does not mean that she actually meditated on scriptural subjects; she had long been accustomed to contemplative prayer, where the soul rests peacefully in the Lord and thoughts may come, or not come, according to His will, but without her doing any deliberate thinking. It means that her mind was saturated with the language and imagery of Scripture, and that therefore she had no difficulty in moving from the recitation of the Psalms in the Divine Office to 'interior' prayer, and from that back to the Psalms. And as she was praying, she was always praying as a daughter of the Church—*Ecclesia Orans* a religious had once called her—and this simple realization of always standing before God as a member of the Mystical Body gives her thoughts about prayer a unity and objectivity that is comparatively rare in modern spirituality. When she prays she has the teaching of the Bible as well as the doctrines of the Church always 'with her'. The Psalms are not pieces to be recited, but to be relived as David had lived them; the *Magnificat* is the exultant joy of our Lady, and when Sister Benedicta recites it she rejoices in her heart with Mary, the Mother of God. On the other hand, when she kneels in silence before the tabernacle, she knows that her prayer is guided by the same Spirit who inspired the Psalms and the Canticles, and that therefore it is as much prayer of the Church as are these, though in a different form. This unity of her teaching, which is but the outcome of the unity of her own spiritual life, is a characteristic of her personality that struck many people; as she progresses in union with God she herself is becoming ever more unified.

This comes out strikingly in another pamphlet, called *The Mystery of Christmas*, an extraordinarily beautiful and profound meditation on Christmas, which affords yet another glimpse of her life of prayer; for the thoughts she sets before her readers are obviously the outcome of her contemplation of the mystery of the Incarnation. She begins with what is popularly termed the 'Christmas spirit', the spirit of love and joy associated with the feast even by unbelievers, and goes on to describe the joy of the Church in Advent, preparing for the coming of the Lord by her longing chants, 'Come, to deliver us'; the joy of the faithful giving each other gifts under the lighted Christmas-tree. But then she strikes a different note and again, in striking this note, closely follows the Church.

> The Star of Bethlehem is a star in a dark night, even today. Already on the second day the Church takes off her festive white vestments and clothes herself in the colour of blood, and on the fourth day in the purple of mourning. . . . Where is now the jubilation of the heavenly hosts? Where the silent bliss of the Holy Night? Where is the peace on earth? Peace on earth to men of good will. But not all are of good will. Therefore the Son of the Eternal Father had to descend from the glory of Heaven, because the mystery of iniquity had wrapped the earth in night. Darkness covered the earth, and He came as the light. . . . To those who received Him He brought light and peace . . . but not peace with the children of darkness. To them the Prince of Peace does not bring peace but the sword. . . . This is a heavy and serious truth which must not be suffered to be concealed by the Child in the manger. The mystery of the Incarnation and the mystery of iniquity are closely related.

As she was kneeling before the Crib in Carmel, the mystery of iniquity was indeed stalking her country. In schools and offices the crucifix was being replaced by the picture of the dictator, Christmas itself should give place to the pagan *Julfest*, innocent people suddenly disappeared, and the dreaded words 'concentration camp' were spoken in a whisper. But if we, of little faith, are horrified by the thought that such things should happen even at Christmas, Sister Benedicta will tell us that it is in the supernatural order of things that they should happen just then.

> The Child in the manger stretches out His little hands. . . . These hands both give and demand: You wise men, lay down your wisdom and become simple as children; you kings, give up your crowns and your treasures and bow down humbly before the King of kings, take upon yourselves without hesitation the troubles and sufferings and hardships which His service demands. You children,

Sister Benedicta of the Cross

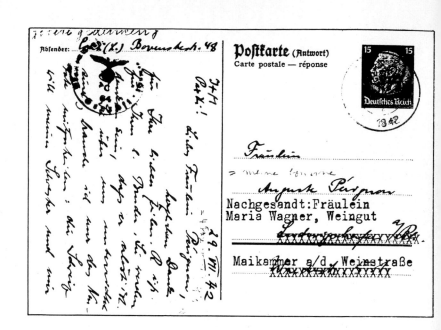

A postcard written four days before her deportation

who cannot yet give anything of your own free will, these Child's hands take your tender life from you even before it has really begun. It could not be used better than to be sacrificed for the Lord of Life. 'Follow Me,' so speak the hands of the Child, as later the lips of the Man. . . . Those who are kneeling round the Crib are creatures of light: the tender, innocent children, the sincere shepherds, the humble Kings, Stephen, the ardent Apostle and the beloved Disciple John, all those who have followed the call of the Lord. But opposed to them is the night of incomprehensible obstinacy and blindness: the scribes who can give information on time and place, when the Saviour of the world is to be born, but who do not draw the conclusion: 'Let us go to Bethlehem.' Herod the king, who wants to kill the Lord of Life. Ways part before the Child in the manger. . . . He speaks His 'Follow Me', and he who is not for Him is against Him. He speaks it also for us, and compels us to decide between light and darkness.

It is a woman of her time who here reflects on the mystery of Christmas and who, guided by the Church and her Liturgy, penetrates into its depths as it affects the world. For her spirituality is never 'convent spirituality'; her consciousness of the unity of the human race in Adam and the unity of the Mystical Body in the Second Adam is too intense to allow of any narrowness, of any artificial division of the life of prayer into 'religious' and 'lay'. 'This is the wonderful thing about mankind,' she writes, 'that we are all one. . . He came to be one mysterious Body with us: He our Head, we His members. If we lay our hands into the hands of the Divine Child, if we say our "Yes" to His "Follow Me", then we are His, then the way is free for His Divine Life to be infused into us. This is the beginning of eternal life in us.' Again she does not shut her eyes to the evils that surround the mystery. In fact she answers explicitly all those who cannot understand that, even after the Redemption, sin and evil remain in the world; perhaps her insistence on this is also a reply to her mother's moanings at the excesses of the Nazis: 'How can men be so wicked?' For her there are no facile solutions. 'The rule of the Divine King turned out to be different from what men had imagined it to be, according to the Psalms and the Prophets. The Romans remained masters in the land, high priests and scribes continued to oppress the poor. Whoever belonged to the Lord carried his

Kingdom of Heaven invisibly within himself. His earthly burden was not taken away from him; on the contrary, many another was added to it, but what he had within him was a winged power that made his yoke easy and his burden light. Thus it is even today with every child of God.'

Here she touches the mysterious paradox of the Christian life, which she herself was destined to live so perfectly: it is signed with the Cross, yet it is not sorrowful; it has its full share of suffering, yet it is overflowing with joy. When Edith Stein followed the call of Jesus into His Church she cut short a brilliant career, she broke away from the traditions of a beloved family, she entered on a life which offered little satisfaction to her natural ambition, but was completely devoted to work and prayer—yet no sacrifice could dim the radiance within her. Then, when the great sufferings came, the persecution of her people, her heart-rending parting from her mother, the total renunciation of her own will and inclinations in Carmel, the Kingdom of Heaven yet remained within her, undisturbed by outward cares and inward afflictions, rather increasing in power and glory. There were even worse things in store for her—but she had laid her hand within the hand of the Divine Child with total abandonment, therefore she could truly say with the Psalmist in the words she loved so much: *Dominus illuminatio mea et salus mea—quem timebo?*

To be a child of God, that means: to be led by the Hand of God, to do the will of God, not one's own will, to place every care and every hope in the Hand of God and not to worry about oneself or one's future. On this rests the freedom and the joy of the child of God. But how few even of the truly pious, even of those ready for heroic sacrifices, possess this freedom. They all walk as if bent down by the heavy burden of their cares and duties. They all know the parable of the birds of the air and the lilies of the field. But if they meet a person who has neither capital nor pension nor insurance, and yet lives without worrying about the future, they shake their heads as if that was something extraordinary. Indeed, if one expects from the Father in Heaven that He will always provide for the income and station in life which oneself considers desirable, he can be very much mistaken. Only then can the trust in God remain unshaken if it includes being prepared to accept absolutely everything from the Hand of the Father.

She herself knew what it means to practise this. It was the perfect abandonment to the will of God that made her own spiritual life so simple. For all men's upsets, all their difficulties and problems with which they so often waste their own time and the time of their directors and friends, arise almost invariably from lack of conformity to the will of God. Men say with their lips 'Thy will be done'—but in their hearts they have a whole series of reservations; they want it to be done in some ways, but not in others. Sister Benedicta, both in her teaching and in her life, took a different view. 'The "Thy will be done",' she writes, 'must be the rule of the Christian's life in its full scope. It must regulate the day from morning to night, the course of the year, and the whole life. It then becomes the Christian's only concern. For all other cares the Lord will make Himself responsible.'

She was thinking not only of external cares.

All sufferings that come from outside [she writes] are as nothing compared with the dark night of the soul, when the Divine light no longer shines, and the voice of the Lord no longer speaks. God is there, but He is hidden and silent. Why is this so? We are speaking of the mysteries of God, and these cannot be completely penetrated. But we may look into them a little. God has become Man in order once more to give us a share in His Life.   The suffering and death of Christ are continued in His Mystical Body and in each of His members. . . . And so a soul united to Christ will stand firm, unshaken even in the dark night of feeling estranged from and abandoned by God. Perhaps divine Providence uses her agony to deliver another, who is truly a prisoner cut off from God.

From this passage it seems that she herself must have experienced what St. John of the Cross calls 'the dark night of the soul', not only the night of the senses, but the night of the spirit, when the soul feels as if she had been completely forsaken by God. She never spoke of it at all; and in view of the words just cited this is not surprising. For she would take this state of interior suffering as simply as she took everything else: as the will of the Father, to which she submitted in silence. That this was her attitude comes out also in a letter in which she writes to a former pupil: 'As regards yourself, do not be put off by coldness and aridity. The chief thing is that the will remains faithful, even when every felt consolation and taste for the spiritual life ceases. You know from your reading that no one is spared such trials, if he really wants to follow Christ. It is only when it is one's own turn that one does not recognize it.' 'Thy will be done'; this will also be the solution of these spiritual difficulties, as it is the true Christian attitude to all external suffering.

Yet Sister Benedicta probes deeper even than this. She asks: 'Can we still say "Thy will be done" even when we no longer have any certainty what God's will requires from us? Do we still have the means of keeping in His ways when the inner light is extinguished?' She herself had been in such a situation at least once, when she was faced with her mother's despair before she entered Carmel. She knows that, even in such apparently total darkness, God does not leave His own without His guidance. If a soul has faithfully followed every day what she believed to be the will of God, then she 'may indeed trust not to stray from the divine will even where there is no longer subjective certainty'. However, we have more to guide us than that: we have our membership of the Mystical Body, and hence obedience to the advice of our spiritual guides as well as trust in the intercession of others will ease the burden. Above all, we have the Eucharist. 'In him who makes It truly his daily bread, the mystery of Christmas, the Incarnation of the Word, will daily be re-enacted. And this, it seems, is the surest way to remain in constant union with God, and every day to grow more securely and more deeply into the Mystical Body of Christ.'

Then she outlines in words that are severe but very true the effects that daily Communion ought to have. From one Holy Communion to the other

one must live in such a way that one will be allowed to come again. It is no longer possible to 'let oneself go', even if only for a little while. One cannot escape the judgement of a person with whom one is in daily contact. . . . So it is also in the daily intercourse with the Saviour. One becomes ever more sensitive to what pleases and displeases Him. If before one had been, on the whole, quite satisfied with oneself, this will now be very different. One will find much that is bad, and one will change it if possible. And one will discover many things that one cannot think are all right, and which are yet so hard to change. And so we shall gradually become very small and humble, as well as patient and indulgent with the motes in the eyes of others, because we are busy with the beam in our own. And finally one learns even to bear with oneself in the light of the divine Presence, and to give oneself up to the divine mercy which can deal with all the difficulties that are too much for our own strength. It is a long way from the smug self-satisfaction of the 'good Catholic' who 'does his duties', reads a 'good paper', etc., but apart from that does what he likes, to a life guided and provided by the hand of God, in the simplicity of the child and the humility of the publican. But whoever has walked in this way will no more turn back.

The way Sister Benedicta sketches here is her own way; it is the way of full co-operation with eucharistic grace, for there are many who go daily to the table of the Lord and yet seem to remain quite unchanged, not, of course, because of the inefficacy of the Blessed Sacrament, but because of their own tepidity and lack of generosity. With Sister Benedicta it had been different. From the moment of her conversion she had co-operated with grace; and now, in Carmel, her truly eucharistic life was bearing its full fruit.

Therefore it is not surprising that she should be very severe when she found any tendency to make light of the Sacramental Presence. Several years later, when she was in Echt, she writes to a former pupil:

I want to answer you as soon as possible, because something in your last letter is worrying me. It is your surprise at the demand of a daily visit [to the Blessed Sacrament]. Yesterday and today, as I was kneeling before the tabernacle, I felt as if I had to make some reparation to the eucharistic Saviour. I will leave aside what Father X. actually did say. Perhaps he would himself be terrified at the consequences you have drawn from his words. What you write can hardly be reconciled with the life and spirit of the Church. It is a dogma of the faith that the Lord is present in the Most Holy Sacrament with His Divinity and Humanity. Certainly not for His own sake, but for ours, in order to be with us until the end of the world. He could do this also in other ways—but this depends on His Will, not on our predilections. We have to accept humbly and gratefully the ways He has shown us and the institutions which He has set up, and which, in His mercy, He has wisely adapted to our human nature. The faith of all Christian centuries (and even of the non-Christian religions) shows that there are 'sacred places' from which spring rivers of grace. Your own experience will confirm it, if you remember the time when you were still simply following your natural feeling. . . . I recommend you to the Queen of the May. She, through whom the Word became Flesh, will also best be able to obtain for us enlightenment on the Word in the species of Bread.

Her gift of counsel shows itself also in much of the correspondence dating from her early years in Cologne. One of her acquaintances, Dr. Ruth Kantorowicz, had told her about her conversion from Judaism, and asked her advice on the subject of entering a convent. Full of joy, she replies:

That your dear father was happy about your conversion is a special grace for yourself and for him. This joy is a sign, is it not, that he himself was near to the light and passed into eternity in the friendship of God? Will you help me to pray for my dear mother that to her, too, understanding may be given?

Now to your questions. Above all I would say to you: Place all care for the future trustfully into the hands of God, and let yourself be guided by Him just like a child. Then you will be sure not to miss your way. As the Lord has brought you into His Church, so He will also guide you to the place where He wants you. Despite your being already thirty-three I would advise you to leave aside the question of a religious vocation for the time being. God's will is not bound by age limits. I was received at forty-two, and others even later. Of course many things are easier if one enters young. This, however, is no longer in our power. You would hardly find a convent which would receive you immediately after your conversion. Most of them ask, for good reasons, that one should have several years' experience of living as a Catholic. And this, it seems to me, is the most important thing for you, too, at present. If your vocation is genuine, it will survive this period of testing. If it is only an illusion of the first enthusiasm, then it will be better that this should be realized beforehand rather than through a great disappointment after entering the convent.

What you write about your education and inclinations would seem to point rather to outside activities such as *Karitasverband* or *Borromaeusverein*. However, I cannot give a definite opinion just from one letter. If you wanted to enter an Order you would have to give up every personal wish about the nature of your activities, and, in holy obedience, leave it entirely to your superiors how your gifts and accomplishments should be used. The daily horary of Carmel leaves very little time for scholarly work. It is an exception that I was given the opportunity for this even in the novitiate.

For the moment I would say to you: remain quietly in your job, as long as you have not received a definite indication from above to turn to something else. Use your spare time to get to know and love God and His Holy Church ever more and more: the doctrine, the liturgy, our saints; but also the ecclesiastical institutions and present-day Catholic life, including its shadows which, in the long run, will not remain hidden from you. If you miss human relationships in Hamburg I would gladly help you to form some.[1]

This letter is very characteristic of Sister Benedicta's balanced personality, containing as in miniature its chief components. Holy zeal, certainly, but tempered by prudence, a patient waiting on the will of God and an appreciation of all natural qualities. At the same time she sounds a warning: very gently she prepares an enthusiastic soul for the defects she is bound to discover one day in the human side of the Church, which at the moment she envisages as the acme of perfection, without suspecting the shadows that cling to it in its militant state. Her own radical quest for perfection had suffered more than one disappointment when she came to realize the difference between the ideal of Catholic life and its reality; now she was concerned to prepare a much weaker soul for the shortcomings she was bound to find. She knew the most efficacious way was not the negative one of warnings, but the positive one of introducing the new Christian to the Divine side of the Church. So she writes in a further letter, just before Advent:

'Before the beginning of Advent I would like to send you a greeting and all kind wishes for this holy season. Your first Advent in Holy Church ought really to be particularly beautiful. Let no external worry prevent you from living in the great ideas of the Advent liturgy. Then the feast will bring you rivers of grace.'[2] Her correspondent was a timid soul, who did not even dare to admit her conversion to her Jewish friends, an attitude totally foreign to Sister Benedicta's frank and apostolic mind. 'I have often asked myself,' she writes in the same letter, 'why you keep your conversion secret. Is there anyone whose feelings you

[1] *Life*, pp. 160f., 6th German edition only. [2] ibid., pp. 161f.

are obliged to spare? Surely it is much more beautiful if one can be quite open. It is true, my brothers and sisters would not understand, but I don't think you need fear attacks. I at least have never experienced any. . . . After all, one never knows whether some little seed may not take root some time!' In the same letter she invited her to spend Christmas at Carmel. When Ruth Kantorowicz accepted the invitation, she initiated her into the mysteries of the Breviary, so that she could follow the Christmas liturgy with deeper understanding. During these conversations in the parlour she continued the guidance she had given the new convert by letter, discussing with her all her difficulties, both spiritual and material. Evidently the consecrated life she was now leading increased in her the gifts of the Holy Ghost, who gave her the opportunity, even behind the grille of Carmel, to use her wisdom by giving this undecided soul much needed counsel.

CHAPTER SEVENTEEN

THE BRIDE OF THE LAMB

THE change wrought in Sister Benedicta by her consecration to God in Carmel was quite striking. While she was in the world many people found her somewhat cool and remote. Here are the testimonies of two quite different persons, the one a university professor, the other a nun, who knew her at different times of her life, the one when she was at Göttingen, the other when she was teaching at Speyer. The professor writes: 'She made a great impression by her beauty, her eyes; but above all by the expression of austerity and remoteness. She would look at you in a cool, searching manner, almost like a judge, giving the impression of an extraordinarily highly integrated personality, resting quietly in herself.' And now the nun, who knew her about ten years later: 'She always seemed to me a world remote and enclosed to which I, a young religious, was not, and did not desire to be, admitted.' Both the professor and the nun use the same word, the one as a noun, the other as an adjective: *Abgeschlossenheit; abgeschlossen*, which has here the sense of being both remote from others and enclosed, detached and sufficient in itself. It is the attribute of the virgin, the garden enclosed which refuses admittance. It expresses a sufficiency that is not yet fulfilled, a detachment that has not yet experienced the mystery of being most itself when most given to others. If the Word is to be made Flesh the Virgin must become a Mother—if the soul is to live Christ in His fullness, the bowl of her contemplation, in St. Bernard's beautiful metaphor, must overflow to others.

It was in Carmel that Edith Stein found this ultimate fulfilment; and again there are two quite different testimonies to the same fact, the one from the Benedictine scholar, Dom Daniel Feuling, the other from a former pupil, the same whom she had disconcerted by demanding that she should write with her left hand when she had injured her right.

The Benedictine, who had also known her in the world, writes of his meeting with her in Carmel: 'As a woman Sister Benedicta seemed to me to have greatly increased in her womanliness. By this I mean two things: one is that Sister Benedicta had achieved in Carmel a union between the two realms of the emotions and the intellect, still more harmonious than the one that had already been noticeable before. The other point is that the characteristically feminine trait, namely that her life as well as her deeper knowledge is enriched and guided by spiritual intuition, had come out much more forcefully than when I had first met her.'[1] Her former pupil expressed the same thing in very much simpler language in a conversation with the present writer: 'She had become much more maternal in Carmel. I was so surprised that I simply had to tell her so. To which she replied: "One never comes to an end in life. This had still to come." Before, I had been unable to find much warmth in her, now she seemed to be far more kind and understanding.'

In the seclusion of Carmel, alone with the Lord and the sisters, the virgin had become a bride, and He who had till then been Christ the Lord—*Christus der Herr*—had become the heavenly Spouse. She confessed herself that the greatest penance for her was the constant change of occupation which never allowed her more than two hours of uninterrupted work, a period that seemed incredibly short. She felt that she had hardly got going when she had to stop again.[2] Except for two short periods as a Red Cross nurse in the First World War, and again after her conversion, her intellectual work had always been given first place in her life. This probably accounts for a good deal of that coolness and remoteness which struck so many of those who came into contact with her. Now, in Carmel, her scholarly pursuits were relegated to a secondary place. It is true that the Provincial had ordered her to be dispensed from other duties to be able to continue it; but choir, meal-time, recreation, sweeping one's cell and all the other routine of convent life remained largely unchanged for her; moreover, if there was an emergency such as illness among the sisters, Sister Benedicta, too, would be called upon to give up her time. It was, in fact, a much more 'feminine' life she

[1] Edith Stein, *Frauenbildung und Frauenberufe*, biographical note, p. 175.
[2] *Life*, p. 157.

was now leading, involving the constant sacrifice of the solitary ponderings of the intellect to the duties of sisterly charity.

Nor was her charity restricted to the needs of the community. The parlour, too, made its demands. Her attitude to her visitors was a little different from that of most of the sisters. She herself writes: 'Most sisters regard it as a penance when they are called into the parlour. And it is, indeed, like going into a different world, and one is glad if one can then once more escape into the silence of the choir and "digest" before the tabernacle what one has received from outside. But afterwards I always feel this peace to be an overwhelming gift of grace, which one cannot possibly have received for oneself, and if someone comes to us exhausted and tired out, and then takes back a little calm and consolation, it makes me very happy.'[1]

It is characteristic of Sister Benedicta that she accepted her vocation as an unmerited grace, of which she had to give as much as possible to others. There may sometimes be a danger for enclosed religious, admired by those who visit them, to regard their sacrifices as something that raises them above the rest of mankind. Sister Benedicta was evidently aware of this, for she continues: 'One can only strive to live the life we have chosen ever more faithfully and purely, so as to offer it as an acceptable sacrifice for all those to whom one is united. The confidence people place in us, the almost terrifyingly high opinion which so many outside have of our life, is an ever renewed spur towards it.'[2]

To her, consecration to God in the religious life meant perfect self-giving, and, through this self-giving, spiritual motherhood. In one of her earlier educational essays on the incorporation of woman into the Mystical Body of Christ, she had written:

Even more perfectly (than in the case of the married woman) the Church is symbolized in the woman who has dedicated her life to the Lord as *sponsa Christi* and has entered an indissoluble union with Him. She takes her stand by His side, co-operating in His work of redemption, as does the Church and her type and origin, the Mother of God. The total devotion of her whole life and being is a living and working with Christ, but this means suffering and dying with Him, dying that terrible death from which springs the life of

[1] *Life*, p. 158.   [2] ibid.

grace for mankind. And thus the life of the bride of God becomes supernatural maternity for the whole redeemed humanity, and for this it does not matter whether she herself works immediately for souls or produces the fruits of grace only by her sacrifice, fruits unknown to herself, and perhaps to all other human beings.

In the community life of Carmel she could at last develop her feminine qualities to the full. And not only feminine qualities; who would have thought that the serious 'Fräulein Doktor' would one day don a red wig over her Carmelite veil and play a 'vagabond of our Lady' who goes on pilgrimage? And not even a serious pilgrimage either; rather one of the Chaucerian kind, stealing and performing all sorts of nonsense in the process. She played this role with such gaiety and childlike *naïveté* that all the sisters were charmed. In another play, about the famous saint of the Order, Simon Stock, she had the title role, in which she was equally successful. For to her Carmel meant community, not a hermit's life, as she wrote some weeks before her profession: 'I had to smile a little at your question, how I had accustomed myself to the solitude. During most of my life I have been far more solitary than here.'[1] In this society of simple women she herself could fully become a woman, as Dom Daniel Feuling saw her, as her former pupil discovered her, intuitive, warm, maternal, a perfectly harmonious spiritual personality. She was truly prepared to make her profession when the Easter bells rang on 21 April 1935.

*   *   *

In contrast to the clothing, profession in Carmel is a private ceremony that takes place in chapter, in the presence only of the nuns. It is an intimate family feast, to which no relatives or friends are invited. Sister Benedicta made her temporal vows about six o'clock in the morning; then Mass was celebrated for her intention, and afterwards the whole day was given over to the rejoicings of the sisters, whose paschal joy was doubled by the happiness of Sister Benedicta's profession.

She did not speak about the graces the Lord had given her on this day, and during the ten days' retreat that had preceded it,

[1] *Life*, p. 163; 160.

but we are at least allowed a glimpse of their reflection. When a young novice naïvely asked her: 'How are you now feeling?' she replied in a voice full of emotion: 'Like the bride of the Lamb.'

The bride of the Lamb. While in the Apocalypse this signifies the Church from early times, the image has also been applied to our Lady, and later, especially in the mystic literature, had been fused with the marriage symbolism of the Canticle and thus been applied to the individual soul. When she had still been in the world Edith Stein had been likened to the *Ecclesia Orans*, the bride of Christ, in her prayer. She herself had written that all prayer is prayer of the Church—now she was truly a bride of Christ, the Lamb, bound to Him by the marriage vows of her profession, and her prayer was in an even stricter sense prayer of the Church, the prayer of the individual bride, as it were, within the Mystical Body of Christ, the Bride *par excellence*.

But she was not only now the bride of the Lamb in the sense that the Church had officially blessed her 'marriage'; the words she spoke to the young sister betray that the outward ceremony had been accompanied by an inner experience. It is neither desirable nor indeed possible to draw back the veil that hides the mysteries of the love of Jesus for His chosen ones; but Sister Benedicta's words leave little doubt that she was given the grace of full mystical union in these days, a realization by experience of the indwelling of Christ in her soul and His love for her, and, from her side, the total surrender to His embrace in a perfect union of wills, that brought her ineffable joy. The words of a friend who visited her a few days later would seem to confirm this. She writes:

Her radiant expression and her youthful appearance in this week of her profession are unforgettable. I think she looked twenty years younger, and I was profoundly touched by her happiness. She must have received very great graces from the Lord—like the saints. I will, however, also tell what she said when she was sitting before me in her crown[1] with her veil drawn back. I said in the course of the conversation that here in Carmel she would certainly be safe. But she replied quickly: 'Oh no, I do not think so. They will surely get me out of here. In any case I cannot count on being left in peace here.'

[1] Of white roses, which the newly professed Carmelites wear during the Octave of their profession.

She said it was clear to her that she was going to suffer for her people, that she was meant to bring many home.[1]

Only a true union with God in the depth of the soul could give a joy that overflowed even into the external appearance at the same time as she foresaw clearly the fate that was in store for her. It might, without irreverence, be compared to the scene of the Transfiguration, where our Lord was clothed with His divine glory and immediately after foretold His Passion. For even, or rather especially, in the most sublime moments of the Christ-life the shadow of the Cross falls on it. But this shadow, far from dimming the light, enhances it, just as the Church marks the paschal season by the constant commemoration of the Cross in her liturgy. Sister Benedicta, young and radiant in her bridal crown, united to Him whom she had loved so faithfully since the day of her baptism, has tasted the peace that no man can take away, and therefore she need not fear those who would one day take away the external peace of her life in Carmel.

*   *   *

Some time after taking her vows Sister Benedicta had thought it right to tell her mother about it. All this time old Frau Stein had been receiving every week her daughter's letter, but had rarely sent a reply. It was left to her sister Rosa to give her the news of the family. But at last her daughter's faithful love touched the mother's heart, and great was Sister Benedicta's joy when she began to answer more regularly and one day she even returned the greeting of Mother Teresa Renata, who was then the novice mistress. This happened after Rosa had given her sister the surprising news that one day her mother had paid a visit to the new Carmelite foundation at Breslau, without telling her daughters anything about it. She was evidently anxious to know the kind of life her Edith had chosen; and the sequel is sufficient proof that the old lady had now become reconciled to her vocation. Perhaps she had felt a little of the contemplative peace that pervades a Carmelite chapel, and had begun to understand how her daughter could be drawn to such a life.[2]

[1] *Life*, pp. 168 f.; 163 f.   [2] Cf. ibid., p. 169; 165

For Sister Benedicta it was a warm ray of light in a world in which the shadows became yet more threatening. Ruth Kantorowicz would have liked to enter Carmel; but the superiors refused on account of the difficult times. So she came to Cologne expecting help from Sister Benedicta, who tried to put her in touch with people likely to give her some occasional work to do. In her own literary work, too, she was feeling the repercussions of the events outside. In the autumn of 1935 she had been asked to do some reviews for a Catholic women's periodical. She wrote the reviews, received the proofs—but the reviews never appeared. At first she was puzzled; but when she was informed that, on account of her Jewish origin, she had been deprived of her political vote, she realized what was the explanation. She was not perturbed. In April 1936 she wrote to a friend who wanted to intervene: 'Please do not worry about it. For a long time I have been prepared for much worse things.'[1] Since it had been her principle, if confronted with a painful situation, to envisage the worst that could happen and prepare herself to endure it, an actual calamity always found her ready. Now she was interiorly prepared even to have to leave her community, so these comparative pinpricks could not affect her. Her soul was united to the risen Lord, for in the same letter she writes: 'Every day I am glad that Paschal-tide lasts so long, and that one can assimilate ever more and more of its inexhaustible riches. It is surely the season of the Church's year when we are nearest to heaven. Moreover, the trees in bloom and the plants shooting up in our garden are, for me, inextricably linked to the great days of grace of my religious life.'[2]

She had been clothed at Easter 1934, and in 1935, the year before this letter was written, she had been professed. Easter, the time of grace *par excellence*, when the Lord had risen from the dead, when the catechumens of the primitive Church were baptized, when the Church throughout the world sings her triple Alleluias and nature in the northern hemisphere awakes from her winter's sleep—Easter was for her, too, the time of blessings. The Lord had risen and the trees and bushes in the convent garden were full of blossom, and her heart rejoiced: *Dominus illuminatio mea et salus mea—quem timebo?* Whatever might be in store for her,

---

[1] *Life*, p. 174; 167. [2] ibid., p. 174; 168.

there was no fear in her heart, because she knew the voice of Him who greeted His apostles: 'Fear not, it is I'; and she knew that to her, too, these words were spoken.

Before the end of the blessed fifty days, however, she received news from home that was more painful even than the political calamities. Her mother had fallen ill, for the first time in her life. Sister Benedicta realized at once that she would not recover and asked for special prayers for her. After a little time Frau Stein rallied sufficiently to write a last greeting to her daughter, for whom it was a blessed thought, indeed, that her mother was no longer bitter about her vocation but that the love with which they had loved each other throughout their lives had survived even this, the hardest, test.

Sister Benedicta's detachment was so perfect that even a St. John of the Cross could hardly have wished her to be more so. But, like his, it was tempered by a deep affection that caused her to suffer silently with and for those dearest to her. As in her joyful Easter liturgy the Church commemorates the Cross, so the Lord set up this Cross in the midst of Sister Benedicta's Alleluias. Towards the end of June Frau Stein got worse; the doctor discovered a swelling in the stomach which he feared was cancer. At her age nothing could be done except to relieve the acute suffering as far as was possible. Her state continued to worsen throughout the summer. In a letter to a friend, who was herself ill at the time, Sister Benedicta writes on 9 August: 'May I ask you to offer some of your own sufferings for my poor Mother? It is now the third month of her illness. In the beginning it seemed harmless and temporary, but then it turned out to be an incurable disease. She has now been lying in bed for many weeks, she can hardly take any food, and of course it is very hard and unintelligible for her that I cannot be with her.'

Edith was the child she loved most of all and her absence from her deathbed must truly have been the hardest of sacrifices for her mother. Though Frau Stein did not know it, God had marked herself, too, with the sign of His Son; for it was for His sake that her daughter had renounced the consolation of assisting her mother in her last illness. Yet it seems that at the moment of death the two women who loved each other with so pure an affection were not altogether deprived of each other's presence.

On 14 September, the Feast of the Exaltation of the Cross, the Carmelites renew their vows. 'For the third time Sister Benedicta took part in this ceremony, in the stillness of the early morning. Afterwards she told a sister with whom she was very friendly: "When my turn came to renew my vows my mother was with me. I distinctly felt her presence." A telegram from Breslau announcing the bereavement arrived on the same day. The hour of the renewal of the vows had been the hour of her mother's death.'[1] This coincidence—if coincidence it was—was a great consolation for her daughter, whose grief was commensurate with her deep love of her mother.

In some of the many letters of condolence she received it had been suggested that Frau Stein had become a Catholic before she died. Sister Benedicta's attitude to this story is significant. She writes in a letter of 4 October: 'The news of my mother's conversion is a totally unfounded rumour. I do not know who started it. My mother has remained true to her faith till the last. But because her faith and her solid trust in her God have held firm from her earliest childhood till her eighty-seventh year, because it was the last that remained alive in her even in her terrible agony, therefore I am confident that she has found a very gracious Judge and is now my most faithful helper so that I, too, may reach my goal.'[2]

Sister Benedicta was well aware of the most comforting doctrine of the Church that to anyone who lives according to the light that is given him God will not deny grace. Throughout her life Frau Stein had lived her Jewish faith to the full; she had brought up her family in the fear and love of the Lord, she had done good wherever she could, she had worked and suffered and kept the Law of her God. Her daughter had no doubt that, though she had not known Him on earth, Christ would know her in Heaven and say also to her: 'Come, ye blessed of my Father . . . for I was hungry, and you gave me to eat; I was thirsty, and you gave me to drink.'

[1] *Life*, p. 175; 168.   [2] ibid.

11

CHAPTER EIGHTEEN

ENDLICHES UND EWIGES SEIN

A FORTNIGHT before her mother's death, in 1936, Sister Benedicta had completed the great work on account of which the Provincial had dispensed her from the ordinary activities of the community after her clothing. The work had been begun while she was still in the world. She had first intended to call it 'Potency and Act', but as the manuscript expanded this title was found to be too narrow, for it had come to deal not only with these restricted notions, but with the whole range of uncreated and created Being.

She begins with the question of 'being' as such, which she approaches through the Thomist concepts of potency and act, since they are at the heart of St. Thomas's philosophy, and, indeed, of all being. Thus the uncreated Being of God, who is pure Act, *Actus purus*, is distinguished from all created being, which presupposes a passive potency as its foundation. She gives a bird's-eye view of the history of the concept of being in philosophical thought, pointing out that its importance, never questioned either in Greek or in medieval philosophy, was destined to dwindle only in modern times, when the first place was given to the problem of knowledge. In making not knowledge, but being the subject of her philosophical life-work, Edith Stein returned to the traditions of European thought; in utilizing the findings of modern philosophers, particularly of course of her own phenomenological school, she followed in the steps of St. Thomas himself, who took what was true wherever he found it, whether in Christian or in pagan sources. 'The re-born philosophy of the Middle Ages and the new-born philosophy of the twentieth century—can they come together in the one river-bed of the *philosophia perennis?*[1] she asks. The greatest difficulty at the moment is, in her view, that 'they still speak in different languages,

[1] p. 7.

and a common language will have to be found before they can understand each other'.

She herself was eminently fitted to approach the problem of a common language, as she had already proved by her translation of St. Thomas's *De Veritate*; and in the present work she constantly defines notions by going back to the original meanings of the Greek and Latin words and brilliantly rendering them into their German equivalents wherever this is possible without giving up the special significance of the Greek or Latin term. She explains which method she will follow in order to make scholastic thought palatable to her contemporaries without falsifying it:

Wherever scholastic arguments are our point of departure, we shall first present them in scholastic terminology. But in order to ascertain that we have grasped the actual sense of the matter, and are not just playing about with words, we shall seek to find our own terms, in which to render the passages in question. We shall be helped in this by investigating the origins of the scholastic concepts, as regards their history, but even more as they originated from the subjects they were coined to describe. . . . While doing this we want to think together with the old masters in a vital manner; but not only with the old masters, but also with those who have resumed the question in their own way in our time. . . . This is the necessary way especially for the present author, whose philosophical home is the school of Edmund Husserl, and whose native tongue, as far as philosophy is concerned, is the language of the phenomenologists.[1]

When Edith Stein became a Catholic she did not give up her early philosophical training: this is her great strength and her importance for modern thought, though, in certain ways, also her weakness. She concludes her preliminary remarks with a paragraph on 'Meaning and Possibility of a Christian Philosophy'.

This is a moot point. The strict Thomists, following their master, separate rigidly philosophy, which deals solely with subjects accessible to unaided reason, from theology; whereas 'both in former as in modern times attempts have been made to build up a philosophy which uses not only natural reason, but also faith as sources of knowledge'.[2] After careful discussion she sides with those who would include the truths of revelation not, of course,

[1] pp. 11 f.   [2] p. 12, n. 18.

as part of philosophy, but as one of the sources of our knowledge with which philosophy has to deal. 'A *Christian philosophy*,' she writes, 'will consider it its principal task to prepare the way for faith.'[1] She rejects the strict division of St. Thomas between theology which rests on divine revelation and 'the philosophical disciplines which are examined by human reason' (*Summa Theol.* q. 1. a. 1. corp.) on the grounds that 'it no longer corresponds to the present-day view [as opposed to the Middle Ages] which has to reckon with a series of completely divided subjects . . . and which assigns to philosophy a peculiar position with regard to all particular sciences.'[2] This peculiar position is due to the special task of philosophy, which is 'to elucidate the foundations of all sciences'.[3]

After these introductory remarks she begins her section on 'Act and Potency as modes of being' with a presentation of the subject according to St. Thomas's early work, *De ente et essentia*, which, following Aristotle, divides all being into material or composite beings, purely spiritual (created) beings, and the First Being, God. In order to elucidate the Thomist conceptions Edith Stein leaves aside for the moment God and angels, as being foreign to modern philosophical thought, and, characteristically, starts with 'something that is quite otherwise near to us, even inescapably near. Whenever the mind of man in its search for truth has looked for an indubitably certain point of departure, it has hit upon this inescapably near fact of its own being.'[4] She traces this going back of the mind to the fact of its own existence from St. Augustine (*De Trinitate*, XV, 12) to Descartes' *Cogito ergo sum*, and from there to Husserl, who based his phenomenological method on

the suspension of judgement . . . in regard to the whole existence of the natural world and the validity of existing scholarship. What is left as the sphere of investigation is the sphere of consciousness in the sense of the life of the Ego: I need not decide whether the *thing* I perceive with my senses does or does not actually exist—but the perception as such cannot be struck out; I can doubt whether the conclusion I draw is right—but the thinking that draws conclusions is an indubitable fact; and so is all my wishing and willing, my

[1] p. 29.   [2] pp. 18f.   [3] pp. 20f.   [4] pp. 34f.

dreaming and hoping, my rejoicing and sorrowing; in short, everything within which I live and am, which presents itself as the being
of the Ego that is conscious of itself.[1]

She then analyses the being of which the Ego is conscious and
finds that it is a temporal being, 'a "Now" between a "No more"
and a "Not yet". But while, in its fluctuating character, it is
splitting itself into being and non-being, there is revealed to us the
Idea of pure Being, which has no admixture of non-being ... which
is not temporal, but *eternal*.'[2] 'Thus,' she continues, 'eternal and
temporal, immutable and mutable being, and also non-being, are
ideas which the spirit finds in itself; they are not borrowed from
elsewhere.'[3] She concludes that 'my present being is ... at the
same time actual and possible; and as far as it is actual it is the
actualization of a possibility that existed before.'[4]

After contrasting the mixed being of man and the pure Being
of God, she states that 'despite the abyss between the two it is
permissible to speak both here and there of *being*'.[5] The analysis
of the two kinds of being is followed by one of the experience of
'becoming' and its relation to 'being'. Here she makes use of the
phenomenological concept of *Erlebniseinheit* (unit of experience)
and analyses such phenomena as 'joy' in their relation both to the
subject experiencing them and the objects that produce them, as
well as the special circumstances that may prevent their full
actualization. With Husserl she distinguishes between the 'pure
Ego' which is the subject of any immediate experience or action,
and a 'transcendent Ego' which lies beyond it and is not necessarily
affected by the experience. She continues to follow Husserl in his
concept of the 'stream of experience' of the Ego which leads her
to a brilliant psychological analysis of the various forms in which
the Ego can recall former experiences and so 're-actualizes' them.
From there she proceeds to follow the memory to times which it
is unable to recall, and finally to the question: 'Has the Ego, too,
had a beginning of its being? ... At several points of its being
there yawns the abyss of emptiness: Did it come from Nothing?
Does it go towards Nothing?'[6]

These ultimate questions lead her to the conclusion that 'it finds
itself existing as living ... itself and its being are ineluctably there,

[1] p. 35.   [2] pp. 36f.   [3] p. 37.   [4] p. 38.   [5] p. 41.   [6] p. 51.

it is "thrown into existence".'[1] She uses this formula of Heidegger advisedly, and, in a footnote,[2] lays her finger on the weak spot of his existentialist philosophy in which the *Geworfenheit* (being thrown) plays such a prominent part.

> With this [she writes] is expressed above all that man finds himself in existence, without knowing how he has come there. . . . But with this the question of the 'whence' has not been abolished. However violently one may try to silence it or to forbid it as senseless, it always rises again irresistibly from the peculiarity of human being demanding a Being that is both the foundation of the former and its own foundation, needing no other, demanding the One who throws that which is 'thrown'. And with this the 'being thrown' is revealed as creatureliness.[3]

With perfect logic the former atheist thinker who had found the truth defeats the protagonist of existentialist pessimism by the strictly philosophical analysis of the human situation which causes her, at the end of this section, to confront the being of the Ego with the eternal Being.

> The nothingness and transitoriness of its own being becomes clear to the Ego, if it takes possession of its own being by thought. . . . It also touches it . . . through fear [*Angst*], which accompanies unredeemed man through life in many disguises . . . but in the last resort as fear of his own non-being. . . . However, fear is not normally the dominant sensation [*Lebensgefühl*]. This it becomes in cases which we describe as pathological; but normally we walk in great security, as if our being was a certain possession. . . . The reflecting analysis of our being by thought shows how little cause for such security there is *in itself*, how far it is indeed exposed to the nothing [*das Nichts*]. Is therefore that security of being proved to be objectively unfounded hence 'unreasonable', is the only reasonable attitude a 'passionate . . . *freedom to death* sure of itself and full of fear [*sich ängstende*]?'[4] Certainly not. For the undeniable fact that my being is transitory . . . and exposed to the possibility of non-being is matched by the other, equally undeniable fact that, notwithstanding this transitoriness, I *am* and am *kept in being* from one moment to the other, and embrace

[1] p. 52.
[2] Her full discussion of Heidegger has unfortunately been left out by the editors.
[3] p. 52, note 10.
[4] Cited from Heidegger, *Sein und Zeit*, p. 266.

a lasting Being in my transitory being. I know myself held, and in
this I have peace and security—not the self-assured security of a man
who stands in his own strength on firm ground, but the sweet and
blissful security of the child which is carried by a strong arm—
considered objectively a no less reasonable security. Or would the
child be 'reasonable' who lived in constant fear that its mother might
drop it? Hence in my being I meet another, which is not mine, but
is support and ground of my unsupported and groundless being.[1]

She then outlines two ways by which to recognize in this
ground of being the eternal Being: one the way of faith, the other
the way of reasoning, which is the way of the Thomist proofs of
the existence of God. There is no doubt about the way she
prefers:

The security of being, which I sense in my transitory being, points
to an immediate anchoring in the last support and ground of my
being. . . . This is, indeed, only a very dark sensing, which one can
hardly call *knowledge*. . . . This dark sensing gives us the Incomprehensible One as the inescapably near One, in whom we 'live and
move and have our being', yet as the Incomprehensible One.
Syllogistic thinking formulates exact notions, yet even they are
incapable of apprehending Him who cannot be apprehended; they
rather place Him at a distance, as happens with everything notional.
The way of faith gives us more than the way of philosophical knowledge: it gives us the God of personal nearness, the loving and
merciful One, and a certainty such as no natural knowledge can give.
Yet even the way of faith is a *dark* way.[2]

This, of course, is true; yet a scholastic philosopher would
probably object very strongly to this preference for 'sensing'
as opposed to proof by reasoning, and to the mixing up of
the spheres of faith and philosophy. It is the preference of the
'modern', and moreover the feminine mind, to which the
objectivity and clear-cutness of Aristotle and Thomas remained
foreign.

The next section deals with essential and real being (*wesenhaftes
und wirkliches Sein*). Edith Stein defines finite being as 'that which
does not possess its being, but needs time in order to reach being'.[3]
In contrast to this the infinite is 'what *cannot* end, because it is not

[1] pp. 55-7. [2] pp. 57f. [3] p. 60.

given its being, but is in *possession of being*, the master of being, even *Being itself*. We call it *Eternal Being*.'[1] She distinguishes between temporal and finite being, because in analysing 'units of experience' she finds factors that are not subject to the flow of time: '*My* joy—this joy which I am feeling at the moment—begins and passes away: *the* joy as such does neither begin nor pass away.'[2] And so she joins Plato and his world of ideas, but rejects the term as too controversial and ambiguous and substitutes the phenomenological neologism *Wesenheiten*, generally rendered in English as 'essences'. She holds with Plato that 'there could not be the experience of joy if the essence joy was not there before'.[3] She thinks that 'the life of the Ego would be a chaos impossible to disentangle, if nothing could be distinguished in it, if the essences were not "realized" in it; through them comes unity and multiplicity, organization and order, sense and intelligibility into it'.[4] She numbers among the essences sorrow, joy, pain, pleasure, but also consciousness, experience, Ego. 'Of course,' she says, 'the essences must not be mixed up with the realities that are named after them. The essence "Ego" is no living ego; and the essence joy no experienced joy. Even greater is the danger of trying to interpret the essence as *notion*. This would be a grave misunderstanding. For we form notions by detaching the characteristics of an object. In this we have a certain freedom: but we do not form essences, we *find* them ready-made. We have no freedom: it is in our power to seek, but not to find.'[5] These essences do not have a temporal, but an immutable and non-temporal being, though not the eternal Being of God. For the being of the essences is an ineffective and hence a non-real being; the essence joy, for example, cannot produce real joy. On the other hand, the Being of God is supremely effective and supremely real. Yet she holds that the being of the essences is no potential being either; though it is not absolutely perfect, it is perfect in its own way in that it can be neither increased nor decreased. 'The *realization* of an essence does not mean that *it* is realized, but that *something* is realized that corresponds to it. The possibility of a real being is *founded* in its being.'[6] So, in her view, the existence of the essences as separate entities is the condition of the existence of the realities

[1] p. 60.   [2] p. 61.   [3] p. 62.   [4] p. 64.   [5] pp. 64f.   [6] p. 66.

corresponding to them: without the existence of the essence 'joy' we could not feel joy. She goes on to contrast the Thomist definition of joy, which relates to the concept of joy, with the phenomenological teaching on the essences which is, of course, something entirely different.

The following paragraphs are devoted to painstaking and often illuminating research into what constitutes the *Wesen* (being, essence—but not *Wesenheit*) of a thing, in scholastic terminology the substance as distinct from the accidents, always in dependence on the language. In fact, a large part of her philosophy, as has been observed before, consists in analysing words in order to arrive at the exact meaning of what they express. It is the essences, she contends, 'which in the last resort give the words their meaning'.[1] And 'that there are such things as essences can be discovered by the ruminating thinker only by ways far removed from the attitude of daily life, and then he has the greatest difficulty to convey his meaning to others'.[2]

This seems difficult, indeed. And for the person not brought up in the phenomenological school the doctrine of 'essences' seems very questionable. For, she writes, 'they are nothing *real*, but the real would not exist—it would be neither real nor possible if they did not exist'.[3] Redness, for example, she calls an essence 'which is imitated in the red colour of every red object'. Hence, of course, comes to mind the well-worn objection to the Platonic doctrine of ideas: What really is the 'essence' redness? Is there also a separate essence pinkness? And is Bordeaux-redness to be distinguished from brick-redness? To put this question is no mere cussedness; for Edith Stein herself later writes about 'joy of a child' as a special 'quiddity', a sub-division of 'essence'. 'The quiddity [*Wesenswas*] "joy of a child" existed in its essential being before all time. . . . When for the first time a child in the world felt joy, then there was realized for the first time the essence and the *quid* [*Was*] of a "joy of a child".'[4] Her investigation of *Wesenheiten* and *Wesen* (essences and beings) is, like so much of her philosophy, based on the linguistic roots of German words, and hence extremely difficult to reproduce in another language. She thinks of the world of essential being (*wesenhaftes Sein*), which corresponds to Plato's realm of ideas,

[1] p. 76.   [2] p. 77.   [3] p. 78.   [4] p. 92.

as a graduated realm, in which the simple essences are the highest
grade. Below them, and formed in their image, are the features
of the composite beings, which she calls *Wesenswas*, best translated as quiddity. Such would be the 'joy of a child' just
mentioned.

After dealing with these two forms of being she gives a short
paragraph to the beings that develop, e.g. the youth who is
becoming a man. Here she thinks it necessary to speak of

two beings which are realized one after the other in the person.
Indeed, we shall have to distinguish according to the essential being,
that which was before the change as something different from what
is afterwards. But in addition we have to presuppose a third, which
comprises, and is the foundation of, the transition from the one to
the other, for this transition is one possible in essence [*wesensmög-
lich*]. Of the comprising and 'founding' essence it will have to be
said that it is real during the whole period of life at every moment,
whereas the partial essences are so only in the time-sections that
correspond to them.[1]

This paragraph shows clearly the subtlety as well as the complicated structure of her analyses, which are both very much in
the tradition of the phenomenological school, though one may
reasonably ask whether they are not farther removed from the
clarity and simplicity of the Thomist philosophy than she herself
realized. In the following section on 'essences' she admits that
her conception of them does not correspond to St. Thomas's
teaching, and is of opinion that it rather approaches Duns Scotus.
After further painstaking analyses she defines them thus: 'In the
realm of what as *essential being* we have been trying to distinguish
from the real being on the one hand, and from the "being in the
mind" on the other, the *essences* are the *elements* from which are
built up the *quiddities* as *composite entities*; they themselves enter
as a basic element into the *full what* of the things.'[2]

She finally links them up with theology: 'Thus the being of
the essences and quiddities is not to be regarded as independent
beside the eternal Being. It is the eternal Being Itself that shapes
in itself the eternal forms . . . according to which it creates the
world in time and with time.'[3] On the basis of her theory of

[1] p. 83.   [2] pp. 98f.   [3] p. 103.

essences, she criticizes St. Thomas's refutation of the ontological argument as 'an unjustified transition from the logical to the ontological order'. 'It [i.e. the ontological argument] deals with the transition from essence to being, and if this transition is inadmissible in the case of all finite beings, no conclusion can be drawn for the infinite Being, because precisely the difference in the relationship between essence and being distinguishes it most from everything finite.'[1]

She then applies her teaching to the doctrine of the Trinity, which she attempts to restate in phenomenological terms.

> Undoubtedly [she writes], in the equation of the divine Being and the divine Essence is expressed the intellectual inseparability of both, and at the same time the *inseparability of essential and real being* in God. . . . How does this inseparability agree with the separability that seemed to be suggested by the Trinitarian theology? Can I separate the Persons and their distinct personal being from the divine Essence, if essence and being are inseparable? I see no other solution than to regard the very *being in three Persons* as *essential being*.[2]

She admits herself that these interpretations are 'parables'—but after all she has said about 'essential being' being different from 'real being', this novel interpretation of the most difficult Christian doctrine seems somewhat risky.

The following section is a very technical discussion of the traditional metaphysical concepts of essence and substance, form and matter, in the light of the phenomenological philosophy. The wide range of her interests shows itself in her discussion of truth, for example, which comprises artistic as well as divine truth.

In her treatment of the *analogia entis*—on which Father Przywara had written a book which had made a great impression on her—she gives a comparison between the relation of the Three Divine Persons to each other and the relation between Creator and creation; this is a very beautiful elucidation of the mystery of the Trinity in the terms of traditional theology. It leads to the section of the book that deals with *The Image of the Trinity in*

---

[1] p. 106, n. 101.   [2] pp. 107f.

Creation. She applies the term image to everything in creation and rejects the Augustinian-Thomist distinction between vestige, relating to the irrational, and image, relating only to the rational creation. After analysing the concept of person in relation to the Trinity she considers it in relation to spirit.

> What [she asks] does spirit mean? . . . The spiritual and intellectual[1] has been characterized as the non-spatial and immaterial; as something that has an 'interior' in a totally non-spatial sense, and which remains 'in itself' by going out of itself. This 'going out of itself' is, again, essentially proper to it. It is the entirely 'selfless'; not as if it had no self, but because it surrenders its self totally, yet without losing it, and in this surrender becomes utterly manifest—in contrast to the hiddenness of what belongs to the soul. In the utter self-surrender of the divine Persons, in which each strips Himself perfectly of His Being and yet preserves it perfectly, each is wholly in Himself and wholly in the others, we have the spirit in His purest and most perfect realization. The Triune Divinity *is* the true 'realm of the spirit', the supermundane [*das Ueberirdische*] as such. All the creatures' spirituality or endowment with spirit means an 'elevation' into this realm, even though in a different sense and in a different manner.[2]

She goes on to apply 'the three fundamental forms of real being' to the Three Persons of the Trinity. 'The psychical being [*das seelische Sein*] would correspond to the Father, from whom everything springs but who is only from Himself, the bodily being would correspond to the Son, as the "born-out" form of the essence [*ausgeborene Wesensgestalt*]; whereas the free, selfless streaming-out deserves once more the name *Spirit* in a special sense.'[3] This threefold division of 'real' being is taken from the philosophy of her friend, Hedwig Conrad-Martius; it corresponds to the old division of man into body, soul and spirit; but its application to the Trinity is certainly novel.

Descending from God to creatures, she investigates the human person and its properties, using again the threefold division body, soul and spirit. She examines the concepts of 'ego', 'soul',

---

[1] *Geistig*—a word practically untranslatable in English, comprising mental, spiritual and intellectual.

[2] p. 333.

[3] p. 334.

'spirit' and 'person', and from there turns to the angels as pure spirits. After summarizing the angelology of the Pseudo-Dionysius, she discusses the possibility of pure spirits, inserting a beautiful passage on nature, grace and freedom.

In her discussion of evil, she contradicts not only St. Thomas, but traditional Christian theology in general by objecting to the teaching that evil is a privation of the good. She writes:

> Evil in its strict and proper sense is only something that springs from free will. The devil has no defective nature, but has perverted his good nature by its unnatural use into evil. Natural reason objects against letting evil pass as a defect or weakness, because it feels distinctly that in evil it is confronted with an effective power. This power is the force of a free spiritual person. The created spirit has this power not from itself. Therefore free will, even that of the highest angel, is no independent last ground of being beside God, nor can he produce anything that is from himself. . . . But he can give a direction to his doing, even one that is opposed to the divine Will. And what we call evil is precisely such a creaturely action of the will that is opposed to the divine Will. As an action of the will it is something that is, indeed it belongs to the highest there is in the realm of creaturely being. But by its direction it is 'negative', opposed to Being. . . . The possibility of evil as the possibility of created grace also, has its roots in the freedom of created spirits.[1]

She thinks that the Christian theologians have not worked out sufficiently the difference between a 'merely natural defect' and 'what is actually evil'. Therefore she concludes that 'Evil . . . is also a being, opposed to its own original nature and direction of its being, a literally "perverted" being.'[2] But if evil is a being, and if *all* being—as she must admit on her own premises—has its origin in God, then evil, too, must be of God. For she had just said that even the highest angel 'cannot produce anything that *is* from itself'—but if evil *is* something, if it is not just a privation of being, where does it come from? Surely the perverted direction of the human or angelic will cannot give *being* to anything? Therefore the Christian theologians say that evil in itself is an absence of being, that, where something evil is

[1] pp. 372f.   [2] p. 373.

realized, the very fact of its existence, *qua* existence, is not from itself; all the 'being' it has is from God, but in so far as it is something evil, it is a privation of being. As St. Thomas says: 'No being is called evil in so far as it is being, but in so far as it lacks a certain being; as a man is called evil in that he lacks the being of virtue.'[1]

The reason for her contradicting the traditional teaching on such a vital point is not far to seek: it is to be found in her phenomenological, non-metaphysical training. Confronted with the 'phenomenon' of evil as it presents itself to the analysing observer —and the strength of the phenomenologist is analysis—he cannot but consider it as something that *is*; whereas the metaphysician, undeceived by 'phenomena', penetrates to the roots of being and sees that even the devil, totally perverted as he is, is yet 'good' in so far as he *is*, because being, *qua* being, cannot be evil. And therefore, even 'the cause of the first sin is not evil, but a certain good (namely the will) with the absence of a certain other good (namely the application of the rule of reason or of the Divine Law)'.[2]

In her angelology, too, Edith Stein leaves St. Thomas and rather follows and develops Duns Scotus. She denies they are pure forms 'because something that is subject to being formed belongs to their structure'.[3] St. Thomas, who considers that the angels are 'pure forms', holds that they are composed of 'act and potency',[4] whereas she thinks this insufficient and posits a 'passive potency' in the angels which enables them to be receptive of further 'formation'. She follows Pseudo-Dionysius in placing the ecclesiastical and celestial 'hierarchies' side by side, and her beautiful pages on the Church as the Mystical Body of Christ are clearly written from the heart of one who has found in the Church her home and the truth she had sought.

Her subsequent considerations of the Trinity and its inner life are far more satisfying than those we have discussed before; here she no longer interprets the doctrine in phenomenological terms, but follows the traditional theological interpretation. The very subtle discussions on the image of the Trinity in the lifeless material world and in non-personal living creatures, however,

---

[1] I q.5 a.3 *ad 2um.*
[2] Ia-IIae q. 75 a.1. *ad 3um.*
[3] p. 378.
[4] I q. 50 art. 2 *ad 3um.*

are not easy to follow; here she utilizes the concepts of soul, body and spirit in *ad hoc* defined meanings which are not always acceptable.

The section on the Image of God in man is full of interesting psychological analyses; but it is by no means clear what she means by soul. 'Man is a spiritual person,' she writes, 'because he stands freely over against not only his body, but also his soul, and only in so far as he has power over his soul, does he have it also over his body.'[1] According to the unanimous Catholic teaching man consists of body and soul; body and soul together constitute the human person.[2] What, then, is this 'spiritual person' that has power over both body and soul? The will, which is one of the powers of the soul, directed by reason, another power, has power to form the human life. How can there be yet another constituent, the 'spiritual person', that stands over against the soul? Here it seems Catholic teaching on the soul and phenomenological analysis (especially Dr. Conrad-Martius's book *Pflanzenseele—Tierseele—Menschenseele*, which influenced her deeply) have both been utilized without distinction and cause a certain confusion.

The next section on 'Steps of Self-knowledge' is built on this phenomenological conception of the soul. The soul is 'the dark ground . . . which rises to the daylight of consciousness in the life of the Ego'.[3] It is 'a thing-like whole with qualities which are made known in its behaviour, and, conversely, can be influenced by behaviour . . . therefore I have the power to co-operate in the formation of my soul'.[4] The soul is a being with many layers, as it were, and man should live from its most interior sphere.

The personal I [she writes] is truly at home in the innermost part of the soul. *If* it lives here, then it disposes of the gathered strength of the soul and can use it freely. Then it will be closest to the meaning of all happenings and open to the demands that are made on it, and will be best prepared to gauge their importance and bearing. But there are few people who live in such recollection. In most of them the I is situated rather at the surface; occasionally, it is true, it is shaken by 'great events' and drawn into its depth; then it will seek

[1] p. 394.   [2] Cf. I q. 75 art. 4.   [3] p. 396.   [4] p. 397.

to live up to the event by behaving adequately; but after a more or
less prolonged sojourn there it will return to the surface. Indeed, what
comes in from outside is often of a kind to allow itself to be dealt
with fairly adequately from a superficial, or at least not very profound, level. It does not require the last depth in order to be more
or less understood, nor is it necessary to respond to it by deploying
one's whole strength. But if a person lives recollectedly in his depth,
he will also see the 'small things' in their wider relationships. Only
such a person can estimate their importance—measured by ultimate
standards—in the right way and regulate his behaviour accordingly.
Only in him is the soul on its way to the final forming and to the
perfecting of its being.... It is from the interior, too, that one's own
being radiates.... The more recollectedly a man lives in the interior
of his soul, the stronger will be the radiation that emanates from him
and exercises its spell on others.[1]

This passage is an excellent clue to her character as well as to
the impression she made on others: that of a soul who was living
habitually in her centre, who saw and judged all things from this
centre, and who would leave this deep recollection that was
hers only if necessity or charity demanded it. This recollection
was not necessarily the supernatural recollection of prayer; for
it had been there even before she became a Christian, and already
had struck people forcibly in her student years. It accounted for
her ability to stay motionless for hours, as well as for her low tone
of voice and her almost complete lack of gesture. It was this
habitual recollection, this refusal to let herself be disturbed, that
impressed people so deeply and gave them the feeling of being
in the presence of a quiet strength on which they could rely and
which would support them, if necessary.

This withdrawal into the innermost part of the soul is no
sterile preoccupation with oneself. 'This it is, that the adepts of
the interior life have experienced at all times: they were drawn
into their inmost part by something that drew them more
strongly than the whole external world; they experienced there
the irruption of a new, powerful, higher life.... Mystical grace
gives as experience what faith teaches: the indwelling of God
in the soul.'[2]

She also finds another approach to the indwelling of God; a

[1] pp. 404 f.   [2] p. 407.

very interesting one, which probably came to her from her own pre-Christian experience. It is based on the relationship between moral obligation and physical strength, the experience that, though one may feel perfectly exhausted, one still finds oneself able to do some work that is demanded by a strong moral obligation. 'The Spirit of God is meaning and power,' she writes. 'He gives the soul new life and enables her to achieve performances to which she would not be equal by her nature. . . . In the last resort every meaningful demand which presents itself to the soul with binding power is a word of God. . . . And if a man willingly accepts such a word of God, he receives by this very fact the divine power to act accordingly.'[1]

This is an interesting idea—but is it true? She gives the example of a completely exhausted doctor who is called to yet another patient at night. He thinks his strength is bound to fail—but then he revives sufficiently to fulfil his obligation. It seems to us that this is a well-known psychological phenomenon that applies by no means only to 'every meaningful demand which presents itself to the soul with binding power'. A criminal, in order to escape the law, may perform feats that far surpass his natural strength; sheer ambition may cause a man to stay without sleep for many nights in order to prepare himself for a competition; he then just 'lives on his nerves', as the popular expression has it. This is even more true of the superhuman powers exhibited by persons in trance. On the other hand, there are cases where even the strongest moral obligation cannot restore the exhausted body. It seems that here the distinction between the supernatural and the natural has been blurred; the ability of a good many people to act with abnormal vigour under strong nervous strain or emotion cannot be made into a sign for the indwelling of God in the soul.

Her thesis that one receives power from God to do what one is obliged to do is far more cogently proved in another sphere, from which her second example is taken.

The command of the Lord: 'Thou shalt love thy neighbour as thyself', binds without conditions and modification. My 'neighbour' is not the person I 'like'. It is everyone who comes near me,

[1] p. 409.

without exception. And again we are told: 'You can, because you shall.' The Lord Himself demands it, and He does not demand the impossible. On the contrary, He makes possible what would naturally be impossible. Saints who trusted in this sufficiently to resolve on loving their enemies in a heroic way, have been made to realize that they had the freedom to love.[1]

What, after all this, is really the image relation between God and man? She bases herself on St. Augustine and on his twofold conception of the image as developed in *De Trinitate*, which is spirit, love and knowledge, and, again, memory, reason and will. She confronts him with a modern thinker, Theodor Haecker, who sees the Trinitarian Image in the threefold division of thinking, feeling and willing, and who regards feeling, not, as traditional theologians, the will, as the seat of love. In a subtle analysis she criticizes Haecker, and with him the whole modern stress on love as an emotion, and vindicates St. Augustine.

Has Augustine simply meant to equate love and the will [she asks]? He calls the desire something like the will and after the manner of love. It becomes love, if that which is desired (the knowledge) has been found. Certainly there is a close relationship between love and will. Who loves feels impelled to keep God's commandments, that is to say to adapt his will to the Divine Will.... Through fulfilling the Divine commandments we obtain a more profound knowledge of God, and through this love grows, in its turn.[2]

But she does not think that one ought to concentrate on one particular psychological or intellectual triad; she considers that the 'three-and-one' is a basic law of the life of the spirit in general. It is a pity that she concerns herself only with St. Augustine and St. Thomas and leaves out of account the whole rich tradition of the Greek Fathers, in whose theology the Image, the *Eikon*, plays such an important part. On the other hand, she finally synthesizes St. Augustine with Haecker and speaks of a

threefold development of the spiritual and intellectual [*geistig*] life outwardly in rational knowledge, feeling and willing, which are yet

[1] p. 410.   [2] p. 414.

one as the development of the mind, and through their being mutually conditioned. We have, on the other hand, a threefold inner life, a being aware of one's own being according to knowledge in the primary form of memory, which is at the same time the primary form of knowledge, a feeling oneself and a voluntary affirmation of one's own being. The inner being of the spirit, its going outward, and the discussion between interior and exterior are the fundamentals of the spiritual life.[1]

After the philosophical she turns to the theological and mystical analysis of the image. The soul 'surrenders herself to the paternal will of God which, as it were, engenders the Son in her anew. She unites herself with the Son and desires to disappear in Him, so that the Father may see nothing in her save the Son. And their life unites itself to the Holy Spirit, it becomes an out-pouring of divine love.'[2] This, indeed, is no longer philosophy, it is mystical theology.

In the section on spirit and soul Edith Stein distinguishes between the soul as spirit and the soul as form of the body. 'As form of the body the soul has that intermediate position between spirit and matter which is proper to the forms of bodies. As spirit she has her being "in herself" and is able to elevate herself in personal freedom above herself and to receive a higher life into herself.'[3] Anticipating the reproach that in this way she splits up the unity of the soul, she explains: 'By this we do not mean to express a parallel existence of spirit and soul in man. It is the one spiritual soul which has a manifold development of her being.' She then analyses the difference between the Divine Image in rational and irrational beings and, on the other hand, its difference in men and angels.

The pure spirits are like rays, through which the eternal Light com-municates itself to creation. Greater is the distance, farther is the way to those spiritual beings which are enveloped in matter and rise like a fountain from a hidden depth. But just this hiddenness, this being like a fountain, give them something of the fathomless inscrutability of the divine Being. And in their detachment they seem to be more self-subsistent than the totally God-borne pure spirits. Finally, precisely through their being tied to matter, they

---

[1] p. 418.   [2] p. 421.   [3] p. 423

have a peculiarly close connexion with Him who descended into the depth of earthly being; with the Word made Flesh.[1]

Her final section deals with this mysterious connexion in the context of human individuality. She begins with a refutation of the Thomist teaching that matter is the principle of individuation. This, however, is not very conclusive, since she seems to understand matter and form in a different—non-metaphysical—sense from St. Thomas. Moreover, she rarely cites St. Thomas himself, but her whole argumentation is concerned with a somewhat simplified manual on Thomism by the Benedictine Dom J. Gredt, which, it seems, had been recommended to her by Father Przywara. She opposes the view that the difference between human persons is due to the fact that 'the souls live in bodies which consist of spatially differentiated matter'—and it almost seems—her language is not quite clear—as if she attributed this absurdity to St. Thomas. Her own philosophical—as distinct from her theological—argument for the 'uniqueness of . . . each human person'[2] is that the 'feeling' of each individual person is to be something unique. 'If we "feel" our own being and that of others as such and such a one, and this such and such as something unique, then this feeling is a special form of original experience and carries with it its own lawful reason.'[3] She follows it up with a scriptural argument. 'Thus we may so understand the verse of the Psalm: *Qui finxit sigillatim corda eorum*[4] that each single human soul has gone forth from the hand of God and bears a special seal.' St. Thomas deduces the same doctrine from the fundamental text: 'God created man according to his image', but she does not cite him here. She again crosses swords with him in her last pages, which deal with the Incarnation. Though she admits that the more widely accepted teaching is that the Word would not have become Man if man had not fallen, she prefers the other view. She writes: 'To whom did the first men owe their being children of God? This was a gift from God . . . but was it given to men independently of the human nature of Christ? I do not think this is compatible with the idea of "head and body one Christ" . . . Perhaps it is even not too bold to say

[1] p. 430.   [2] p. 460.   [3] ibid.
[4] He has formed singly the heart of each. Ps. xxxii. 15, p. 461.

that in a certain sense the creation of the first Man may already be seen as a beginning of the Incarnation of Christ.'[1]

And so the book ends with a view of humanity, and indeed of all creation, as the Mystical Body of Christ; for 'as head of mankind, which itself combines the higher and the lower, Christ is the Head of all creation'.[2]

Her work, despite certain deficiencies, will stand as the bold venture of a deeply religious mind trying to re-think the age-old question of finite and eternal being in the setting of modern philosophy, a search for truth in the spirit of St. Thomas himself.

[1] p. 478.　　　　　[2] p. 482.

CHAPTER NINETEEN

GROWING IN CHARITY

THE great work was finished on 1 September 1936; her mother died a fortnight later. In the weeks before, Sister Benedicta had been much occupied with nursing sick sisters; now a whole avalanche of literary work descended on her, in addition to her vast correspondence. So she has to excuse herself in a letter to a friend: 'If you should really come here, I will gladly tell you more. At the moment I cannot do it by letter. I have had too much to write in these last months and still have. . . . Yesterday we had the Feast of All Saints of our Order, and today began the novena in preparation for the feast of our holy father, St. John of the Cross. These are always days of special gratitude for the undeserved grace of being called into this chosen family of God.' In the same letter she announces the coming of her sister Rosa.

Rosa had been powerfully drawn to the Church, but had sacrificed her desire to become a Catholic for the sake of her mother. Now that Frau Stein was dead she was free to follow the call. She naturally wanted to see her sister, and at the same time to be baptized into the Church; she was expected in Cologne on 15 December. On the night before, Sister Benedicta had an accident.

Mother Sub-prioress was making her private ten days' Retreat and was just making the Stations of the Cross in the dark cloisters. Suddenly she heard a slight cough, as is the custom in Carmel for attracting each other's attention during the periods and in the places where strict silence has to be observed. 'Who is there?' she called into the dark. No answer, but the same sound, as if somebody was in pain, seems to come from the direction of the stairs. Immediately she was at the switch and turned on the light. In three strides she dashes up the first stairs and finds Sister Benedicta lying on the floor on the landing. She had been groping for the switch on the wrong

side of the door and thus had got too near the stairs and fallen down.
With difficulty she was taken to her cell and the convent doctor was
called.[1]

She had broken her left foot and her hand, and had to be taken
to hospital. It was typical of her perfect observance of the Rule
that even in such an emergency she would not break the silence,
but waited patiently till somebody might notice the little coughing
sound that was allowed.

At first there was great consternation that this should have
happened just when her sister was due to arrive; but then everyone realized that the accident had actually been a blessing in
disguise: for instead of having to see Rosa behind the double
grille of Carmel for only a short time every day, she would now
be able to talk to her without restriction in hospital. So Sister
Benedicta had the joy of giving Rosa the last instructions, for
her baptism had been fixed for Christmas Eve. To complete
her happiness, she recovered so rapidly that on that day she could
be discharged from hospital and, her foot in a plaster-of-paris
cast, was allowed to assist at her sister's baptism. As there was
no white robe ready, they used Sister Benedicta's choir cloak, to
the great delight of the catechumen. At the midnight Mass
Rosa made her First Communion. The Carmelites took her to
their hearts at once, and she stayed at Cologne till just before the
New Year.

After this happy interlude Sister Benedicta was once more
inundated with work. *Finite and Eternal Being* had been finished—
but the difficulty was now to find a publisher for it. This would
have been comparatively easy in normal circumstances; but in
Hitler's Germany hardly any firm would dare to risk bringing
out a work by a non-Aryan. So there was a good deal of correspondence, bringing many disappointments, when one house
after another refused. At last the small Breslau firm that had
published her translation of St. Thomas agreed to undertake the
work and sent her their contract in July 1937.

All through this time there was great excitement in the
Cologne Carmel, because the nuns were preparing to celebrate
with great splendour the third centenary of its foundation. The

[1] *Life*, pp. 176f.; 170.

Prioress had had the ambitious project of bringing out a history of the convent and its twelve daughter foundations, and Sister Benedicta was entrusted with the auxiliary tasks: she had to get hold of the relevant documents and to do all the correspondence necessary for that, as well as a vast amount of copying. When the work was at last finished, she had to break up the manuscript into chapters and paragraphs and to make an accurate bibliography. Certainly it was a labour of love for her beloved Carmel—still, for a creative mind like hers it must have had its penitential side to have to content herself with the 'donkey work' and leave the actual writing to another.

Despite the large amount of work involved in her share in these preparations for the jubilee, her private correspondence, especially with souls needing advice and help, was not allowed to be dropped. Ruth Kantorowicz was still her problem child. She had remained in contact with her since she had first asked her help in autumn 1934, and especially since she had come to Cologne, despite the refusal of the Carmelites to accept her. As the position of 'non-Aryans' in Germany deteriorated rapidly, she desired to enter a Carmel abroad, and Sister Benedicta succeeded in getting her accepted as a postulant at a Dutch convent at Maastricht. She herself liked the life, but the community decided that she was unsuitable. Once more Sister Benedicta had to help and write letters on her behalf; for, as she tells one of her friends whom she asks to visit her: 'You can imagine how helpless the poor creature must be out there these days.' She was the more so as she did not even know her own mind, as appears from another letter of Sister Benedicta, written to the same friend of the unfortunate postulant:

I meant to write to you before the beginning of Advent. But then I received a message from Ruth that I should tell you several things, but not before receiving a confirming instruction from her. After that I had a letter which seemed to indicate that I should rather not tell you. But now I feel an urge to tell you on my own responsibility how I see the situation. For I still think you are the person who would be most likely to help her. You will know that Ruth is leaving Carmel in these days and is going to the Ursulines at Venlo. The Sisters at Maastricht will pay her *pension* till she has found something. I have advised her repeatedly to look for work, to learn

Dutch in order to have more possibilities, etc. By way of answer I got only arguments why all this was impossible, that there were only jobs for which she was quite unsuited. I have the impression that she does not want anything else but to wait on the chance that another Carmel may take her. In the New Year she intends to apply again with a recommendation from Mother Magdalene (I suppose in Austria). Externally she has so far clung to Mother Magdalene, and internally she has attached herself so much to the Carmelite way of life that I do not know whether she would still be possible in another Order. You have found her frighteningly helpless even here, and I fear she is even more so now. I feel that now someone ought to take her by the hand and help her to find her feet again in the world. In my last letter I told her that she would stand a much better chance even as a postulant if she were standing on her own feet, than in her present situation which might arouse the suspicion as if she was only looking for a refuge. But one cannot expect a rabbit to behave like a lion. . . . It is Advent, and I do not want to write more than necessary.

In fact the 'rabbit' behaved very foolishly. Her friend was quite ready to visit her, and Sister Benedicta wrote happily: 'This will be a beautiful star in your sad Christmas, when you can celebrate Epiphany together.' But Ruth, who seems to have belonged to the class of people who are their own worst enemies, wrote that she did not want the visit, and Sister Benedicta was 'very sorry for the unhappy little rabbit who deprives herself of help so much needed. Now she herself urgently asks for your visit; today came a new SOS, because they have decided at Maastricht to pay for her livelihood only for another three months. By then she must have found herself some work. I hope that it will now be possible for you to make the journey.'[1]

Another correspondence is equally indicative of Sister Benedicta's love and understanding. In August (1937) she writes to a nun who greatly admired her:

My dear Sister X, this is indeed a great surprise that we may reckon on your visit so soon. . . . But you must not take the matter so very seriously. It is only a little Carmelite novice, to whom you come, not a doctor or a spiritual director. She does not presume to cure your nervous complaints, and would not dream of interfering

[1] Cf. *Life*, pp. 184–7, German edition only.

with your inner life. If you do not want to, you need not tell me a word. I only thought that people who are run down need relaxation in their holidays—for this is the purpose for which God has made the holidays—and I thought it might do you good to let the sun of Mount Carmel shine on you and to breathe in its free air a little more freely than usually. If you wish it, I shall be at your disposal in our parlours, and I should have enough to tell you that would perhaps please you. But if you would rather talk in our chapel to the Queen of Peace and the dear saints of our Order, I shall be equally content. At present we ought simply to wait and see what the Reverend Mother will decide. If she gives the permission, then you will accept it as a gift of God and simply say gratefully: 'Yes, Father.'

The sister could not come, and about a fortnight later Sister Benedicta writes again:

Yesterday I was thinking much of you. After your letter we were all the more sorry that you could not come. But this is only humanly speaking. It is sure to have its deeper meaning. I think it has even done you good to be able to look forward to the visit without restraint. And then this sacrifice has been placed with the many others which you offer every day, and will bear its fruit. If I think of the great concerns of which you write and of many others, known to me of former years, then I think I understand that a high price has to be paid. I gladly take everything with me to the tabernacle.

I should like to make a suggestion with regard to the plan that has failed: If it should turn out again—as was the case four years ago— that only the explicit permission is lacking, but not the will to give it, then why not ask to be given the permission for the next opportunity in advance? But if there should be definite objections, then we will go without seeing each other again *in via*, and look forward all the more to the *visio beata*. . . .

These two letters, as well as those written on behalf of Ruth Kantorowicz, show her own rapid advance on the way of perfection. They were addressed to someone suffering from great nervous strain, to whom she had written a year ago: 'I did not know of your illness. Don't torture yourself by giving me more detailed information. I am not surprised if anyone who is today in a responsible position has a nervous breakdown. . . . In such a case we need not look for other explanations. But of course such things are an instrument in the hand of God, and if we look at them in this way, it is grace.'

The mixture of calm common sense with a thoroughly supernatural outlook is in the authentic line of her own holy mother, St. Teresa. Without appearing to do so, she does in fact give direction: the sister, evidently upset at the disappointment of not being able to come to Cologne, is told to use it for souls. Apparently she did not dare to visit Sister Benedicta because the formal permission of her superiors had not been forthcoming in time; so she is very sensibly advised to ask for a sort of wholesale advance permission to pay the visit when another opportunity should offer. The tone of the letters is gentle, maternal; it is the language of a soul that has arrived at maturity, resting peacefully in the hand of God. She is ready to advise and console, but she is equally prepared to stay in the background, and let our Lady and the saints do the work. She is no longer surprised that human nature is ready to break under strain; this does not seem to be the same voice that once said she could not understand how one could get tired at prayer. The virgin had become a bride and the bride a mother; she was still as hard as ever on herself, but she had learned to understand that human beings are very varied; that human weakness exists even in Carmel, and that the bride of the Lamb must imitate the infinite tenderness of her Spouse. And so, despite her seclusion, she was in contact with many souls whom she helped. She writes in the same letter just quoted: 'The other day we were visited by a little Brother of the Holy Family, who is going to make his profession on 8 September . . . I have been entrusted with quite a number of budding vocations to the priesthood and to the religious life. There is now, indeed, hardly a more urgent need.' St. Teresa had urged her daughters to pray and make sacrifices especially for priests; Sister Benedicta did not only that, but, like St. Teresa of Lisieux, corresponded with them and talked things over with them in the parlour.

All the time the preparations for the conventual tercentenary celebrations were going on—despite the growing dangers; for the Nazis were showing their hostility to the Church, and to the religious Orders in particular, ever more clearly. Sister Benedicta was acutely conscious of the gathering storm; Carmel had not dulled her sense of the realities of the outside world. She writes on 15 October:

> We are so far still living quite undisturbed in profound peace behind our convent walls. Yet the fate of our Spanish Sisters[1] gives us an indication of what we, too, must expect. And if such far-reaching changes occur nearer home,[2] this is a very salutary warning. In any case it is our duty to assist with our prayers those who are now fighting so hard in the front line. We celebrated our jubilee from 30 September to 3 October. The miraculous image of the Queen of Peace from our old convent church of our Lady of Peace was its highest guest of honour. It was exposed on the magnificently decorated high altar; every morning a Pontifical High Mass was celebrated before it; then a sung Mass and several low Masses, three times daily a sermon, and great crowds of people. We must be grateful that such things are still possible.[3]

Sister Benedicta was probably more deeply aware than the other nuns of the contrast between the world, threatened by the forces of Antichrist—Communism in Spain, Nazism in Germany —and the joyous celebrations inside the convent. She took part in them with the loving devotion she had for all that concerned her Carmel; but at the same time she was occupied also with the greater needs of the Church and of souls. She did not hesitate to speak out openly against both the injustice of the régime and cowardice in face of it when she felt it was needed. At this time the government was agitating strongly for the so-called *Einheitsschule*, a secular type of school without any teaching of religion, and it encouraged teachers to join in the propaganda. A sister of one of Sister Benedicta's former pupils had, against her conscience, given way to this pressure. When Sister Benedicta heard of it, she told the frightened girl her opinion in no uncertain terms: 'And even if they had shot you, you ought never to have done it.' Her heart was with those martyred in Spain and persecuted in her own country, offering its sorrows for their support and comfort.

In her desire to help wherever she could, she began with her

---

[1] The civil war was then raging in Spain.
[2] She refers to the attacks on the Catholic schools.
[3] *Life*, p. 184; 178.

own conventual family. A few weeks before the jubilee, in the beginning of September, she had asked for permission to nurse a lay sister who was dying of cancer. This new duty curtailed her correspondence still more. A letter to a nun friend, written a few weeks after the centenary celebrations, gives a glimpse of her life in the convent, punctuated as it was by the demands made on her time by those wanting advice.

Before the beginning of Advent [she writes on 14 November], I should like to send you a greeting. E.N. will have told you that she came in for a little of our centenary celebrations. She will probably turn up again when she has done her exam. She is not yet clear about her vocation. Of course I am advising her not to take any steps until she has full interior certainty. I can understand very well that the great apostolic tasks necessary today urge souls towards external activity. This is indeed necessary—even though the final decisions are made elsewhere.

I affectionately return all the greetings you have sent me. If you should soon write to D., please tell Sister C. that I gladly take all the intentions of her family with me into my prayer. But I hope that I shall be able to send her a greeting myself, before Advent starts. However, it will be difficult by that time to have lowered the mountain of letters waiting to be dealt with. Since the beginning of September I have had to nurse a sick sister. Given our horary, the time which then still remains for other things is negligible. Please, pray a little for my invalid and for her nurse. According to the view of the doctors there is no hope of a cure. But owing to the long time of rest her state has remarkably improved, and so Sister Clara still hopes to get well again. She is our oldest lay sister, who has done a great deal for the house and was an example to all because of her zeal for penance and mortification. Now all intentions are brought to her and recommended to her prayer and suffering.

The picture that emerges from this letter is indeed different from that of Dr. Edith Stein, busy with philosophical studies, admired as a lecturer, travelling from one place to another to address crowds of people, using for her prayer the small hours of the morning and as much time as she can snatch from her other duties during the day. In the eyes of the world her doings are now supremely unimportant: the nursing of a lay sister, following a convent routine that leaves her hardly any time for

writing letters, and being unable to do more for the cause she
has at heart than to pray for it—yet it is just in such an apparently
quite uneventful life that, as she writes, 'the final decisions are
made'.

From the day of her conversion it had been Sister Benedicta's
deepest conviction that the true Christian life is a life of prayer
and sacrifice, and that the apostolic life, too—indeed the apostolic
life before all—is founded on these two. It is surely no accident
that one of the two principal patrons of the missions, St. Teresa
of Lisieux, was a contemplative whose short life had been nothing
but prayer and hidden sacrifice. And she whom the Church calls
the Queen of Apostles spent her days in the house of St. Joseph
at Nazareth, and later with St. John the Evangelist in Jerusalem,
praying and suffering for those whom her Son had chosen to go
out into the world and preach to the nations the Gospel of
salvation.

A few months after taking over the nursing of the sick nun,
Sister Benedicta was entrusted with an office that was to take up
even more of her free time: she was appointed turn sister, that
is to say, she had to provide the link with the outside world, to
accept incoming and outgoing messages, announce visitors and
give orders to the girls who did the shopping and similar jobs
for the nuns, as there were at that time no extern sisters in the
Cologne Carmel. It was a post of trust usually given only to
nuns of proved discretion and reliability; it meant that her
novitiate was drawing to its close; in a few months she would
make her final vows and so become a full member of the
community.

CHAPTER TWENTY

THE GATHERING STORM

ONCE more it was Paschal-time. Once more Sister Benedicta was in retreat, preparing for one of the great events in her religious life, her final profession, which would bind her indissolubly to the Order of Our Lady of Mount Carmel. It seemed that the Lord wished at this decisive time to break the last link with her former life, the life of the philosopher examining 'phenomena' in the search for truth. For while she was spending these ten days in total silence, Edmund Husserl lay dying. God alone knows how much he, who had set her feet on the way that led her ultimately into the Church and into Carmel, was in her prayers during this time of profound recollection. Being a 'non-Aryan', he had been forbidden to teach at Freiburg University. He and his wife had found refuge at the convent of St. Lioba, where Sister Benedicta had been a frequent guest, and where one of his former pupils, Sister Adelgundis Jaegerschmid, was a nun. She kept Sister Benedicta informed on the state of her patient. Once, years ago, when he had been ill, Edith Stein had been sitting at his bedside reading to him from the New Testament; now Sister Adelgundis was doing the same for him, reading the Gospels and speaking to him of Christ. The ways of God are mysterious. The modern philosopher was dying with one of his pupils, now a Benedictine, explaining to him the faith of the Church, and the other, a Carmelite, offering her prayers and sacrifices for this soul so dear to her, who was soon to meet its Maker.

There is something strange about the last days of Husserl. On Good Friday he seems to have had something like a vision, for he moved his arms as if to protect himself from something terrifying. When he was asked what it was, he replied: 'Light and darkness—much darkness, and again light.' Before the end came, on 27 April 1938, he had another mysterious experience.

He told Sister Adelgundis that he had seen something wonderful, and asked her to write it down. But before she had had time to fetch paper and pencil he was dead.[1] First the darkness followed by light, then the vision of something wonderful—may it not be that the prayers of his Carmelite disciple had obtained for him a glimpse of ultimate truth in his last hour? She had come to him as a young student, eager to learn the meaning of things; he had taught her a strict way of philosophizing, unhampered by prejudice and preconceived ideas, looking at all that exists with open eyes and seeking to attain to its essence; and in following his teaching she had discovered another Teacher, and accepting His word she had found the Truth she had sought. The pupil had outstripped her old master, who nevertheless had followed the development of his disciple with affectionate interest—and now, perhaps, her prayers were allowed to smooth his way into eternity.

Six days before his death, on the Thursday of Easter Week, Sister Benedicta had made her final profession; and on 1 May, once more the Sunday of the Good Shepherd, she received the black veil, a very special Carmelite ceremony. As on the day of her clothing, a large number of her friends had come to assist at the impressive service. When the preacher had finished his sermon the black veil was blessed by the bishop and placed on her head, together with a crown of white roses. *Veni sponsa Christi, accipe coronam*, recited the bishop, and the nun responded: *Suscipe me, Domine, secundum verbum tuum*. Once more she was lying on the ground, her arms stretched out in the form of a cross, while the choir was singing the *Te Deum* and all the bells of the little convent church were ringing in thanksgiving that another soul had made her final surrender to God, to be a holocaust of love for the adoration of Him and the salvation of men.

A little note she wrote shortly after the ceremony to the parents of a former pupil of hers who had died several years before is characteristic of her love and solicitude for those in the world:

Dear Frau X [she writes]. Very many thanks to you and your dear husband for the beautiful present, for your kind note, and above all

[1] cf. Oesterreicher, *op. cit.*, p. 96.

for your visit. It was a special joy to me that you were present at the feast. Surely your dear husband, too, will find his way here some time. I do not know whether it is possible for you to travel together. If one has a business this is always difficult. .... I expect that in the great 'do' the other day you did not get a souvenir except the profession picture. Therefore I enclose something today. Wishing you every blessing for the coming lovely feast days, I am, in the love of Jesus and Mary, yours gratefully, Sister Teresa Benedicta of the Cross.

For Sister Benedicta her Carmelite vocation was a great and undeserved grace, which she tried to share as much as she could with those outside. This is not always the way of enclosed contemplatives, many of whom avoid contact with the 'world' as much as possible. This attitude, too, has its justification; souls can certainly be helped by prayer only, without any other means. Yet it seems as if in our days the trend is going increasingly towards a form of contemplative life which includes also a more active apostolate, whether by writing or by personal contacts through retreats, instructions and other means of influencing souls directly. Sister Benedicta was truly a woman of our time, in the world as well as in the convent, and, with the full approval of her superiors, she used these means to the full. Also, she had been living too long in the world, and was altogether too open-minded, not to realize that the gulf between convent and world is not so deep as it sometimes appears; that there can be holiness in the world and a good deal of imperfection in the convent. She wrote to a lady who greatly venerated her:

I should not like to hurt you, but I really must tell you that something in your last letter, as also sometimes on other occasions, has caused me embarrassment: it is this, that you emphasize so much the supposedly immense distance between you and me. I should feel like a Pharisee if I quietly accepted these statements, for I can find no objective reason for them. Certainly you are not the only person whom our grille fills with awe. But surely this grille does not mean that outside, 'in the world', everything is bad, and within all is perfection. We know how much human misery is still hidden under the habit, and therefore it is very embarrassing if people burn incense before us. God is merciful and gracious beyond all comprehension and abundantly rewards even the mere resolve to

13

consecrate oneself entirely to Him. When you are here, you sense
something of the peace of His house, and this we certainly do not
grudge you. But you must not attribute to a poor human being
what is in reality the gift of God.[1]

It was, and still is, a necessary reminder. Sister Benedicta knew
from her own experience that it is possible to lead a life of great
perfection in the world; if this were not so, by far the greater
number of Christians would be condemned to mediocrity by
their very state of life, and our Lord said to all: 'Be ye perfect.'
On the other hand, she had no doubt realized in Carmel that
neither the grille nor the habit are infallible means of protection
against the weakness of fallen nature; one need only read the
story of St. Teresa of Lisieux to realize how much pettiness and
downright injustice there can be even in the strictest Order.

Sister Benedicta knew well that the tendency to admire religious
disproportionately for no other reason than that they are religious
may quite often be due to a person's own failure to use the
means at his disposal for his sanctification; and so a tepid Christian
may think of life in the world as necessarily involving mediocrity,
and conversely, life in the cloister as necessarily entailing perfection. It is true, Sister Benedicta herself was destined to find her
perfection in the cloister, under the sanctifying influence of
community life; but she knew that grace is omnipresent and
needs neither grilles nor habits, only the wholehearted co-
operation of the will. Edith Stein had known it, and Sister
Benedicta had not forgotten it. Later in the year, when Hitler's
persecution of the Church was becoming more evident, and
many religious were driven from their houses, she wrote to a
fellow nun who had momentarily to live outside her convent
(though not owing to the persecutions): 'Certainly it is difficult
to live outside one's convent and without the Blessed Sacrament.
Still, God is within us, the whole Blessed Trinity. If we only
know how to build within us a well-closed cell and to retire
there as often as possible, then we shall lack nothing, wherever we
may be. In this way the priests and religious in the prisons must
contrive to live. For those who grasp this properly, it becomes a
time of great grace. This we have heard from many quarters.'

[1] *Life*, p. 190; 181.

This doctrine of the inner cell had already been taught by St. Catherine of Siena; indeed, it is indispensable for all who cannot live in a material cell. Only seven years ago, after she had left Speyer, Edith Stein had written of how very hard she found it to live outside a convent. In Carmel, under the influence of its doctrine of utter detachment, she had learned to rely more and more on the will of God alone. If God's will for her was the enclosure of Carmel, she gratefully accepted it; but if this should be taken away, she would also be content. While she was writing these lines, on 20 October, she must have foreseen that she herself would have to practise one day what she was teaching now. There was no misreading the signs of the times, at least not for a clear-sighted mind like hers.

One of her godchildren, the wife of a Jewish lawyer, became a frequent guest at the parlour, pouring out her fears and worries and planning emigration. Then the repeated elections brought tension even to the peaceful Carmel. Things came to a head in 1938. In view of the often-made excuse that ordinary Germans were totally ignorant about the real character of the régime until, during the Allied occupation, they were told about the horrors of the concentration camps and other misdeeds of their leaders, it is interesting to read what Sister Benedicta's Prioress writes in her biography. If anyone could have remained ignorant of what was going on in Germany at the time, then surely it was an enclosed nun. But she writes quite frankly: 'On 10 April 1938 things looked much more serious. The principles of National Socialism and the government of Hitler had so clearly proved hostile to Christ and God, that even the most unsuspecting German could no longer be in doubt about the goal at which they were aiming. At the same time the power of those in office had developed into a brutal reign of terror at which everyone was trembling.'[1]

In these circumstances it was difficult, indeed, for the nuns to know what to do. Many monasteries of both men and women had already been closed, and the religious been literally driven into the street. Some well-meaning people had advised them not to vote at all; but they had never done that before, since they had permission to leave their enclosure for the purpose. So if they

[1] *Life*, pp. 191 f.; 182.

did not go out this time, it would arouse the suspicion of the authorities. The majority of the nuns were of opinion that they should vote for Hitler so as to avoid any repercussions, for it was well known in Germany that the voting now was not secret, and failure to give one's vote to the Führer might have the most serious consequences. In addition, the nuns contended that it did not matter anyway how they voted; the result of these elections was a foregone conclusion. In fact, everyone knew it was going to be about 98 per cent for the Führer, and it was a common joke that one day they would find that 102 per cent of the electorate had voted for him.

'This view, however, was violently opposed by Sister Benedicta. She, otherwise so gentle and quick to give way, could hardly be recognized. Again and again she urged the sisters not to vote for Hitler, no matter what would be the consequences for the individual or for the community. He was an enemy of God and would drag Germany to ruin with him.'[1]

Sister Benedicta's was certainly the more heroic attitude, and her prediction came true. Yet heroism in itself is not always necessarily the only possible way of action for a Christian. The nuns were certainly right in saying that their vote, whatever it was, would not make the slightest difference to the predetermined outcome of the so-called 'elections'. Nor was such a mere formality as voting for Hitler under duress equivalent to apostatizing from the faith. Hitler had, in fact, a Concordat with the Holy See which, it is true, he was breaking right and left; but German Catholics were not forbidden to vote for him, and in the circumstances the nuns might well be excused for their refusal to run into danger without real necessity. But Sister Benedicta was one of those radical natures to whom such political considerations are foreign. Though she was now a Christian contemplative of the purest water she had never quite understood the age-old wisdom of the Church who is anxious to come to terms even with hostile governments in order to allow her children to practise their faith in peace, and who demands resistance even to death only where the alternative is apostasy. Because her own soul was so obviously cast in the heroic mould, she found it hard to understand the considerations of prudence.

[1] *Life*, p. 192; 183.

In this particular case her position, moreover, was different from that of the other nuns: because she was of Jewish origin her reactions against the Nazi régime, who considered the Jews as enemy number one, must necessarily be more violent than those of her 'Aryan' fellow nuns.

The political discussions had caused some disturbance in the peaceful Carmel, and on election day there was considerable confusion among the sisters. This got worse when, on the morning of polling day, before eight o'clock, just as the first group of sisters were going to set out for the polling station, representatives of the election committee carrying an election urn were announced in the parlour. This had never happened before, and the Prioress did not fail to express her astonishment to the gentlemen. They pretended, however, that, knowing the Carmelites are not allowed to leave their enclosure, they wanted to make it easier for the sisters by collecting their voting papers in this way. The superior once more stressed that the voting, though secret, was a public act, which they so far had never failed to perform in order to give a good example to the populace; this the gentlemen had now prevented. Resistance was useless, she had to give in. The voting was done in alphabetical order. At the end the officer in charge declared: 'Not all of you have been voting. Anna Fitzeck is missing.' 'She does not have a vote.' 'Why not?' 'She is mentally deficient.' A short pause. Then came the dreaded question: 'And Dr. Edith Stein?' 'She is not entitled to vote.' 'Certainly. She was born in 1891. She must be entitled.' Then the calm answer: 'She is non-Aryan.' The gentlemen recoiled. Then one of them snapped: 'Write down: she is not Aryan.' Whereupon they made a quick departure.[1]

When Sister Benedicta was told about the scene she was heart-broken and asked to be transferred to another convent. She would have liked best to go to Palestine, to the Carmel at Bethlehem; for she felt most poignantly that her presence at Cologne endangered the whole community. The sisters, however, thought she was being unduly pessimistic and would not hear of her leaving them. So she carried on with her work.

[1] Cf. *Life*, pp. 192f.; 183.

Despite the growing difficulties the Breslau publishers were trying to bring out her book. In October she wrote to a friend:

Last week there have been piles of proofs. Now there is once more a pause. Since things are so irregular, it is impossible to foresee when the opus will appear. In fact at least the first volume should be finished by Christmas. Perhaps Fräulein P. might enquire at Borgmeyer's place when the book will be out? I think that might give them a little incitement to go on printing. But she need not order a copy from the booksellers. For we (that is to say the Order) will be paid back in copies the money we have contributed to the costs of printing, and have then to see how we can sell them.

In the same letter she writes: 'Last Friday my brother said good-bye to me, before emigrating to America. It was just the fifth anniversary of my entering, and our first meeting since then. Perhaps for ever. Everything is in the last stages of dissolution. Please help with your prayers.'

It is strange to read in the same letter her calm, business-like directions for pressing on with the printing of her book and her brief account of her brother's visit, her staccato sentences quivering with suppressed emotion. Two other letters, the first written on the same day, the other a few days after, show how her life was still going on in its accustomed manner despite the gathering storm. In the former she deals with a question of mystical theology which a Dominican nun had put to her:

Is the life of mystical graces reserved to the few? Your confrère Garrigou-Lagrange has tried to show . . . that it is only the development of the three theological virtues, and that all Christians are called to it. That means to what is essential to it, namely union with God. This in itself, he says, is not extraordinary; only its occasional accompaniments such as ecstasies, visions and the like. The fact that actually only few attain it, is explained by obstacles on the human side. The holy parents of our Order[1] are not quite of this opinion. At least both emphasize, for the consolation of those not endowed with mystical graces, that the decisive fact is the conformity with the divine will. However, our Holy Mother has considered the vocation to Carmel as equivalent to a vocation to contemplation. The same surely holds good for any other contemplative Order. I

[1] St. Teresa and St. John of the Cross.

think, in any case, it is a safe way to do oneself all one can to become an empty vessel for divine grace.

Here Garrigou-Lagrange's position is over-simplified (it does not seem that she had ever studied his larger works on the subject); but it is hardly to be expected that she could have had time to expound these problems more thoroughly at the moment, as becomes abundantly clear from the next letter, addressed to the friend of Ruth Kantorowicz on 31 October:

When your kind letter of 29 September arrived we were just having lots of excitements: triduum for the Little Flower and a diamond jubilee. Shortly after, the feast of our Holy Mother, which was also that of our dear Reverend Mother. Added to this piles of proofs, because the great work is now really being printed. Hence I could not comply with your request for a note before. On 1 August we received a postulant for the office of extern sister, a dear child, but unfortunately unsuitable for the work. . . . Ruth is still 'maid of all work' with the Ursulines at Venlo. Several possibilities which turned up came to nothing. The other day she had been asking after you. It is always a good work if you write to her . . . even better if you could visit her again. On the 26th Fr. Przywara gave a talk to the Graduates Association here and visited us the following morning for the first time. In Carmel the usual autumn cold is making the round at the moment. For some time two Sisters have had to take it easy, hence the others have some additional work. You cannot imagine how active is our contemplative life. But yesterday we had a Quiet Day which we could really spend at the feet of the King. On All Souls' Day we shall both remember our mothers. This thought is always a great consolation for me. I am firmly convinced that my mother now has power to help her children in their great distress. I wish you much progress in the Carmel of the divine Will.[1]

These letters are typical of Sister Benedicta; they show her deeply sensitive nature completely mastered by an iron will. Without this will she could never have been able to concentrate sufficiently to write a closely reasoned philosophical work amidst the tragedies of her time; without her deep sympathy with human suffering she could not have helped those who fled to the parlour or who wrote to her from a distance, with her advice and

[1] *Life*, pp. 193 f., 6th German edition only.

understanding. Yet both her philosophical detachment and her human feeling were rooted in her utterly supernatural attitude to life; they both sprang from the mystery after which she had desired to be called, from the Tree of the Cross.

*   *   *

Shortly after these letters had been written, on 9 November, pogroms broke out all over Germany. Jewish-owned shops and private dwellings were plundered, the Jews and 'non-Aryans' themselves, easily recognizable by the yellow star which they had for some time been compelled to wear on their clothing, were murdered, synagogues were burnt down. Sister Benedicta was transfixed with horror. 'This is the shadow of the Cross falling on my people. This is the fulfilment of the curse which my people has called down on itself. Cain must be persecuted, but woe to him who touches Cain. Woe also to this city and this country, when God shall revenge what is today done to the Jews.'[1] Whoever has walked among the ruins of Cologne after the last war cannot but feel that this was a prophecy destined to be fulfilled.

The pogroms ceased after a few days of terror, but now it was clear to all that not only was no Jew any longer safe in Germany, but that the mere presence of a 'non-Aryan' was dangerous for those associated with him or her. With a heavy heart the Prioress and her nuns at Cologne realized that Sister Benedicta had to leave them. Her original plan to go to Palestine was no longer feasible, since the government there no longer allowed immigration of German Jews. The best solution seemed to be to approach the Dutch convent at Echt, which had been founded from Cologne in the nineteenth century, and with whose Prioress Sister Benedicta had already been in correspondence on the occasion of the centenary celebrations. When her superior cautiously wrote that Sister Benedicta needed a 'change of air' the sisters at Echt understood and immediately invited her to join them.

Sister Benedicta had always been particularly fond of the silence of Advent, when the sisters lovingly and joyfully prepared

[1] *Life*, pp. 194 f.; 184.

for the Coming of the Lord. This year things were different. It was still the time of the Coming of the Lord; but it was also a time of preparation for herself to leave. The arrangements were not easy; the necessary papers had to be obtained, a photograph had to be taken for her passport. 'The photographer who was to take it arrived in the afternoon, and Sister Benedicta, who wished on no account to leave the enclosure before it was time, stood in the open enclosure door. She wore her usual poor habit. When the Reverend Mother who was present saw the darned scapular it seemed to her too shabby. Quickly she took her own scapular from her shoulders and threw it over Sister Benedicta, who thanked her with a loving look of her beautiful eyes. Thus the last, strikingly true likeness was taken.'[1]

It is truly the picture of Benedicta of the Cross, a woman 'of sorrows and acquainted with grief', like her Master. The shadows round her eyes and mouth tell of a life of penance and suffering; but the calm, though sorrowful eyes, and her clear brow are those of the contemplative who has 'overcome the world', and whose peace no man can take away.

Christmas came, and the feast of joy was this year one of sorrow—at least in the natural sphere. Some of the nuns were hopeful: the parting would not be for ever. Sister Benedicta saw more clearly. But her insight was equalled by her courage. She, too, was 'the strong woman', as her mother had been before her. The esteem in which she had been held by the community showed itself clearly in these last days. One of the older sisters, with tears running down her cheeks, thanked her for the wonderful example which she had given them from the first day of her presence among them. But this was too much for her humility. 'How can you say such a thing?' she retorted. 'I must thank God that I was allowed to stay with you.'[2]

Carmel had, indeed, been the fulfilment of her life. It had given her the last purification, the perfection of her humanity in the total union with God and the communion with her sisters. She had known from the first that not even the grille of Carmel would protect her from the rage of the powers that were bent on the complete destruction of her race; and now she, like so many thousands of her people, had to go into exile.

[1] *Life*, p. 195; 184.   [2] ibid., p. 195; 185.

On New Year's Eve, 1938, the enclosure doors opened, and alone, accompanied only by the sorrowful prayers of her sisters, she stepped out into the dusk, where the car of a doctor who was a great friend of the Carmelites awaited her. As a last consolation she had asked to be taken to the shrine of Our Lady of Peace, a small church that had once belonged to the first German convent of Discalced Carmelites. Here she knelt, before the statue of the Mother of God, for her last prayer before she left her country for ever.

'Peace I leave with you: my peace I give unto you: not as the world giveth give I unto you. Let not your heart be troubled, neither let it be afraid.' Wherever she went, this peace would go with her; for neither exile nor war itself can touch this deepest region of the contemplative soul where the King of Peace rules supreme.

CHAPTER TWENTY-ONE

BEGINNING ANEW

WHEN Sister Benedicta arrived at Echt in the evening
she went at once to her cell, and from there to the
recreation room, where, according to the then
Prioress, she showed herself remarkably gay. Evidently she felt
that the intolerable strain of living under a dictatorship had been
lifted, at least momentarily, and she did her best to adapt herself
at once to her new community. The next day she asked to be
shown the graves of the old Sisters of Cologne, who had once
fled to Echt during Bismarck's *Kulturkampf*, in order to pray
there.

The life of the sisters at Echt, though of course fundamentally
the same as that of the Carmel at Cologne, was yet in some ways
different from the one to which she had been accustomed. It
was slightly stricter; the Office was monotoned, not chanted; the
taste of the nuns perhaps less 'educated' than that of the Cologne
ones. It was from Echt that Sister Benedicta wrote the letter,
cited before, in which she speaks about the demand of charity
'to adapt oneself even to the unwritten customs of the house and
the taste of the community'. But its spirit was deeply supernatural.
Only a few years before Sister Benedicta's coming Gertrude
Erzberger, daughter of a German minister of finance, had lived
there an intensely sacrificial life which had left its mark on the
community.

By now Sister Benedicta had come to know from experience
how easy it is for a Carmelite to go to sleep during meditation,
especially as she did not sleep too well at night. So the Prioress
spoke to her about it, advising her to use a book to prevent it. But
as Sister Benedicta was long past the stage where books can be a
help to prayer, she humbly replied that she had been told to pray
from the heart, and so her superior acquiesced.

The adaptation to her new life was made easier by her being

able, during the first months, to continue the work that had absorbed her energies in her last year at Cologne: the correction of the proofs of *Endliches und Ewiges Sein*. She worked on them with all the painstaking accuracy that marked everything she did, at the same time taking part in all the community duties, except recreation, from which she was dispensed when her literary work made attendance impossible.

These last years were to be lived ever more clearly under the sign of the Cross. On Passion Sunday, barely three months after her flight from Cologne, she asked permission from her Prioress to offer herself as a sacrifice of atonement.

Dear Mother [she wrote on the back of a used card, in the spirit of holy poverty so strictly interpreted in Carmel], please may Your Reverence allow me to offer myself to the Heart of Jesus as a sacrifice of expiation for true peace: that the reign of Antichrist may perish, if possible without a new World War, and a new order may be established. I should like to do this even today, because it is the twelfth hour. I know that I am a nothing, but Jesus desires it, and He will certainly call many others to this in these days. Passion Sunday, 26 March, 1939.[1]

If a soul of such mettle makes such an offering, it is usually accepted. When she went to Carmel she went deliberately as a victim, offering herself for her people. Now, as her clear mind saw that war was almost inevitable, she intensified her offering by this formal act, including in her intention not only her race, but the world, that needed a new order.

A small but costly sacrifice, laid on her soon after she had made her offering, was that an author's joy at seeing her *magnum opus* finally published and acclaimed by the world, was not to be hers. In the same year she has to tell a friend rather wistfully: 'The great opus is at a standstill. In the first months here I received the last galley proofs of the second volume and the first page proofs of the first. Then everything stopped, because the publishers lost courage. All efforts to keep it going have come to nothing. I can do no more than commend it all to the Lord.' In fact, the publisher had informed her that the work could not possibly appear under her name, but suggested that it should be

[1] *Life*, p. 223; 212.

published under that of another religious, acceptable to the Nazi authorities. This, of course, was an impossible proposition; and so Sister Benedicta had the great disappointment of having her manuscript returned to her.

> After the proof-correcting has stopped [she writes], I have asked to be given work in the house. It was very necessary; we are only eighteen (in July we lost one dear Sister who died of a very painful cancer), only few are young and fully fit, and hence they are badly overworked. Since the middle of June I have been second Turn Sister, and am responsible for the refectory. In addition there is the common work in a big rural household; the laundry, fruit-picking and bottling—this year's harvest was more than plentiful—spring-cleaning, etc. Add to this our seven hours of daily prayer, so there is rarely any time left for the writing desk.

As she was not so quick at the domestic chores as the other sisters, she sometimes had to ask on Saturday afternoon, the time when the Carmelites are cleaning their cells, to leave recreation a little earlier so as to have finished her work in time for meditation. For she always wanted to be exactly in time for the community duties; when the other sisters were a little late she would, of course, say nothing; but the expression on her face, they say, told them of her disapproval.

If she was slow with her broom, she scored in another way: many of the sisters at Echt were Germans, who had never bothered to learn Dutch. Now the authorities of the Order had just enjoined that in all the Dutch convents Dutch should be spoken in chapter and at recreation, and that the vernacular prayers, as well as reading at meal-time, should be in Dutch. The other German nuns, less gifted than Sister Benedicta, were somewhat slow at learning the new language; but she quickly grasped it and made a point of meticulously observing the new regulation which the others were finding irksome.

Despite her full time-table she still managed to do some writing, in addition to her correspondence which was as large as ever. On 30 May she writes to a former pupil who had sent her a pamphlet of a Carmelite Father who had left the Order:

> As to yourself, be not disturbed by coldness and aridity. The chief

thing is that the will remains faithful, even when all sensible consolation and taste for the spiritual life are absent. You know from your reading that no one who seriously desires to follow Christ is spared these trials. Only we do not recognize it when our turn comes. Many thanks also for the pamphlet you sent me. Of course we had already heard a good deal about it. Now I have also read it —with distaste, as you can imagine. But I am grateful for it, since it spurs me on yet more to make atonement and satisfaction, especially by absolute faithfulness to my vocation. Now, however, I should be very grateful to you if you would allow me to destroy the pamphlet. It might affect others quite differently from the way it affects me. I should not like to be responsible for that. Our dear Mother, too, would like that best. I could tell you a good deal about these 'confessions'. But I can hardly write it. I should only like to make one point, which will hardly have escaped you. Everything supernatural is completely left out. He seems quite unaware of the fact that the essential of a religious vocation is 'the call by our Lord Jesus Christ', as our Constitutions put it. Everything is misinterpreted as human activity, in faithful adherence to the axioms of official psychology. The name of Jesus is never mentioned. It abandons Christianity completely. I am glad that I have just started work on the life and writings of Sister Marie Aimée de Jésus, in order to write a short biography. This is the best antidote. For in this life the working of God can be seen and touched at every point. Thursday, 1 June, we have the clothing of a little lay postulant who arrived at this house on the same day as I; she is also a convert from Germany. On the evening of 2 June I am allowed to make my ten days' retreat. Please pray a little for that, also for our sick and for many other intentions, especially my relatives.

In those days German priests and religious had every incitement to fall away from their vocation; the state was proclaiming a new *mystique*, the religion of the 'Aryan' race, and the duty of every pure-blooded German to transmit his inheritance to as many sons and daughters as possible. Celibacy was almost a crime against the race and the fatherland; priests, monks and nuns failed in their first duty by remaining unmarried. No wonder that from time to time—though very rarely, indeed—one of them succumbed to the temptation and apostatized, sometimes also yielding to the urge to make his experiences known to the world, sure that he would find a willing public. It is not difficult to imagine how deeply affected Sister Benedicta must have been every time she heard of such a case; for from the very beginning of her life as a Christian the supernatural had been paramount in her thought as well as in her whole being, and now more than ever her religious life was, and was meant to be, a total sacrifice.

A few months later she could report that she had finished the biography of Sister Aimée de Jésus. It is a little book full of devotional spirit, but hardly differs from the usual kind of convent biography. It is strange that she, so critical in all philosophical matters, who did not fear to contradict St. Thomas and even St. Paul himself, should accept without examination all the legendary features of this sort of literature. The explanation is probably that she was a philosopher, and therefore felt that she had not only the right but the duty to leave no problems unexamined that came within her range of interests; whereas she felt she should accept with childlike trust the marvels of popular accounts of saints' lives and similar subjects of which she had never made a special study. Nevertheless, it has to be admitted that these later hagiographical ventures do not come up to the high standard of her work on St. Elizabeth; a fact also due, no doubt, to the circumstances in which she had to work, far removed from the possibilities of independent inquiry.

That she herself found comparatively little intellectual satisfaction in this kind of work becomes clear from her correspondence. But she had already begun to study the saint whose teaching is marked by total abnegation, and a letter to a close friend, a nun in a teaching Order, dated 13 March 1940, is revealing, both of her own state of mind at this time and of the growing influence of St. John of the Cross. She writes:

Now I will at once begin to answer your questions. By 'pure love' our holy father John means the love of God for His own sake, coming from a heart that is free from all attachment to any created thing, to itself and other creatures, even to all consolations and similar things, which God may give to the soul, and any special devotions, etc.; from a heart, that is to say, that no longer desires anything save that God's will be done, and which lets itself be guided by Him without any resistance. *The Ascent of Mount Carmel* deals extensively with what oneself can do in order to get there; *The Dark Night* with the way in which God purifies the soul. The

result of both is described in *The Living Flame of Love* and *The Spiritual Canticle*. (Actually the whole way is to be found in each work, only that one or the other stage is emphasized respectively)....
Should we aim at pure love? Most certainly. For this we have been created. This will be our eternal life, and here below we must try to approach it as closely as possible. Jesus became Man in order to be our Way there. What can we ourselves do? Strive with all our powers to be empty: our senses mortified; the memory as free as possible from images of this world, and our hope directed towards Heaven; reason emptied of all natural searching and musing and directed towards God in the simple gaze of faith; the will (as I have already said) lovingly devoted to the divine Will. This is very simple to say, but the work of a whole lifetime would not suffice to reach the goal, if God did not do most of it. We may, however, trust Him that He will not withhold grace if we do faithfully the little we can. Little, if considered absolutely, but for us it is very much. Moreover, we must take care not to want to judge how far we ourselves have got. This is known only to God.

All this, of course, is pure St. John of the Cross. The emptying of memory, reason and will from all that is not God is his way by which to ascend Mount Carmel, though, since it is a letter to someone whose vocation was teaching, Sister Benedicta might perhaps have profitably made the necessary adaptations to her friend's state of life rather than give a mere repetition of his doctrine. She then goes on to an exegesis of Psalm xviii, for which her correspondent had asked, especially verses 13 and 14.

What we know of ourselves [she explains], of our faults and trespasses, is but the lit-up surface. The depth from which they come is largely hidden from us. God knows it and can purify it. The *ab alienis* is, I think, open to being understood in different ways. I think especially of our share in the guilt of others. But one could also think of what is introduced into ourselves by others. *Delictum maximum* probably does not refer to any particular sin. It seems to me rather to point to the greatness of the divine mercy and omnipotent power of redemption for which nothing is too great.

Then, passing on to the special passages from the Lady Office which that nun was reciting:

Emissiones tuae paradisus—in the language of Eastern imagery the perfume emanating from the bride is probably meant. Without imagery: Mary is full of graces and virtues. They emanate from her like a perfume pleasing to God and enriching us. It is good that you put questions to me. I think only if I am set a task. Otherwise my intellect is mostly at a standstill. But I am glad if it is wound up and may still be of use to somebody. During Lent it has been allowed to do something very beautiful, namely to compose a Mass and Office in honour of our Lady Queen of Peace for the Carmel at Cologne[1] which wants to ask for a feast of the first class in Rome.

'Our share in the guilt of others.' This is an unusual interpretation of the verse, but it gives a key to her thought in these days, when she felt that what was happening to the Jews was in some way the judgement of God on His people, and that she, too, had a secret share in this guilt, in the mystical solidarity of the Chosen People, and had to expiate for them. But no guilt is too great for the divine mercy; this was the ground of her hope that her sacrifice might be accepted. Part of this sacrifice was surely that her intellect was 'mostly at a standstill'. She certainly loved the simple life of Carmel and accepted it with her whole heart; but there can be little doubt that her natural desires sometimes went back to the life of the intellect, the animated give and take of philosophical discussion, the long hours of uninterrupted thought that she had given up for God. At Cologne she had still had the satisfying task of writing *Endliches und Ewiges Sein*—but this was now finished, without any hope of being published, and there was at the moment no incentive to undertake any other work on a large scale. She had just explained to her friend how the understanding must be emptied; for her, too, the time had come to be more and more detached from all intellectual pursuits, to leave her brilliant mind without the food to which it had been accustomed, so that she might be perfected in the science of detachment which she was soon to teach to others.

God, however, did not leave her entirely without human comfort. In 1939 her sister Rosa had come to Cologne, where she had been living at the Carmelite convent outside the enclosure. From there she had gone to Belgium, where she had

---

[1] Dedicated to our Lady under this title.

the misfortune of falling into the hands of a swindler pretending to be the foundress of a new Carmelite Third Order. Sister Benedicta immediately set to work to get her out of this situation, a difficult undertaking, owing to the war and the fact that Rosa was without financial support; for 'non-Aryans' were not allowed to take money or valuables out of the country, and all Rosa had been able to take across the frontier was her furniture and clothes. When Sister Benedicta finally obtained a permit for her to come to Holland, she had to leave even these behind in Belgium. So she arrived at Echt in the summer of 1940 with no more than a few clothes; but she equalled her sister's detachment from all material things and could laugh at her own misfortunes. The nuns greatly loved and esteemed her, not only for her domestic qualities and her sound judgement—she was as practical as her sister was not—but also for her deep piety, which drew her constantly to the tabernacle. Every Sunday and feast day the two sisters had the consolation of spending an hour together in the parlour; besides, they would speak to each other at the turn, a kind of revolving open cupboard in which letters and parcels are placed, and so Sister Benedicta was always kept informed on the state of the persecution of the Jews. She was naturally very sensitive on this subject, and 'she took it badly if anyone made an unfavourable remark about them. Then she would say that all was slander and maintained that "just as all sorts of things are said about the Jesuits, so it is also with the Jews".'[1]

Her baptism had really deepened her attachment to her people; after all, our Lord Himself was a Jew according to His Humanity, and faith in Him was meant to be the fulfilment of the faith of Abraham, Isaac and Jacob. No wonder that the great women of the Old Testament should have appealed to her particularly, above all Esther, the beautiful queen who risks the anger of the king to intercede for her people, whose situation then, threatened with wholesale extermination in Persia, was poignantly similar to their present predicament. For one of the 'great' recreations, she produced a dramatic monologue called 'Esther', which she performed herself and which impressed the community profoundly. Unfortunately she herself afterwards burned the text.

Yet her intense concern with the fate of the Jews brought a

[1] *Life*, p. 198; 188.

certain element of unrest into her own life and that of the community. Rosa kept up the connexion with converts from
Judaism and then reported to her sister at the turn what she had
heard outside. Sister Benedicta, despite her detachment in other
things, would be very upset; moreover, the Prioress rightly
feared for the security of her own convent if the Jewish connex-
ions became too widely known. So she decided on a step which
would profit both the convent and Sister Benedicta's peace of
mind: she removed her from the turn and ordered her to continue her scholarly work, so that she would be less preoccupied
with the Jewish question.

* * *

In 1941 Holland was well in the grip of the German occupation;
night after night the raids on England were made from the
Dutch coast. While the Carmelites were singing their Matins and
Lauds, the air only a hundred miles away was filled with the
noise of Heinkels and Dorniers taking off on their missions, and,
as the last bombers returned empty of their loads, the small
hours of the morning found the nuns again in choir, making their
meditation. The contemplative life was going on amidst the
terrors of total war, and Sister Benedicta obediently immersed
herself in the depths of mystical theology, bringing her starved
mind and her phenomenological method to bear on the abstruse
doctrine of Pseudo-Dionysius. The essay which was the outcome
of this occupation was destined for a new phenomenological
periodical that was being brought out in America. She was at
work on it for a great part of 1941 and finally sent it to the
United States in September of that year, though she had misgivings whether it would arrive, as she tells a friend on one of
those little postcards to which most of her correspondence with
Germany was now reduced, all bearing the stamp of the Nazi
censor. The essay did arrive, however, but was not published in
the phenomenological journal; it was finally printed in the
Dominican review, *The Thomist*, in 1946.

Professor Rudolf Allers, who translated it, says in an introductory note: 'The reader acquainted with Husserl's phenomenology will recognize his influence in the present article. It

seems to have been the intention of the author to make use of
certain ideas, developed within Husserl's school, for the elucidation of metaphysical and theological problems.' This phenomenological basis gives her work on Christian mysticism its
special interest, but at the same time it is also responsible for its
limitations and evident defects. She herself was well aware that
this new sphere of work presented many difficult problems. A
letter written in May 1941 to a Carmelite in Cologne, who had
entered eight weeks after herself, throws much light on them:

> I think that it is very good for you to have something definite to
> work on. It seems to me that the beginning is good. I am sure that
> these books have not come into your hands by chance. The dear
> Mother knows what happened in the case of my work in this respect;
> how, at the appropriate moment, I used to remember exactly what
> I needed and then received it from somewhere.

After giving some advice on books to be consulted, she continues:

> For the rest, the chief thing is, of course, the assistance of the Holy
> Spirit. I shall gladly ask for it, together with you, and I shall also be
> very grateful if you will do the same for me; for I, too, cannot trust
> in anything else. I am moving in the new sphere of work like a small
> child just learning to walk. The Holy Spirit must help you not only
> with the work, but also with overcoming new crises, which might
> easily arise from it. For no work of the intellect comes into the world
> without heavy labour. It also always tends to absorb the whole
> person, and for us it is not possible to allow this. It is in itself a good
> thing that our daily horary and duties prevent our being 'eaten up'
> by it. But, of course, the balance cannot be established without
> tension.[1]

This letter shows clearly that she realized the difficulties con-
fronting her in this new sphere of work. It also shows a danger
that had always been present to her on account of her phenomenological training, but which was now increased by a somewhat one-sidedly supernatural outlook. Her friend and fellow
pupil of Husserl, Adelgundis Jaegerschmid, has admiringly
written: 'Edith, like our master Husserl, did not need many
books, the learned apparatus which to us ordinary mortals is the

[1] *Life*, pp. 205 f.; 194 f.

indispensable tool of our trade.' But books are needed especially when one approaches a new subject; the Holy Ghost certainly assists anyone in his work for God, but He very rarely supplies those needs for which a person is perfectly capable of catering by his own natural efforts. It is a dangerous proceeding to leave the selection of one's bibliography to what one takes to be Providence; and although in the experience of most writers (by no means only religious ones), once they have started on a subject the apposite material will come their way often in the most amazing and quite unforeseen manner—this does not absolve an author from systematic search. While Sister Benedicta had in certain ways become a disciple of St. Thomas, she never became one in the careful utilization of all the knowledge available for her own work. Husserl's habit of working by analysis *ab ovo* had remained with her, and this phenomenological method was not invariably an advantage when dealing with mystical theology. The letter also hints at the interior tensions and struggles which this scholarly work in Carmel entailed, and which probably were another cause of certain deficiencies. The constant interruptions, the necessity of leaving what she was doing at the first tinkling of the bell, the very little time she had to give to it, made work on her own subject difficult enough. But to approach an entirely new field under these conditions, deprived, moreover, of all competent advice for the year was 1941, and international contacts were completely broken—must have presented insurmountable difficulties. The quality of her scholarly work necessarily suffered from all this. But the loss of the work was transformed into gain for her spiritual personality. As Father Nota, S.J., expressed it in an article which appeared in *De Linie* (Amsterdam, 1 August 1947) to commemorate the fifth anniversary of her death: 'Edith Stein's person is more important than her work.' When she went to Carmel, she went deliberately to offer herself for the salvation of others. The work for which she had come was self-sacrifice, not scholarly achievement. Therefore, though her intellectual activity continued, it was no longer the main thing, and the tension between Edith Stein the philosopher and Sister Benedicta the Carmelite was resolved by continual growth in holiness rather than by the transformation of the philosopher into a theologian.

This growth in holiness was evident especially in an ever increasing, childlike obedience, which struck her superiors more than anything else, and which is particularly to be admired as her intellectual superiority might have tempted her more than others to follow her own views. Though she had been dispensed from most of the community activities in order to gain more time for her literary work, she had been given one task very congenial to her, namely, to teach Latin to the novices. She wrote in November 1941: 'On 30 October the first of five postulants was clothed, the second is to follow on 11 November; the other three only entered in October. All are very good and a great joy to us. So much young life in the house—this is an extraordinary grace for a small and so far rather old family. I am allowed to teach the little ones Latin, and am glad that I get to know them in this way.' This teaching work was a happiness to her and a source of edification to the community; the Prioress admired the 'heavenly patience' which she showed on these occasions, when she devoted herself to the work as if she had nothing else to do. It was indeed a joy to her to introduce these ardent young souls to the splendour of the liturgical worship of the Church, to which the knowledge of Latin was the essential preliminary. She knew how to draw out the deeper meaning from the Psalms and other parts of the Old Testament, and to show their relation to the life of the soul; while she was introducing the postulants entrusted to her to the mysteries of Latin and of the divine Office, she had once more a welcome opportunity for using her great educational gifts in the service of souls.

There was also another reason why she loved this work. It made her

think of our early days in the Order and the marvellous guidance which the way to Carmel always implies. Perhaps the history of the souls in Carmel is even far more marvellous. They are deeply hidden in the Divine Heart. And what we sometimes think we understand on our own will always be only a slight reflection of what remains God's mystery until the day when all things will be made manifest. The hope for the light that is to come is my greatest joy. Faith in the secret history of souls is also needed to uphold us when what we

are shown externally (both in ourselves and in others) is apt to
discourage us.[1]

There is an element of wistfulness in this letter—the wistfulness
of autumn that holds memories of spring. She had been in
Carmel not quite eight years when these lines were written, but
they sound as if she had been there a lifetime; more, as if she
knew that the end was not very far away—the end which would
at last reveal the light which she could as yet see only 'as through
a glass, in dark manner'. In watching the young postulants she
seemed to be reliving in memory her first weeks and months
in Carmel, that first Advent and Christmas when she had been
overflowing with joy because she could truly sing with the
Psalmist: 'I rejoiced at the things that were said to me: We shall
go into the house of the Lord.' There must have been disappointments, too—for there were things 'both in ourselves and in
others' that were 'apt to discourage' her. While she was still
living in the world, she had been easily shocked at the shortcomings of others, even at merely physical weaknesses such as
the inability to pray for many hours in a hot church. In the close
community life of a small Carmel, faults and weaknesses show up
quickly and clearly, more than in a big monastery where safety
lies in numbers. Sister Benedicta, with her ardent zeal for perfection both in herself and in others, must have felt it particularly
hard when she discovered that the religious life is not so much
achievement as striving for perfection, and that even in Carmel
the way is often far from smooth. But at the same time the
human disappointment which she must often have felt made her
realize that the history of a soul looks different in the eyes of
God; He alone knows the secret efforts as well as the obstacles
that every soul must overcome. The somewhat stern 'Fräulein
Doktor' of Speyer and Münster has mellowed and matured;
she has come to realize the deep mystery of every loving soul—
not only of those in Carmel, surely—and, having learned to
withhold her own judgement, is ready to wait for the day when
the hidden meanings will be revealed.

This increasing mellowness and simplicity finds its spiritual
expression in a deep and very Carmelite devotion to the Holy

[1] *Life*, p. 206; 195.

Child of Prague, which she interestingly links up with European history.

> Yesterday [she writes in 1942], before the little picture of the Holy Child of Prague, the idea suddenly came into my mind that He wears the Imperial Coronation robes, and that it certainly was no accident that His activities should have begun in that very city. For centuries Prague has been the seat of the old German or rather 'Roman' Emperors and makes a majestic impression such as no other city known to me can equal, not even Paris or Vienna. The little Jesus appeared just at the moment when the political glory of Imperial Prague came to an end. Is not He the 'secret' Emperor who, one day, will end all troubles? For it is He who holds the reins in His Hands, however much men may think they govern.

Her learning, her perfect trust in God, as well as her intense concern with the events of her time, are all gathered up in this little passage which allows a glimpse of her prayer, in which all these natural and supernatural elements were welded into one harmonious whole.

CHAPTER TWENTY-TWO

MYSTICAL THEOLOGY

THE outcome of Sister Benedicta's occupation with mysticism, to which the last years of her life had been devoted, were two studies, one brief, the article on Pseudo-Dionysius already mentioned, the other much longer, her work on St. John of the Cross.

For some time she had been greatly interested in the mysterious writer whose works had been attributed to St. Paul's convert Dionysius (Acts xvii. 34) throughout the Middle Ages, large parts of which she had translated. Her article, *Wege der Gotteserkenntnis* (Ways to know God), is a study of his teaching on the various modes by which creatures may attain to a knowledge of the Divinity. It begins with what he calls 'symbolic theology', that is, knowledge of God conveyed in images, in order, as she writes, 'to conceal the holy from the desecrating eyes of the multitude and to reveal it to those who, striving for holiness, have freed themselves from childish habits of thought and have acquired the lucidity of mind necessary for the contemplation of simple truths'. She then gives a fine account of Dionysius's interpretation of such scriptural images as fire, as a metaphor of the divine Essence as well as of angelic beings, and the mixing bowl of Wisdom. 'The mixing bowl,' she writes, 'is a symbol of divine Providence; food and drink are images for various forms of instruction . . . the question is: to what does "symbolic theology" attempt to lead us through images gleaned from the world of experience? This goal is manifold and may perhaps best be covered by the name of the "kingdom of God".' Now if the sacred writers—and others as well—represent God, the angels and the supernatural world in general by means of images, they must themselves know God, for 'to shape something into an image one must know the original'. 'What, then,' she asks herself, 'is the foundation of this presupposed knowledge of God? There are several sources from which a knowledge of God may be drawn: natural knowledge of God, faith as the "ordinary" way of supernatural knowledge of God, and finally a supernatural experience of God as the "extraordinary" way of a supernatural knowledge of God.'

This distinction between the two latter forms of knowledge shows clearly that her way of approach is phenomenological rather than theological. Her view of the role of faith in the spiritual life will be discussed at greater length a little further on. Here we would only point out that, whatever school of thought may be followed—whether we hold with Garrigou-Lagrange that the mystic life is in the 'normal way' of sanctity, or with Poulain that it is an 'extraordinary' way—the mystic life, or, as she calls it, the 'supernatural experience of God', cannot be simply distinguished from faith as the extraordinary from the ordinary way, since as long as we live on earth, deprived of the Beatific Vision, we live necessarily by faith, even though we may have attained to the highest mystical state possible.

Sister Benedicta first studies the 'natural knowledge' of God which man can gain from nature, a subject that is more accessible than the other two to the phenomenological method. In a brief survey she analyses our world, which is a meaningful whole 'speaking' to us in a thousand voices, revealing its being as a whole and in every one of its parts, and none the less remaining a mystery for ever. It is the same world which by all it manifests and conceals, points beyond itself to Him who, through it, 'reveals Himself mysteriously'.

From this natural knowledge of God she goes on to the sacred authors, the 'theologians', as Dionysius calls them, who use the language of images because 'they have the gift of understanding the image-language of God (sc. in creation) and of translating it into human language so as to lead others to God by the way of symbolic theology'. Above this natural knowledge that makes use of the symbols of creation is the knowledge of faith, which is 'dark knowledge in that the conviction it entails is not founded on insight into the truth accepted in faith'. After a very summary treatment of faith which she defines simply as 'the acceptance and retention of supernatural revelation', Sister Benedicta leads the reader to 'supernatural experience of God', which she sub-divides into 'Revelation and Inspiration' and 'Personal and Mediate Experience of God'. In the former section she discusses the relation between inspiration and the consciousness of being inspired on the part of the recipient of divine Revelation with reference to the famous case of the unconscious prophecy of Caiaphas. She then analyses the prophetic consciousness.

What gives to the prophet the certitude that he is standing before God? [she asks]. Seeing with the eyes or with the imagination does not necessarily belong to it. All this may be absent, and yet the inner certitude may be there that it is God who speaks. This certitude may be based on the 'feeling' that God is present; one feels oneself touched by Him who is present in one's innermost being. This is what we call 'experience of God' in the strictest sense. It is the kernel of all mystical experience, meeting God as one person meets another. A sensible vision, such as that of Isaias, may be added to this, as an inessential accompaniment.

This passage shows clearly that her intellect tended to investigate even theological and spiritual questions with the equipment and from the point of view of the phenomenological philosopher; but this equipment was sometimes insufficient for the task. From the point of view of the theologian the passage just cited is open to serious criticism. The prophetic visions of the Old Testament cannot be treated as ordinary mystical experiences. Their certitude is based neither on 'seeing with the eyes or with the imagination', nor on 'the feeling that God is present', for both these criteria are entirely subjective. In fact, this certitude is a mystery that cannot be explained, as has been constantly affirmed by theologians from St. John Chrysostom onwards.[1]

The next section deals with 'Personal and Mediate Experience of God'. Here she gives a fine description of the deepening relationship between God and the soul. 'Each higher stage is a richer and deeper self-revelation and self-surrender of God to the soul; for the soul it is an ever deeper and more comprehensive penetration and knowledge of God, which demands from her an ever more perfect surrender.' Here she evidently describes her own experience, the mutual love and self-giving between God and the soul, which is the essence of the contemplative life. But when

---

[1] Cf. Fr. Sutcliffe, S.J., in *The Catholic Commentary on Scripture*, p. 414.

she attempts to relate this experience to faith her interpretation
becomes doubtful. She says of this experimental knowledge of
God in the mystical life that it 'must be counted among the
supernatural experiences and is *therefore*[1] distinguished from faith.
All forms of supernatural experience—but particularly the
personal acquaintance—are related to faith in the same way as,
on the natural level, one's own experience is related to mere
knowledge by information.' A little later she continues: 'Faith
may furnish a bridge for this transition. But if we imagine this
transition from natural knowledge to supernatural experience of
God as happening without the mediation by faith, that is, as a
gift of grace to a former unbeliever, and if this experience is
accepted . . . then the whole will have much more strongly the
character of an interior revolution and transformation.' There
follows a sensitive description of the various ways in which people
accept or reject the 'symbolic theology' of the Scriptures—in fact
the phenomenological method which Sister Benedicta uses
throughout lends itself far better to descriptive analysis than to
interpretation, which is properly the sphere of theology.

She examines the reasons for unbelief and comes to the
conclusion that:

> in most cases . . . the unbeliever is also himself responsible for his
> blindness. Nobody can live in such conditions that no testimony
> whatsoever of God would reach him. If he refuses it entrance into
> his mind and does not at least take some pains in following up the
> views of which he has come to know, it is his own fault; if at a
> later time there results a total incapacity for knowledge, . . . all these
> effects are ultimately his own doing. This is, obviously, even more
> the case when there is not only actual lack of faith, but definite
> atheism by principle, or hostility against God.

And so 'symbolic theology may, eventually, succeed in hiding
God rather than in revealing Him'. For, as she truly says, 'to
him who does not accept God's word as the word of *God*, it
turns into a dead word. It no longer points beyond itself in a
living manner. . . . The heathens may find a confirmation of
their idolatry in some of the images, the dialecticians discover

[1] Italics mine.

contradictions between different passages; the educationists and moralists be scandalized by many things, because their minds remain obtusely ignorant of the hidden meaning.'

Here she lays her finger on the paradoxical fact that the Bible, the inspired revelation of God, has so often been made to prove heretical opinions, and, on the other hand, been dissected by the critics until nothing is left but a shambles of contradictions. If the Word of God is to make sense, it must be accepted as His word; as soon as it is seen not with the eyes of faith but examined by mere unaided reason of fallen man it turns into 'a dead word'. Therefore Divine revelation needs a key—and from here she regains her point of departure, the Dionysian theology.

It may also happen [she writes] that a sort of 'office of the keys' is conferred on individuals or groups which have received the gift of Scriptural exegesis. This point of view makes possible an understanding of the Areopagitic 'hierarchies'. God reveals Himself first of all to the pure spirits whose natural capacity of understanding is greater than ours and in whom the Divine Light does not encounter any inner obstacles. To these spirits is given the office to transmit the light they receive, and their office is taken over and continued by the 'Ecclesiastical Hierarchy' in the degrees of the human order. . . . It is their duty to accept the Divine mysteries with a purified mind and to take charge of them. This also implies preaching and interpreting the Divine Word. Corresponding to the different modes and degrees of hiddenness, there are different modes and degrees of unveiling, degrees of office and of difference in the extent to which a person is forbidden or allowed approach.

This passage gives simply and clearly one of the leading ideas of Dionysian thought, which the Areopagite himself had wrapped in his characteristic deliberately obscure language, that makes it difficult to penetrate his meaning. In the last short paragraph Sister Benedicta gives the reader a quick glimpse of another 'theology', far surpassing the way of 'symbolic' theology. 'All speaking about God presupposes God's speaking. His most real speaking is that before which human speech is silenced, that which no human words can comprehend nor the language of images express.' She concludes: 'The foregoing discussion presents a set of problems in a first survey as it results when one attempts to proceed with a minimum of theological presuppositions.' This obviously deliberate procedure accounts for the insufficiencies in her presentation.

Her other work concerned with mysticism, the *Kreuzeswissenschaft* (Science of the Cross), was written at the request of her superiors in honour of the four hundredth anniversary, in 1942, of the birth of St. John of the Cross. It was almost finished, but lacks the last polish, since she was unable to put the final touches to it. This lends the book its particular poignancy, and at the same time makes it especially distasteful to view it with a critical eye. Yet matter for criticism there is, and it needs to be discussed, for these very defects of her thought are essential to a true portrait of her. This is the portrait of a philosopher who had found the faith, who became a contemplative of the purest water, but whose thought, as distinct from her prayer, remained the thought of a philosopher and hence insufficient to tackle the questions and difficulties arising from her occupation with mystical theology. Therefore it is not surprising that Sister Benedicta, embarking on such an abstruse subject with hardly any help from books and from theological advisers, should not have accomplished her difficult task as well as she might have done in different conditions.

In her preface she lays down both her method and her aim:

In the following pages the attempt has been made to grasp John of the Cross from the unity of his being, as it is expressed in his life and in his works, from a point of view that makes it possible to envisage this unity. Hence we do not give a description of his life nor an exhaustive evaluation and presentation of his teaching. But the facts of his life and the contents of his writings have to be utilized in order to penetrate to this unity. The documents are cited extensively, but after they have been heard the author attempts an interpretation. It is in this that she offers what she believes to have grasped of the laws of intellectual and spiritual being and life, after a lifetime of effort. This applies particularly to her theories on spirit, faith and contemplation which have been inserted in various places, especially in the section 'The soul in the realm of spirit and the spirits.' What is said there on the ego, freedom and person, is not derived from the writings of our holy Father John. Though certain points of contact may be found, such theories were remote not only from his leading intention but from his mode of thought. For only modern philosophy has set itself the task of working out a philosophy of the person such as has been suggested in the passages just mentioned.

She goes on to cite her main sources, apart from the works of the saint himself. They are only three: the two books by Père Bruno de Jésus Marie, *Saint Jean de la Croix* and his small summary, *Vie d'Amour de saint Jean de la Croix*, and the somewhat questionable and certainly not traditional work by Jean Baruzi, *Saint Jean de la Croix et le problème de l'expérience mystique*. She uses neither of the two standard works of the two opposing schools of mystical theology, Père Poulain's *Grâces d'oraison* and Père Garrigou Lagrange's *Perfection chrétienne et contemplation*, which latter treats the subject with particular reference to St. Thomas and St. John of the Cross, nor Jacques Maritain's *Degrés du savoir* with its large section on the Carmelite saint; neither does she refer to such important works of theologians of her own Order as Père Gabriel's various studies of St. John of the Cross, which appeared in Rome in 1936 and 1938, or to Père Paschal's important article on the saint in the *Dictionnaire de théologie catholique*. It is quite probable that, owing to the war, she could not lay hold of these and had to content herself with what happened to be available at the moment. Unfortunately her work suffered gravely from this lack of contact with contemporary thought on the subject.

But it is not only this defect that makes for incompleteness. In the preface just quoted she says that 'only modern philosophy has set itself the task of working out a philosophy of the person'. Now St. John of the Cross was not a philosopher but a theologian; therefore with him it can be no question of a philosophy, but of a theology of the person. And though there did not exist in his time a philosophy of the person in the sense in which modern thinkers understand it, there certainly existed a theological concept; for practically all the Trinitarian and Christological controversies of the fourth and fifth centuries of our era were concerned with exactly this: what was meant by the three Persons of the Trinity in the One Divine Essence, and the One Person of the Son in the two natures. Apart from these more strictly theological discussions, the ordinary human person, too, was a subject of Patristic thought: the structure of the soul itself, the image and the *hegemonikon*, its relation to spirit and body, all these constituents of human personality were discussed by both Greek and Latin Fathers, whose views were in their turn systematized by St. Thomas and the Schoolmen. The strange thing is that Sister Benedicta herself had dealt with most of these concepts in *Endliches und Ewiges Sein*; she had analysed the image of God in the soul, and had mentioned the theological concept of person. But she had treated it all in philosophical contexts—where it was far less appropriate—and took no notice of the fact that the doctrine of the Image had become one of the main bases for the interpretation of the mystical life.

Her work begins with a profound analysis and justification of the term *Kreuzeswissenschaft*, in which she seems to give unconsciously a portrait of her own soul:

> If we speak of the Science of the Cross, this is not to be understood as science in the ordinary sense: it is no mere theory. . . . It is indeed known truth—a theology of the Cross—but it is living, actual and active [*wirkliche und wirksame*] truth: it is placed in the soul like a seed, takes root in her and grows, gives the soul a certain character and forms her in all she does or leaves undone, so that through this she herself shines forth and is recognized. . . . From this form and force living in the depth of the soul is nourished the philosophy of this man and the way in which God and the world present themselves to him.

And, a little further on:

> Where there is truly living faith, there the doctrines of the faith and the great deeds of God are the content of life, everything else must take second place and is formed by them. This is holy objectivity [*heilige Sachlichkeit*]: the original interior receptivity of the soul reborn of the Holy Ghost. Whatever is brought to her, this she accepts in the proper way and depth; and it finds in her a living, mobile power ready to let itself be formed, and unhampered by false inhibitions and rigidity. . . . If the mystery of the Cross becomes her inner form, then it becomes the science of the Cross.[1]

And again: 'The Crucified . . . demands from him [the artist] as from every man, that he should follow Him: that he should

[1] pp. 4f.

form himself, and suffer himself to be formed, into the image of the Cross-bearer and the Crucified.'[1]

Despite their calm objectivity these pages vibrate with a personal feeling that betrays her own profound experience of the 'science of the Cross'. When they were written she was already on the last stages of her way to Calvary, and whenever she leaves the philosophical and enters the personal sphere this becomes apparent. For her the Cross was never some mystery of the faith passively accepted, but a living reality, the seed of which had first been cast into her soul when she met its strength-giving power in the widow of her teacher Reinach, and from then onwards grew until it was also outwardly revealed in her name, Benedicta of the Cross. And now she lovingly traces its development in the life of the great Doctor of Carmel, who, she suggests, was first instructed in its mysteries by Our Lady of Sorrows beneath the Cross; for 'who', she asks, 'could be so well versed in this science and so deeply penetrated by its value as the wisest of Virgins?' She herself used to pray for long hours before the image of the *Mater Dolorosa* at Beuron, and one of her most revealing poems is dedicated to her:

Juxta Crucem tecum stare!

Today I stood with you beneath the Cross,
And felt more clearly than I ever did
That you became our Mother only there.
Even an earthly mother faithfully
Seeks to fulfil the last will of her son.
But you became the handmaid of the Lord;
The life and being of the God made Man
Was perfectly inscribed in your own life.
So you could take your own into your heart,
And with the lifeblood of your bitter pains
You purchased life anew for every soul.
You know us all, our wounds, our imperfections;
But you know also the celestial radiance
Which your Son's love would shed on us in Heaven.
Thus carefully you guide our faltering footsteps,
No price too high for you to lead us to our goal.

[1] p. 6.

> But those whom you have chosen for companions
> To stand with you round the eternal throne,
> They here must stand with you beneath the Cross,
> And with the lifeblood of their bitter pains
> Must purchase heavenly glory for those souls
> Whom God's own Son entrusted to their care.

This poem had been written on Good Friday, 1938, and expresses what she knew to be her own vocation; the same vocation that she now sought to retrace in the life of St. John.

So she follows his early years, his mortifications and sufferings as a boy, and his renewed encounter with the Cross in his later study of Scripture. 'The prophecy of His [Christ's] death,' she writes, 'confronts the disciples with the image of the Crucified and still confronts everyone today who reads or hears the Gospel. It contains a silent demand for an adequate answer.'[1] This challenge of the Passion of Christ becomes especially urgent in the days when the Church commemorates it in her Liturgy 'in poignant words and tunes which draw us irresistibly to live the suffering with Him'.[2] We know how deeply she entered into the meaning of the Holy Week ceremonies at Beuron; and at Carmel, too, though stripped of much of their liturgical splendour, these days meant for her a real reliving of the Passion. In describing their effect on St. John of the Cross, she tells of her own experience.

She then traces the message of the Cross, as it must have confronted him during his studies, through the Old Testament prophecies to St. Paul. In glowing words she speaks of the 'Word of the Cross' as the Gospel of St. Paul, which makes it clear that her understanding of the great apostle has deepened since the days when she criticized him for his 'Judaizing' views on the place of women in the Church. In a short section on St. John's attitude to the sacrifice of the Mass she stresses particularly the saint's prayer to be preserved from mortal sin and yet to feel the contrition for such. 'To be pure from guilt, and yet to feel the sorrow—is not this the true union with the spotless Lamb who took upon Himself the sins of the world, is not this Gethsemani and Golgotha?'[3] It was the same spirit in which she

---

[1] p. 11.   [2] p. 12.   [3] p. 17.

wanted to be a sacrifice for the sins of her people, the same
desire that had led her into Carmel.

Apart from these forms in which the message of the Cross
comes to all Christians, she describes the visions St. John had of
the Cross, and the cross that was laid on him in palpable form
during his imprisonment at Toledo. 'To be helplessly delivered
up to the wickedness of embittered enemies, tortured in body
and soul, cut off from all human consolation and even from the
sources of power in the sacramental life of the Church—could
there be a harder school of the Cross?'[1] In a few months this
was to be her own fate, as it had already been the fate of so many
priests, nuns and laymen alike. As she was writing these words
she knew her own danger only too well; for she wrote in April
1942: 'Humanly speaking, my sister Rosa and I are in a rather
insecure situation.' But she continues: 'We leave everything
trustingly to Providence and quietly go about our duties.' She
was living in the very atmosphere she was describing: in the
atmosphere of the Cross, which means not only suffering, but
suffering accepted in total abandonment to the will of God, which
may even include the utter spiritual desolation of Golgotha which,
in the language of St. John of the Cross, is the dark night of the
soul. With this ends the brief first part of the work, the message
of the Cross (*Kreuzesbotschaft*), which is followed by the main
part, the doctrine of the Cross (*Kreuzeslehre*).

She begins this with a very illuminating comparison between
the Cross as a sign and the Night as a symbol; the one having
acquired its meaning by its history, without any inner connexion
between itself and what it signifies, the other being a natural
symbol of the spiritual reality it serves to express. Her penetrating analysis of the twofold meaning of the night symbol is
one of the finest examples of the phenomenological method
applied to mystical teaching, whose symbolism lends itself
particularly well to that method because of the interpenetration
of spiritual and material realities.

The night is something of nature: the opposite of the light, envelop-
ing us and all things. It is not an object [*Gegenstand*] in the true sense
of the word: it does not stand over against us, nor does it stand upon

[1] p. 24.

itself.[1] Nor is it an image, in so far as this means a visible form. It is invisible and formless. And yet we perceive it; indeed it is much nearer to us than all objects and forms, it is much more closely related to our being. Just as the light causes the things and their visible qualities to stand out, so the night swallows them up and threatens to swallow us up, too. What is drowned in it is not just nothing: it continues to exist, but indistinctly, invisibly and without form, as the night itself, or like a shadow or a ghost, and hence threatening. At the same time our own being is not only outwardly threatened by the dangers that are hidden in the night, but it is also inwardly affected by it. The night takes away the use of our senses, it impedes our movements, paralyses our faculties; it condemns us to solitude and makes our own selves shadowy and ghostlike. It is a foretaste of death. And this has not only a natural, but also a psychological and spiritual significance. The cosmic night affects us in a similar way as that which is called *Night* in a metaphorical sense. Or conversely, that which produces similar effects in us as the cosmic night is metaphorically called Night. Before we try to grasp what this is we have to realize that even the cosmic night has a double aspect. The dark and uncanny night has as its contrast the gentle, magic night, flooded by the soft light of the moon. This night does not swallow up the things but lights up their nocturnal aspect. All that is hard, sharp or crude is now softened and smoothed; features which in the clear daylight never appear are here revealed; voices, too, are heard which the noise of the day tends to drown. And not only the luminous night, the dark night, too, has values of its own. It makes an end of the noise and bustle of the day; it brings quiet and peace. All this has its effects also in the psychological and spiritual spheres. There exists a nocturnal, gentle transparence of the spirit in which it is freed from the busy-ness of the day, and loosened but also collected, so that it can be drawn into the deep relationships of its own being and life, in the natural and the supernatural world. And there is a deep and grateful rest in the peace of the night. Of all this we have to think if we would understand the night symbolism of St. John of the Cross.[2]

This beautiful passage is cited in full, not only because it shows so well what illuminating results the phenomenological method

---

[1] It is impossible to translate her typical analysis of the meaning of the word by going back to its roots, *gegen* and *stehen* ('against' and 'stand'), though the English-Latin word *object* affords a parallel, consisting of *ob* and *jacere* ('against' and 'throw')—something that is thrown over against.

[2] pp. 33 f.

can produce if handled with the skill of a Sister Benedicta, but also because it seems to describe a state of soul and of prayer well known to herself. Even before she became a Christian she appears to have experienced a similar state when she wrote in her essay on the *Philosophical Foundations of Psychology*: 'There is a state of resting in God, of a complete relaxation of all mental effort . . . where one no longer acts, but abandons all the future to the divine Will.' The descriptions of those who knew her best always stress the almost rigid attitude of her motionless body at prayer, expressive of a soul at rest before her Maker. So it seems as if, from the very beginning of her Christian life, she had been drawn to a form of prayer which was not so much formal discursive meditation, but a resting in God, often accompanied by a transparence of the mind in which her soul would become aware of 'the deep relationships of its own being and life, of the natural and the supernatural world'. Or, as Abbot Walzer expressed it: 'Surely innumerable thoughts ascended and descended in her soul, like heavenly messengers on a Jacob's ladder. Ardent desires and generous plans would follow; but just like her exterior, almost rigid attitude, so also her interior remained in the repose of a blissful contemplation and rejoicing before God.'[1] Something like this she found in what now, following St. John of the Cross, she calls 'a deep and grateful rest in the peace of the night'.

After these preliminaries she turns to the works of the mystical doctor himself. After giving her own excellent translation of St. John's Canticle of the Dark Night, she gives an account of his teaching on the 'active night' as the 'night of the following of the Cross' (*Kreuzesnachfolge*) according to his *Ascent of Mount Carmel*, and on the passive night as 'being crucified' (*Gekreuzigtwerden*) according to the *Dark Night of the Soul*. She follows the saint in his teaching on faith as the only adequate means of union with God, lucidly and succinctly explaining his criteria for the transition from meditation to contemplation, and his views on visions, revelations and other extraordinary phenomena. This part of the work consists chiefly in citations and résumés from St. John's works without any commentary of her own, as do the following sections on the purification of the faculties; in

[1] *Life*, p. 151.

their clarity and brevity they form an excellent introduction to the *Ascent of Mount Carmel* and the *Dark Night* and greatly facilitate their understanding.

In a few pages on the natural activities of the soul and her supernatural life of faith, she discusses the state of the soul who has abandoned formal meditation. She 'no longer needs to meditate in order to learn to know and love God. The way is far behind her; she rests at the goal. As soon as she begins to pray she is with God and gives herself lovingly to repose in His presence. Her silence is dearer to Him than many words. This is what one calls today *acquired contemplation*.'[1] This description is somewhat vague, and she takes no notice of the discussion on the subject of 'acquired contemplation' between the different schools of spirituality, but quickly turns to the 'passive night of the spirit', which she describes in much the same way as the preceding sections of St. John's doctrine, though her verbal citations become longer as the subject increases in difficulty.

It is between her account of the *Dark Night* and the *Living Flame of Love* that she inserts a chapter developing her own ideas, which she calls: 'The Soul in the Realm of Spirit and the Spirits' (*Die Seele im Reich des Geistes und der Geister*). In it she presents her view of the soul, its structure, its relationship to God and created spirits, and the connexion between faith and contemplation. From the point of view of mystical theology it is perhaps the most controversial and least satisfactory part of her work. For she attempts to discuss the structure of the soul in this context without referring at all to the traditional teaching on the Image of God, in which the soul was created, and which is the seat of contemplation. Instead of this she gives a phenomenological analysis of the various types of soul, e.g. the sensual man, the seeker after truth, and so forth, which offers hardly any help to explain the mystical life.

But perhaps the most serious defect of her attempt at interpreting St. John of the Cross in terms of her own thought is her insufficient definition of faith, which is at the root of her particular view of the relationship between faith and contemplation. She defines the virtue of faith as 'the power to assume as real what

[1] p. 103.

one does not perceive as present, and to suppose to be true [*für wahr zu halten*] what one cannot cogently prove by rational arguments'.[1]

It is regrettable that she should have substituted this explanation, which she seems to have taken from a catechism, for the classical definition of faith in the eleventh chapter of the Epistle to the Hebrews: 'Faith is the substance of things to be hoped for, the evidence of things that appear not.' It is the more incomprehensible, since she had herself translated St. Thomas's *De Veritate*, in which this definition is elaborated at length, and she herself frequently cites from this very chapter of St. Thomas's treatise in other contexts. Basing himself on this definition, St. Thomas calls faith *Quaedam inchoatio vitae aeternae*, a certain beginning of eternal life. Sister Benedicta indeed cites this definition, though she adds: 'but only a *beginning*',[2] whereas St. Thomas certainly did not mean to stress beginning, but 'eternal life'. On the other hand, she speaks of faith as a seed: 'It has been placed within us like a seed through sanctifying grace; under our devoted care it is meant to develop into a large tree bearing magnificent fruit,' continuing: 'For it is the way which is to lead us to union with God even in this life, even though the highest perfection belongs to the next.'[3] So it would seem from this that faith can actually be transcended even on earth—just as the tree is no longer the seed—a view evidently not shared by St. Thomas or by St. Paul who, after speaking about seeing here 'through a glass, in a dark manner', wrote: 'And now there *remain* faith, hope and charity.'

St. John of the Cross only follows the traditional teaching in stressing over and over again that faith 'alone is the proximate and proportionate means whereby the soul is united with God; for such is the likeness between itself and God that there is no other difference, save that which exists between seeing God and believing in Him'.[4] Sister Benedicta of course knew these and many other similar passages very well. But, taking her stand on her insufficient conception of faith, she found them incomprehensible and, in order to bring St. John of the Cross into line with her own ideas, she indulged in a veritable *tour de force*. In this she was no doubt influenced by the critical methods of Baruzi,

---

[1] p. 158.   [2] Her italics.   [3] p. 151.   [4] *Ascent*, Book II, Chapter IX, 1.

to whom, as she herself writes in the preface, she owes many suggestions.

> It is conceivable [she thinks] that John may have been anxious sharply to distinguish his own teaching from illuminism (as is evidently done in many passages) and to bring the mystical development into the closest possible relation to the *normal way of grace*.[1] The comparison of the older editions with the manuscripts and the comparison of the manuscripts among themselves has proved that such an intention has been at work in the editing of his writings. *The Living Flame of Love* and *The Spiritual Canticle* are extant in two manuscript versions. The later versions show the desire to prevent misunderstandings by toning down bold expressions and by adding explanations.[2]

Sister Benedicta gives no definite opinion whether the alterations were made by St. John himself or by other people, but she seems to incline to the latter view. She thinks, however, that in view of the differences of the versions we cannot get an answer from St. John of the Cross himself, on whether he thought the mystic union was *in via normali sanctitatis*, and she therefore proposes to turn to St. Teresa for an answer. In her works she finds that the indwelling of God in the soul by the union of love is different not only in degree, but in kind from the indwelling by grace, and so she assumes that this must have been St. John's real thought—his other view was stressed only because of the Inquisition.

This seems inadmissible. The root of the matter is that St. John of the Cross was a theologian as well as a mystic, who knew how to base his mystical experience on the principles of theology, whereas St. Teresa was giving descriptions of mystical states without attempting to put them on a theological basis. The whole problem of mystical contemplation in its relation to faith in St. John of the Cross is admirably resolved by Père Poulain. He writes in his *Grâces d'oraison*:

> All depends on the more or less wide interpretation one gives to the term faith. In the large sense, it means all supernatural knowledge below the Beatific Vision. But between the faith taken in a more

---

[1] Her italics.   [2] p. 155.

restricted sense and the intuitive vision, there is an intermediary, namely the infused knowledge which one calls faith enlightened by a gift of the Holy Ghost. Faith in the strict sense believes solely on the testimony of another, that is to say God. Infused knowledge goes further; it begins to cause a soul to see with more or less clarity. Mystical contemplation is an act of infused knowledge. Now St. John of the Cross takes the word faith in the first, that is to say in the large sense; and so he can say that mystical contemplation is in the domain and line of faith.[1]

It is due to Sister Benedicta's unfortunate lack of the requisite technical knowledge that she took the term 'faith' in a restricted sense where it was used in a large sense, and, moreover, was not conversant with the traditional teaching on the place of the gifts of the Holy Ghost in the mystical life, so well elucidated, for example, by John of St. Thomas. If she had had this indispensable equipment she would probably not have spoken of the basic difference between faith and contemplation, and the possibility of contemplation without faith. This latter she had already asserted in her essay on Pseudo-Dionysius, and she reiterates it now:

God can grant to the soul a dark, loving knowledge of Himself even without a preceding exercise of meditation. [This, of course, is obvious.] He can place it suddenly into the state of contemplation and love, he can *infuse* contemplation. This, too, will happen not without connexion with faith. As a rule it will be granted to souls who have been prepared for it by living faith and by a life of faith. But if an unbeliever should be seized by it, then the teaching of faith which he had not yet accepted would yet help him to know by what he had been seized. And the faithfully loving soul will always return from the darkness of contemplation to the secure clarity of the doctrines of the faith, in order to understand from there what is happening to her.[2]

From this it appears that she thinks it possible that a man without faith could be granted infused contemplation. Now it is, indeed, possible that a person not belonging to the Catholic Church, or even not a Christian at all, should receive this grace. But if he did receive it, the condition for it would nevertheless

[1] Chapter XV, 43.　　　　[2] p. 163.

be faith, though this faith would be 'implicit', as St. Thomas calls it, for example, in the *Secunda Secundae*.[1] It may be that here she was thinking of her own prayer before she became a Catholic, which has been discussed before and in which contemplative traits seemed unmistakable. Another questionable point is that she opposes 'the secure clarity of the doctrines of faith' to the 'darkness of contemplation', and this with explicit reference to St. John of the Cross himself.[2] Now if there is one theme that the mystical doctor reiterates over and over again it is, as already observed, that faith is the one and only adequate means of reaching contemplation, and for the precise reason that both are obscure. St. John of the Cross would never speak of 'the secure clarity of the doctrines of the faith', for these doctrines are themselves obscure, else they would not belong to faith but to knowledge. Sister Benedicta seems in fact here to have misinterpreted—or mistranslated—the passage in question: 'Oh that Thou wouldst but give me these truths which Thou teachest me formlessly and darkly, and which are veiled in Thy articles of faith, clearly and formally revealed in them, according to the entreaty of my desire.' There is no question here that the soul wants to return from the darkness of contemplation to the clarity of the doctrines of the faith. Her desire is to leave the obscurity of both faith and contemplation, and to have the dark doctrines at last revealed in the Beatific Vision. This becomes even clearer in the next paragraph, where the saint writes: 'Wherefore the truths that are infused into the soul through faith are as it were in outline, and when they are in clear vision they will be in the soul as a perfect and finished painting, according to the words of the Apostle. . . . When that which is perfect is come [that is, clear vision] then that which is in part [namely, the knowledge of faith] shall be done away.'

This chapter has been discussed at length because it is somewhat surprising that the thought of such a brilliant mind as Sister Benedicta's should prove so comparatively unsatisfactory when it approaches mystical theology. Her lack of acquaintance with the relevant theological literature accounts for much. But there seems another reason as well. It is that she herself was a contemplative, and that she necessarily tended to interpret her

---

[1] Q. II art. 7 *ad 3um*.   [2] *Spiritual Canticle*, explanation of stanza II.

own contemplative experience not as a theologian, but as the phenomenological philosopher which she had remained. As such she would be struck by the difference of the 'phenomena' of accepting the doctrines of the Church by faith and meditating on them in discursive prayer, and the experience of the Divine Presence in contemplative prayer. As she was analysing these 'phenomena' in the same way as she analysed everything else according to the method she had learned from Husserl, they seemed so different that she felt she could not assign them to the same root of faith. The same 'phenomenological' difference would account for her divorcing the mystical life from the life of grace when she writes about the 'difference in principle of the union by grace and the mystical union', though 'it is not excluded that the life of grace *may*[1] prepare the way for mystical union'. The traditional teaching is, of course, that the mystical union is the consequence (whether 'normal' or 'extraordinary', according to the different schools of mystical theology) of the life of grace, apart from which it does not exist.

She ends this chapter by uniting the mystical experience to the mysteries of Christ:

> In the passion and death of Christ our sins have been devoured by fire. If we accept that by faith, and if we accept the whole Christ in faithful self-giving, that is to say by choosing, and walking in the way of the imitation of Christ, then He will lead us 'through His Passion and Cross to the glory of the Resurrection'. It is exactly this that is experienced in contemplation: the passing through the atoning fire to the blissful union of love. This explains its twofold character. It is death and resurrection. After the Dark Night, the Living Flame of Love shines forth.[2]

After this interlude in which she set forth her own views, Sister Benedicta resumes her analysis of the works of St. John of the Cross. She now does the same for *The Living Flame of Love* as for the *Ascent* and the *Dark Night*; she gives a very sensitive summary of the teaching of the saint, again illustrated by many well-chosen citations. In dealing with these exalted states her own language sheds the sometimes didactic style of the philosopher and reflects the ardours of St. John's mystic love.

[1] p. 160. Italics mine.   [2] p. 165.

'One feels,' she writes, 'how the veils are being lifted for the
saint, and how everything becomes transparent for him in
order to illumine the secret intercourse between God and the
soul.'[1]

She then analyses the *Spiritual Canticle*, dealing especially with
the relation between the two versions in which it has been
preserved. She ascribes the changes in the second version and
the way in which the saint interprets his poem to his desire to
safeguard his work 'from the vigilant eye of the Inquisition and
the suspicion of Illuminism', and she greatly prefers the poem
itself to the interpretation. She refers to the saint's own words
in the prologue that: 'Since these Stanzas, then, have been
composed under the influence of a love which comes from
abounding mystical knowledge, they cannot be fairly expounded,
nor shall I attempt so to expound them, but only to throw upon
them some light of a general kind.' She comments: 'He declares
that his own explanations are not binding. When we have read
these explanations, we are sincerely grateful; for the contrast
between the poetical and mystical fervour of the Canticle and
the totally different style of the interpretation are here far more
deeply perceptible than in the *Ascent* and *Night*.'[2] This is a very
unusual judgement. The chief reason for it seems to be that the
saint has followed very closely the traditional teaching of
mystical theology, a procedure she ascribes to his fear of the
Inquisition. She finds fault with his division of the spiritual
progress into purgative, illuminative and unitive ways, and with
the clear line of demarcation he draws between the last stage of
the mystical life here on earth and the Beatific Vision—a line
which every Catholic theologian must necessarily draw, though
in a poem his language might be less unequivocal. It is unfortunate that Sister Benedicta here follows the arguments of Baruzi[3]
and thinks that all this points to the intention of 'representing
the mystical development of the soul in as traditional and
unsuspicious a manner as possible'; and she considers that the
explanations of the *Spiritual Canticle* give the impression of a
'Dictionary of its language of images'. She calls this 'allegory'
an artistic form which 'is in the taste of the time, a characteristic
of the poetry of the Baroque. John knew the poetry of his time

[1] p. 195.   [2] p. 206.   [3] Second edition, pp. 28 ff.

very well and had been formed by it. . . . But if in the interpretation he strings one explanation of a word to the next, and sometimes gives several quite different explanations of the same image . . . he goes beyond what is required by the allegory as such and mars the impression of the poem by resolving the unity into a multitude of details.'[1]

It is hard to understand such cool and critical language about what is generally considered to be one of the priceless gems of mystical writing, and even more so when such language comes from a Carmelite. But Edith Stein was fundamentally a critical mind, who refused to accept opinions without investigating them, and as Baruzi's arguments seemed to her conclusive, she had no hesitation and sacrificed the interpretation of the *Spiritual Canticle* almost *in toto*. Fortunately this did not prevent her from giving an excellent account of the book itself, ending with a summary which shows how deeply she herself was affected by the theme she was treating: 'Thus the bridal union of the soul with God is the goal for which she has been created, bought through the Cross, accomplished on the Cross, and sealed with the Cross for all eternity.'[2]

The pages that follow, *Kreuzesnachfolge* (Following the Cross) have remained unfinished. They are in a very true sense her swan-song. Nothing of herself, of her own suffering—it all went into the description of the sufferings and death of St. John of the Cross. We read there: his union with God 'was the fruit of an interior purification, in which a richly gifted nature loaded itself with the Cross and delivered itself into the Hand of God to be crucified; a spirit of intense power and vitality had made itself a prisoner, a heart full of passionate ardour had found rest in radical abnegation'.[3]

This description is, with some modifications, a description of herself. She, too, delivered her richly gifted nature to be crucified in Carmel, she sacrificed her powerful intellect, and instead of a new career that was offered her in another country, she chose the Cross. Thus she traces in St. John the harmony between his teaching and his life—just as in her own life her conduct had never belied her faith.

'In the life of the Lord,' she writes, 'the happiest hours were

[1] p. 209.   [2] p. 241.   [3] p. 261.

surely those in the silent night, in solitary converse with the
Father. But they were only the breathing space after an activity
which placed him in the midst of the crowds of men and offered
him daily and hourly the mixture of human weakness, meanness
and wickedness like a drink of vinegar and gall.'[1] She applies
this to the life of St. John; and her own life before she entered
Carmel was not without the same experience. After dealing all
day long with her pupils and students she, too, used to spend a
good deal of the night in prayer, especially in the very early
hours of the morning. With deep feeling she describes the last
sufferings of the saint, his struggle for the Teresian ideal at the
last Provincial Chapter he attended at Madrid, the humiliations
he accepted from his own brethren in perfect submission and
obedience to the Will of God. 'Humanly speaking,' she writes,
'his lifework lay in ruins as he went on his way to Penuela[2]—as
in the case of the Saviour, when He let Himself be bound and be
led from the Mount of Olives to Jerusalem.'[3]

In the description of the last days of the saint she follows the
work of Father Bruno;[4] but her account has a special poignancy,
for these last pages were written with her own violent death
already in sight. 'Brother Diego was holding the saint in his
arms as he was passing away, unnoticed. Suddenly the Brother
saw a light round the bed. Only then did he realize that the saint
in his arms was no longer alive. "Our Father has gone to heaven
in this light," he said to those present. When he then, together
with Fr. Francis and Fr. Matthew, laid out the sacred remains,
a sweet scent went out from them.' With these words the
manuscript breaks off. . . .

---

[1] p. 265.
[2] The monastery assigned to him at the Chapter at Madrid.
[3] p. 271.   [4] Saint Jean de la Croix, pp. 361 ff.

CHAPTER TWENTY-THREE

AVE CRUX!

SISTER Benedicta would have liked to be permanently settled in Echt, but in view of the uncertainty of her position the Prioress did not consider it opportune. This was a great disappointment for Sister Benedicta, but she humbly submitted and expressed her resignation in a beautiful note to her Prioress, written while she was occupied with her book on St. John of the Cross:

> Dear Mother. If Your Reverence looked at the letter of P. . . . you will know what his views are. I would not like to do anything more in this matter. I place it in Y.R.'s hands and leave it to Y.R. whether Y.R. wants to get a decision. I am content with everything. One can only gain a *Scientia Crucis* if one is made to feel the Cross oneself to the depth of one's being. Of this I have been convinced from the first moment and have said with all my heart: *Ave Crux, spes unica!* Your R.'s grateful child B.

In April 1942 Sister Benedicta had written: 'We leave everything trustfully to Providence and quietly go about our duties.' Preparations for her transfer to the Swiss Carmel at Le Paquier had been begun at the end of 1941, and were being followed up while she was writing *Kreuzeswissenschaft*. She was well known to one of the novices at the Swiss Carmel, on whose vocation she herself had had considerable influence. So the Carmelites there were soon willing to receive her, but she wanted to take her sister Rosa with her. A place was eventually found for her with a Swiss convent of Third Order Carmelites. But it all took time, and time was precious indeed. For in the spring of 1942 the Gestapo ordered her and Rosa to appear at their office at Maastricht. Possibly they had become suspicious when they had applied for visas to Switzerland, or Rosa's relations with Jewish converts had attracted their notice.

When they entered, Sister Benedicta greeted the SS officers with 'Praised be Jesus Christ' instead of the official 'Heil Hitler!' 'Later she explained to the Reverend Mother that she had felt impelled to this—humanly speaking—imprudent behaviour, because she realized that this was not a matter of mere politics, but of the age-old fight between Jesus and Lucifer.'[1] It probably was imprudent—though the outcome would hardly have been different had she said 'Heil Hitler!'; but it is refreshing to meet such fearless confession of Christ in the face of the dreaded Gestapo, before whom far too many in those days went pale with fear. Sister Benedicta need not excuse herself; it was the act of a Christian woman, and we would love and respect her less had she whispered a cowardly 'Heil Hitler!'

The Gestapo were not disposed to treat her gently. They shouted at her because her identity card did not bear the big red J, and because the name 'Sarah', which all women of Jewish origin had to add to their first names, was missing. She and her sister were ordered to write to the police bureau at Breslau and to ask 'most humbly' that these omissions be rectified. They were then issued with a 'David's Star' of yellow cloth which all Jews had to wear.

In May they had to appear again before the Gestapo, this time at Amsterdam, as well as before the Jewish Council, and had to fill in piles of questionnaires. During one of these interviews a friendly Gestapo officer from Cologne told them about the heavy air raids on the city, and that the old church of Our Lady of Peace had been destroyed. Did she remember how, years ago, when the persecutions of the Jews started, she had said that all this would one day be revenged most terribly? What she certainly remembered was her prayer before the statue of Our Lady of Peace in that New Year's night of 1939, when she was taken across the frontier into Holland. This little sanctuary, too, was now gone—had our Lady herself forsaken her country?

Yet Sister Benedicta's faith and peace remained unshaken, and deeply impressed others. On her way to one of these interviews with the Gestapo a business-man whose sister was a benefactress of the Carmel met her at the station, where they had to wait almost an hour for the train. So he had ample opportunity to

[1] *Life*, pp. 208 f.; 198.

talk to her and observe her. He was an unemotional Dutchman, with 'no nonsense about him'. He afterwards said to himself: 'Today I have spoken to a saint.'

In June she wrote to the Carmelites at Cologne: 'For months I have been wearing on my heart a slip of paper with the verse from Scripture: Matthew x. 23.[1] There are negotiations going on with Le Paquier, but I am so deep in our Father John of the Cross that everything else is indifferent to me.'

It is quite possible that she might have been saved even then, had she consented to do something 'illegal' and simply gone into hiding in another convent, as many other 'non-Aryans' managed to do. A young priest suggested it to her. She was horrified; it might have serious consequences for her convent. He did not think that ought to stand in the way—it would result in nothing more than a fortnight's unpleasantness for the nuns. Sister Benedicta would not hear of it. Another priest made the same suggestion. To him she replied that in Protestant Germany Catholics had a reputation for lying, she would not add to that. If she could not be saved with the full knowledge of the political authorities, she would rather suffer.

How comparatively little she allowed her peace of mind to be disturbed is shown by an amusing little incident. On 16 July she received the visit of a newly ordained priest. It was the Feast of Our Lady of Mount Carmel, and owing to the war they could not have the customary celebrations. Sister Benedicta quickly took advantage of his presence and asked him whether he would not like to conduct a little service for them. He could not very well refuse. Her next proposal was that it would be so nice if he could also give them a sermon. The young Father had never before preached one; but this was no obstacle for Sister Benedicta. She walked out of the parlour, and after a few minutes returned with a Breviary, and spent the next half-hour practically making the sermon for him. So the nuns had their celebration as she wanted it, and she was allowed to enjoy on this Carmel feast, the last of her life, at least a faint reflection of its former glory.

Then the storm broke. On 11 July all the Christian communions in Holland, including the Catholic bishops, had sent a telegram to the Nazi authorities, in which they protested against

---

[1] 'When they shall persecute you in this city, flee into another.'

the persecution of the Jews, and requested that at least the Christian 'non-Aryans' should be exempted from the deportations. The Germans agreed to make an exception for all those who had belonged to a Christian community before January 1941. This, however, did not affect the inhuman treatment of the other Jews, and so the Christian communions decided to issue letters condemning this, and referring also to the exemption they had obtained. The Nazis, received information of this plan and asked that the telegram should not be mentioned, as it was of a confidential character. The Archbishop of Utrecht, however, regarded this condition as undue interference on the part of the secular authority in ecclesiastical matters, and refused to change the text of his pastoral, which had already been sent to his clergy. People in Holland were anxiously wondering what the consequences of this would be.

Sister Benedicta's anxiety increased when, on 28 July, she received the news that one of her brothers and his family had been taken to the concentration camp of Theresienstadt, though she accepted it with quiet resignation. Four days before her deportation she knew that for her, too, the end was near. She writes on a postcard:

As you have been kept informed about us I need only tell you the latest: Switzerland will open its gates to my sister and myself, since the only enclosed convent of our Order at Le Paquier, Canton Fribourg, is prepared to accept me, and a Third Order Carmelite convent, one hour's distance from there, my sister. The two houses have made themselves responsible to the aliens police to keep us for life. But it is very doubtful, indeed, whether we shall here receive the permission for emigration. In any case it would take a very long time. I should not be sorry if it were not granted. It is no small matter to leave a beloved conventual family for the second time. However, I take it as God wills it.

On this open card, addressed to one who did not belong to her most intimate friends, she only mentions the very natural reluctance to be once more uprooted. But this, surely, would have counted little with her, whose whole being was penetrated by her sense of the supernatural. She had offered her life for her people as early as 1938, soon after she had come to Holland.

Now the Lord was going to take her at her word and allow her to consummate her sacrifice.

*   *   *

On 2 August, as a reprisal for the pastoral of the bishops, all non-Aryan Catholics were arrested throughout Holland. At five o'clock in the evening, as the sisters had just gone into choir, the Mother Prioress was summoned to the parlour, where two officers asked to see Sister Benedicta, who had just been reading out the points for the meditation. The Prioress was sure that it must have something to do with the proposed emigration to Switzerland and went out to call Sister Benedicta. Then she hopefully posted herself before the door of the parlour to wait for the outcome of the conversation. She soon realized that the visit of the SS officers had a much more sinister purpose. One of them ordered Sister Benedicta to leave the convent within five minutes. She replied: 'I cannot do that; we have strict enclosure.' The officer then told her to remove the grille and come out. To which absurd suggestion she made the spirited reply: 'You had better show me how to do that.' 'Call the Superior,' ordered the SS man.

When the Prioress came into the parlour, the SS man insisted to her that Sister Benedicta had to leave the convent within five minutes. On being told that this was impossible, he gave her ten to pack up her things—a rug, a mug, a spoon and food sufficient for three days. A protest, pleading that Sister Benedicta had already permission from the authorities in Switzerland to go there, was met with the threat of reprisals against the convent if they would not let her go at once. While this conversation was taking place in the parlour, Sister Benedicta was hastily packing up the most necessary things in her cell, assisted by several other nuns. When she was leaving the enclosure, her sister Rosa, who was also being deported, was kneeling at the entrance to receive the last blessing of the Prioress.

One of the out-sisters had rushed to ring up the sister of the Dutch business-man who had met Sister Benedicta at the station on a previous visit to the Gestapo. She arrived just in time to see her and Rosa coming out, and walked with them a few steps despite the threats of the two Gestapo men, who were on the other side of the street. A little group of angry people had gathered outside the convent. When, at last, the Germans started crossing over to separate Sister Benedicta forcibly from her friend, they shook hands hastily. The latter walked back, her face streaming with tears, while Sister Benedicta and Rosa entered the police van to join the other victims who were already in it.

From Echt they were all taken to the local police authorities.[1] They left again the same evening in two police vans, carrying thirteen and seventeen people respectively. They were due at their next destination, Amersfoort, the same night; but the driver lost his way, so that they arrived there only at three o'clock in the morning. So far the German SS soldiers had been comparatively kind to the prisoners; but at Amersfoort they were treated very brutally. Cursing and swearing, the SS men hit them in the back with their rifle butts and drove them into dormitories without any food.

Three days later the nuns at Echt received a telegram asking for warm clothes, rugs and medicine to be sent to the concentration camp at Westerbork, where they had been taken in the meantime. On the same day the Ursulines at Venlo received a similar message on behalf of Ruth Kantorowicz, this timid friend of hers whom she had so often to encourage, and who would now need her strength more than ever before. So the nuns sent two men from Echt with the things required for the camp. This was fortunately guarded by Dutch police, who allowed the sisters to meet the messengers outside, and did not open the letters they sent or received. Sister Benedicta was grateful, indeed, to have the greetings and prayers of her sisters, the last link with the world outside. She told the men that she had found many friends and acquaintances in the camp, and gave them an account of their experiences in a quiet voice, passing over her own sufferings almost completely. With shining eyes she told the visitors that all the nuns in her hut—they were ten—were still wearing their habits, and that they were determined to do so as long as at all possible. Indeed, everyone in the camp was glad that there were Catholic priests and nuns with them, who were their only hope and support. She herself was

---

[1] The following account is based on *Life*, pp. 223 ff.; 212 ff.

happy to be able to help them as much as she could with words of encouragement and prayer.

She assured the men that the Mother Prioress could be perfectly at peace as far as she and her sister were concerned. They had time for prayer all day long, being interrupted only three times to fetch their food. They had no complaint either about food or about their treatment by the soldiers.

She was indeed at peace, for she had long learned to live forgetful of herself, loving God and her neighbour. It was here, in the camp of utter human misery and despair, that she grew to the full stature of Christian charity. The simple statement of a Jewish business man who had the good fortune to escape deportation and death is the most eloquent testimony of the height she had reached.

Among the prisoners who arrived on 5 August Sister Benedicta made a striking impression by her great calm and composure. The misery in the camp and the excitement among the newcomers were indescribable. Sister Benedicta walked about among the women, comforting, helping, soothing like an angel. Many mothers were almost demented and had for days not been looking after their children, but had been sitting brooding in listless despair. Sister Benedicta at once took care of the poor little ones, washed and combed them, and saw to it that they got food and attention. As long as she was in the camp she made washing and cleaning one of her principal charitable activities, so that everyone was amazed.

When she was not occupied with these, the contemplative side of her was allowed to show itself. The mother of a future Dominican gives the following account:

The great difference between Edith Stein and the other sisters lay in her silence. My personal impression is that she was most deeply sorrowful, but without anxiety. I cannot express it better than by saying that she gave the impression of bearing such an enormous load of sorrow that even when she did smile it only made one more sorrowful. She hardly ever spoke, but she often looked at her sister Rosa with indescribable sadness. . . . She was thinking of the sorrow she foresaw, not her own sorrow, for that she was far far too calm, she thought of the sorrow that awaited the others. Her whole appearance, as I picture her in my memory sitting in that hut, suggested only one thought to me: a Pietà without Christ.[1]

[1] *Life*, p. 256; 6th German edition only

Once her attitude at prayer had reminded a Benedictine monk of one of the Orantes of ancient Christian art; now Benedicta of the Cross was being transformed into an image of the Mater Dolorosa whom she had loved so much. At her profession the virgin had become a bride, now her course was complete, she had truly become a Mother—a Mother tending little children whose natural mothers neglected them; a sorrowful Mother, suffering with and for her children, who, like herself, would soon be driven into the gas chambers to be 'liquidated' like vermin. Rachel weeping for her children, as the Church sings on the feast of the Holy Innocents.

On 6 August she wrote to her Prioress:

J. & M. Pax Xti! Dear Mother. The Mother of a Convent came last night with suitcases for her child and will take this little note with her. Tomorrow morning the first transport will leave (Silesia or Czechoslovakia?). The most necessary things are woollen stockings, two rugs. For Rosa all warm underwear and whatever she has in the laundry. For both towels and face flannels. Rosa has no toothbrush, no crucifix and rosary. I should also like the next volume of the Breviary. (Up to now I have been able to pray marvellously well.) Our identity cards, racial certificates and bread coupons. A thousand thanks and love to all. Your Reverence's grateful child B.

On 7 August one of her former pupils, then recently married, stood on the station platform at Schifferstadt. She heard herself called by her maiden name and, looking round, she recognized her former teacher Edith Stein standing at the window of a train and calling to her: 'Give my love to the sisters at St. Magdalena. I am travelling eastwards.'

In August also, Sister Adelgundis Jaegerschmid received a little scrap of paper, scribbled in pencil: 'Greetings from my journey to Poland. Sister Benedicta.'

* * *

After that no more. For, on 9 August 1942, the Vigil of St. Lawrence, Edith Stein and her sister Rosa disappeared into the gas chamber at Auschwitz.

'A sacrifice of expiation for true peace.'

BIBLIOGRAPHY

WORKS:

Edith Stein's *Werke*, vols. 1–3, 1950 ff. Nauwelaerts (Louvain) Herder (Freiburg) ed. by Dr. Lucie Gelber and Fr. Romaeus Leuven, O.C.D. containing:

Kreuzeswissenschaft (vol. 1)
Endliches und Ewiges Sein (vol. 2)
Des hl. Thomas von Aquino Untersuchungen über die Wahrheit (vol. 3)
Beiträge zur philosophischen Begründung der Psychologie und der Geisteswissenschaften, Jahrbuch für Philosophie und phänomenologische Forschung, 5 vol., Halle a.d.S. 1922.
Eine Untersuchung über den Staat, ibid., 1925.
Husserls Phänomenologie und die Philosophie des hl. Thomas, Husserl-Festschrift, Halle a.d.S. 1929.
Frauenbildung und Frauenberufe, Schnell and Steiner, München, 1949.
Das Gebet der Kirche, Bonifacius-Druckerei, Paderborn, n.d.
Teresia von Jesus, Kanisius-Verlag, Konstanz, 2. ed. 1952.
Margareta Redi, Rita-Verlag, Würzburg, 1934.
Das Weihnachtsgeheimnis, Karmel Maria vom Freiden, Köln, 1950.
Der Intellekt und die Intellektuellen. 'Das heilige Feuer', July–August, 1931.
Natur und Übernatur in Goethes Faust, MS, Husserl-Archives, Louvain.
Die Bestimmung der Frau, MS, Husserl-Archives.
Der Eigenwert der Frau in seiner Bedeutung für das Leben des Volkes, MS, Husserl-Archives.
Ein auserwähltes Gefäss der göttlichen Weisheit, Sr. Marie-Aimée de Jesus. MS, Husserl-Archives.
Ways to Know God (Wege der Gotteserkenntnis), in 'The Thomist', July 1946, Baltimore.

BIOGRAPHICAL STUDIES:

Schwester Teresia Renata de Spiritu Sancto, *Edith Stein*, 6 ed., Glock & Lutz, Nürnberg, 1952. Engl. translation, Sheed and Ward, London and New York, 1952.
Edith Stein, par une Moniale Française, Editions du Seuil, Paris, 1954.
John M. Oesterreicher, *Walls Are Crumbling*, The Devin-Adair Company, New York, 1952.
Erich Przywara, *Edith Stein zu ihrem zehnten Todestag*, in 'Die Besinnung', Nürnberg, 1952, S.238ff.

INDEX

Allers, R., 66, 195
analogia entis, 155
angelology, 158
Aristotle, 148, 151
Augustine, St., 148, 162

Bach, J. S., 48
Baruzi, J., 207, 215, 220f.
Bergson, H., 27
Bernard, St., 137
Beuron, 17, 56ff., 65, 95f., 121, 209f.
Bismarck, 187
Bolzano, B., 12
Brentano, F., 12
Bridget, St., 125
Britain, 18
Bruno de Jésus Marie, O.C.D., 207, 222

Catherine of Siena, St., 79, 96, 125, 179
Cato, 88
Chrysostom, St. John, 203
Conrad of Marburg, 87
Conrad-Martius, H., 30, 32, 34f., 120, 156, 159

Descartes, R., 148
Duns Scotus, 154, 158

Elizabeth, St., of Hungary, 66, 69f., 86f., 191
empathy, 20, 26
Erzberger, G., 187
essences, 152ff.
Esther, 57, 74, 194
Eucharist, 80, 123, 132ff.
evil, 157f.

faith, and contemplation, 202ff., 214ff.

feminism, 28, 62, 75, 83f.
Feuling, D., O.S.B., 47, 73, 137, 140

Gabriel of St. Mary Magdalen, O.C.D., 207
Garrigou-Lagrange, R., O.P., 182f., 202, 207
George, S., 25
Goebbels, J., 93
Goethe, J. W., 21, 26, 72
Grabmann, M., 52
Gredt, J., 164

Haecker, T., 162
Heidegger, M., 50, 53, 64, 150
Hitler, 93f., 96, 178ff.
Husserl, E., 11ff., 15, 20ff., 33, 48ff., 77, 147ff., 175f., 195ff., 219
Husserl, Frau M., 24
Husserl Archives, 23, 50

Image of God, 155f., 159ff., 208, 214
intellectuals, 84f.
Israel, mystery of, 7

Joan of Arc, St., 79
John, St., the Evangelist, 174
John, St., of the Cross, 108, 111, 131, 144, 166, 182, 191f., 201, 206ff., 222, 224
John of St. Thomas, O.P., 217
Joseph, St., 174
Judith, 57, 74

Kant, I., 11
Keller, G., 26
Koyré, 73

Le Fort, G. von, 88f.
Lehmann, M., 18f.
Lipps, T., 20, 27

233